Fishing

The History of the Leintwardine Fishing Club

Barney Rolfe-Smith

Fishing in Time

Published by Stonebrook Publishing

Stonebrook House

Downton on the Rock

Ludlow, SY8 2LH

First Edition 2011

ISBN 978-0-9568972-0-6 Hardback

ISBN 978-0-9568972-1-3 Paperback

This book is number

....

of a limited edition of

400 copies. First 100 hardback

By the same author:

Notes on Bringewood Forge and the Downton Walks, 2009,

ISBN 0-954-31947-8

2

This book is dedicated to Janet

TROUT

GRAYLING

CONTENTS

Chapter		Page
	Acknowledgments, Foreword and Introduction	6-9
1	The River Teme	12
2	The Right To Fish	15
3	The Developing Reputation of The Leintwardine Fishery	21
4	The Origins of the Club	30
5	The Early Years, 1848-1870	36
6	Andrew Rouse Boughton Knight, 1870-1909	43
7	Edward Meredith, Keeper, 1849-1907	75
8	Charles Rouse Boughton Knight, 1909-1920	100
9	Transition, 1920-1946	124
10	Herbert Rushton Sykes, 1946-1951	133
11	Sydney Slater Guy, 1951-1967	142
12	Postscript, 1967-2011	155
	INDEX OF SOURCES	161

APPENDICES

ONE	LFC Members, 1848-1967	162
TWO	Bibliography	190
THREE	The Grasshopper	197
FOUR	Lord Coventry's Fishing Journal	204
FIVE	Archdeacon William Lea, *A Day at Leintwardine*	210
SIX	Officers of the Club, 1848-2011	219
SEVEN	The River Keepers, 1848-2011	221
EIGHT	List of Maps and Illustrations	225
	INDEX	227

ACKNOWLEDGMENTS

After half a lifetime following the flag around much of the old British Empire, I was lucky enough to find a home on the Downton Estate. I was soon aware of a delightful river flowing through a picturesque gorge and offered my services to Tom Wall of Natural England as a volunteer warden for the National Nature Reserve that nestled there. It was not long before the history of Downton captured my interest and with Tom Wall's encouragement and help I produced a booklet *Notes on Bringewood Forge and the Downton Walks*. My research had re-introduced me to Sir Humphry Davy's *Salmonia* and several other books that eulogised the Teme at Leintwardine and I knew there was a story there.

Many people have been very generous in helping me to produce this book. Daniel McDowell, the current Chairman of the Leintwardine Fishing Club, took a risk in handing over the Club archives to me and allowing me a completely free hand to write what I wished, and it is therefore to him I owe an enormous debt of gratitude. Another Club member and a good friend, Laurence Parker, has given a huge amount of his time to introduce me to the river and to other club members as well as acting as a sounding board for my more outlandish ideas.

Edward Harley very kindly gave me access to his archives at Brampton Bryan and without that access this book would have been impossible. The Record Offices of Worcester, Hereford and Shrewsbury are all staffed by generous and helpful people and I thank them for their endless patience. Daniel Lockett, Curator of Ludlow Museum was instrumental in providing material that led to an important breakthrough in my narrative. I have been allowed access to several private archives, both large and small; although the holders wish to be unnamed I would like to make public my thanks for their generosity. John Williams of the Leintwardine History Society has been unstinting in his practical support and advice. I owe a great deal to Pam Hatherly for her very particular assistance. Club members Cliff Gammon, Hugh Hughes, and Merlin Unwin have all helped enormously with material and advice. Many individuals have provided help ranging from photographs, papers, books or contacts, amongst these I would like to thank Linda Bromage, Michael Barr, Alan Morris, Sue Hubbard, David Edwards and Caroline Amphlet.

The books from which I have quoted are listed in Appendix Two. Acknowledgments for photographs or pictures used can be found in the List of Illustrations. The website used for reading much of the published fishing literature is www.archive.org, an invaluable and freely available source which I would recommend to anyone. www.measuringworth.com is the site used for comparing costs or wages with modern times and www.thepeerage.com for some genealogy details.

Barney Rolfe-Smith

FOREWORD

It is a great honour to write the foreword to *Fishing in Time*. It may seem surprising that no previous member of the Leintwardine Fishing Club has sought to record its illustrious and, at times, precarious history – the reason being, no doubt, that fishing the Club water was seen to be a more interesting occupation. Nevertheless, there is a great story to be told and this book gives a unique insight into an ancient and highly-regarded Club that has always been, and continues to be, devoted to fishing for grayling and trout – at all times in the most sporting fashion.

This book will have broad appeal, not only to those lucky enough to have fished the rivers of the Marches, but also to local historians and those interested in the development of the sport within this country. For those who have family or other connections with the Club, the comprehensive list of members will be of particular interest.

The links with influential and important anglers, many of whom travelled from far and wide to fish the Club water, are well described. Likewise the 'local scene' and the strong relationship with Leintwardine and the neighbouring villages are much in evidence. It is very appropriate that the Club continues to allow the villagers of Leintwardine access to a section of the water below Leintwardine Bridge.

One of the most refreshing aspects of the Club is the way that the spirit of sportsmanship and enthusiasm which so pervades the book still manifests itself strongly today. Barney Rolfe-Smith has brought together in depth historical research combined with his fine ear for a good story to produce a remarkable book about a remarkable Club.

Edward Harley

Brampton Bryan

The front page of a list of members from the Club archive.

Leintwardine Fishing Club.

1863—64.

HONORARY MEMBER.

ANDREW ROUSE BOUGHTON KNIGHT, Esquire,
Downton Castle.

MEMBERS.

JAMES ACKERS, Esquire,
Prinknash Park, near Gloucester.

B. ST. JOHN ACKERS, Esquire,
Lincolns Inn, London.

C. VILLIERS BAYLEY, Esquire,
Privy Council Office, London.

HENRY BROWN, Esquire,
4, Douro Villas, Cheltenham.

COLONEL COLVIN, C. B.
Leintwardine.

CAPTAIN FRANK CORBETT,
Greenfield, Presteign.

OVER.

FISHING IN TIME

"Thus shall memory often in dreams sublime

Catch a glimpse of the days that are over.

Thus, sighing, look through the waves of Time

For the long faded glories they cover."

Edward Hamilton

INTRODUCTION

At one stage this book was to be entitled A Tale of Knights, a Lady and a Grasshopper. This was not an attempt to mislead readers. The book is the story of the Leintwardine Fishing Club but it is also rather more than that. This is a true story of the relationship between two estates, a club, a village and the river that connects them. It is based in part upon the collection of papers and minute books which the Club has retained. The Club archive, sadly, is in no way complete and it has been necessary to explore local archives and record offices. Fortunately, the river, and later the Club, established a countrywide reputation for excellence and thus a considerable quantity of fishing literature has helped to provide a fuller picture.

In consequence it is hoped that the reader will find this is not a dry rendering of members' records and their catches but an insight into a club of some consequence and its development over the Victorian and Edwardian eras and into modern times. The Club still thrives today and is now one of the very few in this country and perhaps elsewhere that can claim such a long and continuous heritage. In passing it is interesting to note that one consequence has been the promotion of a small village in north Herefordshire to national if not international prominence. How many foreign tongues will have stumbled over the first pronunciation of the village name until hearing it spoken? 'Lent-war-dine'.

The village today has a thriving history society and its support and archives have been invaluable. An additional aim has been to increase the Leintwardine History Society's body of knowledge in return. Above all the intention has been to produce for the Leintwardine Fishing Club members of today, and for the descendants of those of the past, a history of the Club that is as accurate as I can make it 'warts and all'. There is one caveat: when primary resources are scarce one can never do enough research to satisfy all the questions and it is quite clear that this may not be the complete story but I am confident that it comes close.

A club is an entity that is more than its members; it relies upon the landowners and the owners of the fishing rights, and their agents and lawyers; it employs river keepers and under-keepers and night-watchmen; it needs labourers and artisans to maintain the river structures and the river banks. Its concerns are for the river, the fish, their food and the predation by poachers, pests and pestilence. It needs the nearby village for housing or fishing 'boxes', inns and hotels for lodging and sustenance and places to meet and celebrate. It needs the carters to carry and carriages to fetch, housekeepers to cook and small boys to carry the heavy creels. So this story is as much about them as it is about a famous and exclusive club.

To those readers wondering about the title of this book, as some already have, I perhaps owe an explanation as it is entirely an indulgence of my own. Fishing had to be there in the title. As I carried out my research I was constantly reminded of the metaphors used that associate the passing of time with streams: *"Time's fleeting river.."* (Shelley, 1820); *"Time, like an ever-rolling stream.."* (Watts, 1799) and many more. When I laid out sheets of notes, quotes and angling ephemera in date order on the floor of my study coincidences of people and places rose to the surface of this stream of paper. Each visit to an archive felt like a fishing expedition into the past. I knew what I hoped to find but was it there and would I find it? As for the rest; Thymallus (the grayling), Thyme (the fish is supposed to smell of water-thyme), Teme (the river). Finally there was the hope that readers could discover for themselves some connections with both the people of the past and the places associated with the Leintwardine Fishing Club whether they fish or not.

It is a significant and interesting story that celebrates a fine clear river, some excellent fish and a picturesque countryside. That these few miles of river in the Welsh Marches and the Club that fishes upon them have become so embedded in the sporting folklore of this country is also remarkable and deserves explanation. One reason has to be the singularity of the river and this is probably the best place to start.

The source of the Teme

The Teme at Milebrook, 6 miles above Leintwardine

CHAPTER ONE

THE RIVER TEME

The River Teme has its source in Wales at a height of about 460 metres above sea level in the Kerry Hills on the slopes of Cilfaesty Hill and Bryn Coch, which lie about six kilometres south of Newtown. Draining as it does the rough and rural grassland, numerous peaty streamlets trickle uncertainly through this ancient vegetation of sedges and mosses to form the very beginning of the Teme. This dalliance lends certain acidity to the waters and few nutrients, but not for long. Soon the young Teme is dashing across and through the silts and gravels that are to influence and flavour its constitution. Through riffles and pools it speeds past cobbles and pebbles. Then as if to catch its breath the pre-teenage Teme chooses to explore, in season, storm flow channels, cut-off pools and back channels. It then enjoys a quieter mood meandering past meadows flanked with alder, oak, and willow. Its developing body is ready to muscle aside mighty mounds of gravel into banks and ridges. Its strength when roused erodes and gouges and rebuilds its boundaries at will.

The river flows eastwards, falling steeply to Knighton where perhaps it earned its Celtic name 'Lent', meaning torrent, before flowing into England and then more gently past Brampton Bryan. The Teme now tastes the ancient shale and mudstone and adds these more calcareous ingredients to the now increasingly nutritious waters as they approach Leintwardine. A kilometre or so below Brampton Bryan the Teme is reinforced by the River Clun, the confluence being just before the site of the ancient Roman military settlement of Branogenium. A few metres further downstream is Leintwardine Bridge, where that famous Roman highway Watling Street once forded the river. Here we can begin our story, for it is here that the Fishing Club waters start.

Leintwardine, called *Lenteurde* in the 1086 Domesday Book, meaning the 'enclosed settlement by the Lent', conjoins in its name both river and people. It would be too much to expect that fishing would also feature in the name, but it would be beyond belief for anyone viewing the river at this point not to imagine that since the time of the Romans and their mercenaries, if not even earlier, the river waters have yielded fish to the fisherman. For thousands of years the rise of fish to the fly in this place has signalled to the people of Leintwardine a source of food and perhaps solace. The flash of silver and at times the sound of a heavy splash would summon even the most incurious passer-by to the water. For the fisherman, the mere glimpse of this pellucid stream tells all he needs to know. There are fish here aplenty! We should wonder why.

It is probably the very variety of flow and geology that help to make the River Teme officially special. It was designated as a Site of Special Scientific Interest (SSSI) throughout its 122 kilometre length in 1996. The citation states *'The notified channel is of special interest as a representative, near-natural and biologically-rich river type associated with sandstone and mudstones'* and goes on to say, *'These attributes and the high water quality, support significant river plant, fish and invertebrate communities'*. The Environment Agency describes the Teme as *'a nationally outstanding example of a large river with rich and varied plant, invertebrate, fish and otter communities'*. Once past Ludlow the river starts to gather the clays and silts that characterise an alluvial river. The Teme is more ponderous now, perhaps stately is a kinder word, for we know that it still has a quick temper and happily inundates fields at will. It is maturing into middle age as it approaches Tenbury Wells before finally joining the River Severn just below Worcester, having descended some 446 metres to just 14 metres above sea-level.

However, it is the young adult river that particularly concerns us, that stretch between Brampton Bryan and Ludlow. It is here that all the conditions seem to combine to produce very favourable fishing waters particularly for salmonids (this group includes trout and grayling). Here the river is in its prime, but not all of it has been available to be fished and the availability of this 'best' water is restricted even further to the game fisherman. Several factors are responsible for the resulting exclusivity, mostly consequent upon the actions of the landowners.

Leintwardine Bridge

A current sketch map showing the Leintwardine Fishing Club water

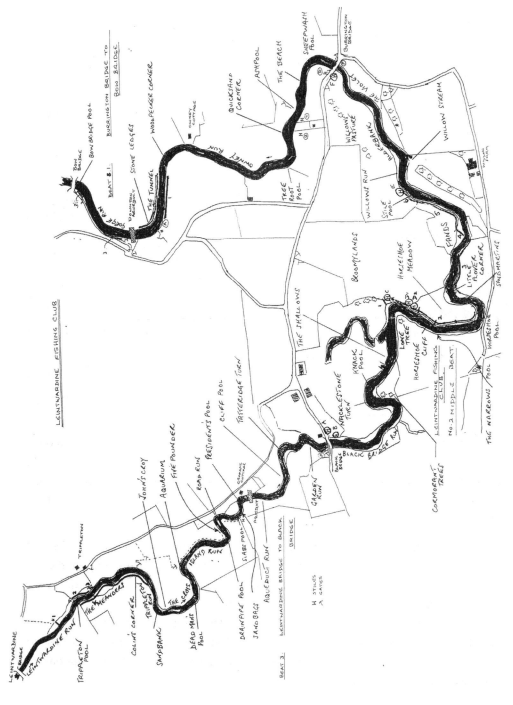

CHAPTER TWO

THE RIGHT TO FISH

It is not necessary to delve too deeply into history for a broad understanding of the development of the estates that border the Teme between Leintwardine and Ludlow, and their right to fish the river. The three private estates along this stretch, Brampton Bryan to Ludlow, are essentially the same today as they were four hundred years ago: the Harley Estate, the Downton Estate and Oakly Park. A very brief and simple résumé will give some idea of the complexities involved concerning fishing rights and boundaries. Very few documents exist to prove the fishing history and several land agents and lawyers have attempted to follow the transfer of fishing rights without total success.

My understanding of their efforts is as follows: Edward Mortimer, who was crowned Edward IV in 1461, had as his ancestral home Wigmore Castle and the ownership of the 'Honour of Wigmore' which included the forests of Bringewood, Mocktree and Deerfold. Following his coronation these lands became Royal Chases which included the rights to the game within. It is reasonable to assume that this included fishing rights. It would appear that the Teme itself delineated the boundaries of Bringewood and Mocktree with other lands, which may have meant a sharing of rights in those areas. A much later tithe map[6] of 1847 shows the parish boundary just below Burrington Bridge criss-crossing the river and in other places running down the middle, all of which has added to the complexities.

The Harley Estate, at Brampton Bryan, dates from the 14th century and is one of the oldest estates in England to have remained in the same family. This estate was among the first to be created from the former Mortimer estates through which the Teme flows.

Oakly Park originally lay within the Bringewood forest but by 1478 appeared to become a separate entity, probably for breeding deer, but still owned by the Crown. Oakly Park remained in Crown hands until 1635 when it was acquired by the Herbert family. By 1751 the Herbert family was linked by marriage to the Clives. Robert Clive bought Oakly in 1767 on his second return from India.

The Downton Estate was a more complex creation. During Elizabeth's reign, the Earl of Essex, Walter Devereux, was awarded the lease of Bringewood and he ordered the building of the ironworks, Bringewood Forge, on the Teme, which became operational about 1580. Gradually the Crown lost interest in the three forests and by 1638 they had been acquired by the Earl of Lindsey. When he was killed at the battle of Edgehill the forests passed to the Earl of Craven who proceeded to draw up plans to enclose various areas, and it is his map of 1662[1] that has helped us identify some of the boundaries of Bringewood and Mocktree.

The Manor of Downton in 1665 lay within the Forest of Deerfold and the Crown leased Downton to Thomas, son of Sir Robert Harley, and the fishing below Leintwardine Bridge was included in the lease. At some time towards the end of the 17th century the Earl of Craven sold Downton to Richard Knight, 'The Iron Master', and leased Bringewood Forge (1698) to him. The sale of the Downton Manor, however, excluded Trippleton, its adjacent 102 acres and its section of fishing on the left bank, as that had already been sold to Thomas Harley. Thomas then let Trippleton to a Mr Edwards on a 99-year lease (ending 1799). Eventually Thomas bequeathed Trippleton to the Harleys of Brampton Bryan.

Richard Knight's business continued to thrive and he was clearly in a position to take advantage of the impecunious state in which many landed gentry found themselves; he could provide the cash they required if they sold their land. He soon added the manors of Burrington, Elton, Leinthall Starkes, Leintwardine, and Whitton to that of Downton, and by so doing needed to come to an arrangement with the Harley Estate to tidy up matters with regard to the fishing rights. The result was a deed, of which an abstract[1] is available, of an exchange of lands between Richard Knight (the Iron Master, and Richard Payne Knight's grandfather) and Edward Harley (2nd Earl of Oxford and Mortimer) in 1741. The deed clearly sets out the division of fishing rights on the Teme below Leintwardine Bridge. Upstream from Criftin Ford the fishing rights went to Harley, and downstream to Richard Knight. Sometime later the Downton Estate bought Trippleton and, so the Knights believed thereafter, the fishing rights as well. The deeds have not been found. However, this was not the last attempt at settlement of the fishing rights and the situation would remain fluid until the 20th century. At this point in the story a short explanation of the involvement of the Knight family with the Teme will help us understand the eventual development of a club and its connection with Downton.

At the time of Richard Knight's death in 1745 the Downton Estate comprised some 10,500 acres, the second largest estate in Herefordshire, and included the Teme from Black Bridge through the Downton Gorge and as far as the neighbouring Oakly Park, owned by Edward Clive, who was soon to be created Lord Powis. The Downton Estate then passed briefly to Knight's eldest son, another Richard, a lawyer, who first lived at Dinham House in Ludlow and then bought Croft Castle. However, he died in 1765 and had no male heir. The Iron Master's second son, the Reverend Thomas Knight, who had lived at Wormsley Grange, was already dead, and this meant that *his* eldest son and Richard Knight's grandson, Richard Payne Knight aged 15, now stood to inherit the fortune once he came of age.

In the absence of his father, the young Richard Payne Knight was guided by his uncle, Edward Knight. The day-to-day management of the Downton Estate went to another

Richard Payne Knight, 1751-1824.

uncle, Samuel Nash. Payne Knight's education flourished under his Uncle Edward's direction. He was an earnest student with a passion for scholarship and developed considerable powers of concentration; as a young man, he made several tours of the continent and rapidly became noted for his largely self-taught classical learning. No doubt he became familiar with the valuable connections his uncle and family had built up throughout the Midlands; Edward had already visited many of the gardens of the gentry, and had started to develop a noted collection of paintings. Payne Knight could hardly avoid developing similar tastes and aspirations. It is unsurprising, therefore, that having reached his majority Payne Knight had the knowledge, maturity, and of course the means, to put his ideas into practice. Built principally to his own design, over the years 1772 to 1778, the mansion at Downton was the first manifestation of his vision.

His interest at Downton, once he had completed his asymmetric house, was to ensure that the area of the gorge below and nearby the Castle retained the sense of wild natural beauty that he so much admired. The river was essential to that vision and he keenly appreciated the assets nature, and his grandfather, had bequeathed to him. Whether that included a desire to lure fish to his hook seems unlikely. He created walks through the gorge but these seem to have been for the benefit of visitors rather than anglers. He wanted his guests to experience intimacy with the natural world: the beauty of unfolding views, encounters with the roaring and tumbling waters in the narrow gorge. Payne Knight enjoyed some sport in his youth and certainly followed the hounds. There are indications that he was keen to preserve the shooting on his estate but there are no direct references that indicate any personal interest in fishing. It is likely that he did appreciate the desire in others to fish, and perhaps that anglers too could appreciate the 'Picturesque' as it can be no coincidence that the stretch of Teme immediately in front of the Castle, where the meadows stretched directly from the front door to the water's edge, were always reserved for Castle guests to fish and were never let out. He was so pleased with the effect he had created in Downton Gorge that he commissioned Thomas Hearne to paint his favourite views in 1785. The one shown here is of Castle Bridge and, perhaps coincidentally, illustrates an excellent spot for fishing.

Castle Bridge by Thomas Hearne c 1785

Richard Payne Knight's election to Parliament in 1780 and his election to the Society of Dilettanti in 1784 naturally took him to London and further widened his circle of friends and acquaintances. There can be little doubt that Payne Knight would have extolled the virtues of his part of the River Teme to his friends in London and elsewhere. Although he may not have been that interested in the fishing, some of his friends would definitely have been encouraged to come and visit and to bring their rods.

The owners of all three estates were not unresponsive to the needs of anglers and most would allocate stretches of water for particular uses. Stretches of water close by the main house would be the 'House' water reserved for family and personal guests. At Downton this was from Castle Bridge to Forge Bridge. Below Forge Bridge and downstream to the boundary with Oakly Park at Tin Mill the water was given over to estate workers and tenants. Upstream from Castle Bridge to Bow Bridge, ie. through the gorge itself, the water was either let as part of the Estate shoot or later given to an individual, usually a personal friend, to manage the fishing of his own group of friends. It follows that the water furthest from the house might be suitable for others to use: from Bow Bridge to the western extent of the estate at Leintwardine.

It is becoming clear that almost by natural selection the conditions to support a club fishery — a thriving fish population, a good clean river, and the provision of access for the angler without interfering with the privacy of the landowner — happily come together in the five miles of water between Leintwardine Bridge and Bow Bridge. When this portion of river first came to be publicly recognised as a 'fishery' is uncertain. None of the pre-1800 maps found so far identify the stretch of water starting at Leintwardine as a 'fishery'. The first to do so are the early Ordnance Survey maps for this area which were published in 1833 and presumably surveyed a year or so before that. Even so the exact extent of the fishery at that time is not clear; judging by the positioning of the label 'Leintwardine Fishery' it is referring to that section of river from Leintwardine Bridge as far as Criftin Ford Bridge (now Black Bridge). We could conclude from this that the fishery already had a well-established reputation in order to qualify for inclusion on the map. It is a reasonable assumption that in earlier days the monks of Wigmore Abbey, only a short walk away, would have made sure that they had a regular supply of fish during their tenure from 1179 until the dissolution of the Abbey in 1530. Thereafter the fishing rights would probably have followed the various changes of ownership until the situation described above when the Knight and Harley Estates both owned land bordering the River Teme, with the Downton Estate having the lion's share.

We could conclude that until the production of more widely available maps and the availability of fishing literature, generally after 1800, the fishing on this part of the Teme would be known only to those who lived close-by, and although well-regarded by those who used it, the fishing would have been largely private and unknown further afield As we shall see, that was soon to change.

Downton Castle by James Sheriff c 1780

Mr Humphry Davy, 1778-1829

CHAPTER THREE

THE DEVELOPING REPUTATION OF THE LEINTWARDINE FISHERY

One of the first widely published references to fishing on the Teme for sport or recreation may have come from a Ludlow doctor, one Richard Bowlker, who wrote a book *The Universal Angler, or That Art Improved, in All Its Parts, Especially in Fly-Fishing* published in London in 1766 in which he lists the Teme as one of the 86 *'principal rivers'* in England (an earlier version of this book may have been published in Ludlow in 1747). It is clear from his chapter on the use of maggots, page 146, that he finds them particularly useful on the Severn, Wye and Teme for catching grayling. He further describes using maggots, or *'gentles'*, as they were known then, for catching grayling of two pounds weight in the river near Oakly Park.

Another author, Thomas Pennant, a fellow of the Royal Society, naturalist and antiquary, in the third volume of his book *British Zoology* , published in 1766, looks at reptiles and fish and in his section on grayling declares that they are to be found in the *"Tame near Ludlow"*; in his description he notes that the grayling is *"a fish of elegant form; less deep than that of trout: the largest we ever heard of was taken near Ludlow, which was above half a yard long, and weighed four pounds six ounces, but this was a very rare instance"*. As we see later this particular quote is picked up and repeated again and again by different authors discussing the subject of grayling or Ludlow or the Teme.

The Reverend William Barker Daniel published in 1801 his second volume of *Rural Sports*, in which he deals with fishing matters. He has clearly read Pennant's book. It would seem he chose to copy both the style, and perhaps some of the detail, of Samuel Taylor's 1800 publication *Angling in all its Branches* which also claims the Teme *"abounds with fine trout and grayling"*. Daniel describes the principal rivers in each county and for the *"Teme or Temd"* notes that, *"This river abounds with excellent Grayling and Trout."* Later in his section on grayling he writes, *"In length the Grayling seldom exceeds sixteen inches. Mr Pennant mentions one taken near Ludlow above half a yard long and weighing four pounds six ounces as a rare instance."*

An individual now entered the scene who was eventually to have a most profound effect on the promotion of the Teme as a fishery. To understand how this man, Sir Humphry Davy, became involved with the Teme it is necessary to describe how he came to know Downton.

When Payne Knight joined the Society of Dilettanti Sir Joseph Banks was the Secretary. Banks went on to become the President of the Royal Society in 1778 until 1820. In 1791 Banks was looking for someone to advise the Board of Agriculture on farming in Herefordshire and consulted Payne Knight who recommended his brother Thomas

Andrew Knight, who was then living at Elton Hall and who was already developing his own reputation as a botanist and agriculturalist. In 1805 Thomas Andrew was elected fellow of the Royal Society. Shortly after Thomas Andrew was introduced to the Society he met Mr Humphry Davy, *"a young philosopher who had distinguished himself by some discoveries in chemistry and the eloquence of whose lectures had made all the fine people in London run after him"*. This description[2] was written by Frances or Fanny, Thomas Andrew's daughter, who was later to become Mrs Stackhouse Acton. She went on to describe Davy as *"a shy young man who blushed and held his head down when he was spoken to and ..... From this time (1805) till his marriage in 1812 he always spent a week at Easter and an-other in August for grayling fishing,*

Thomas Andrew Knight, 1759-1838

either at Elton or at Downton where we removed in 1808. He is said to have been spoiled by the way he was courted by great people, but to us he was always unaffected and affectionate, and there was a combination of poetry and science in his conversation that was peculiarly attractive and which I have never met with in any other person".

Fanny's memoirs make a further, but later, reference, to **Sir** Humphry Davy: *"In the autumn of 1811, a visit from Sir Humphry Davy caused me some amusement. To his surprise, my father* (Thomas Andrew Knight) *heard that Sir Humphry and party had established them-selves at the little Inn at Leintwardine* (possibly The Lion), *instead of coming to the Castle as usual, and a messenger was at once despatched. The next morning Sir Humphry appeared in person to answer the note, and after some hesitation he said that 'a lady was of the party'."* Fanny goes on to say of this lady: *"She was showy in person.....handsomely dressed and high-ly rouged.....no other conclusion could be come to but that she intended to bestow herself and her fortune upon him and we suspected that the latter was the most attractive to him."* Davy and Mrs Apreece were married the following spring. Fanny, despite this disparaging description, clearly had a high regard for Davy and no less than three engravings of Fanny's drawings are included in one edition of the book, *Salmonia*, written by Davy towards the end of his life, a book we shall discuss later.

We should return now to the chronological development of the reputation of the Leint-wardine Fishery by giving as an example the extract shown below from *The Times*, of London, 17th February 1815. The agent who placed this advertisement was convinced that any gentleman reading the paper could not fail to give it their every attention and that any fisherman would not only recognise the names of the rivers mentioned but also the desirability of being able to fish them.

"GENTEEL RESIDENCE, LEINTWARDINE, HEREFORDSHIRE. – To be LET, or SOLD" and the advertisement goes on to describe the location as follows, *".....the situation of Leintwardine is justly esteemed pre-eminent, being an agreeable distance from those justly admired rivers, the Teme and the Clun, which appear beautifully meandering at the foot of the lawn, abounding with the most favourable fish; the views from thence are extensive and varied, and for variety of sporting no spot can be more desirous....."* One military gentleman, General Banas-

Banastre Tarleton,

1754-1833

tre Tarleton, responded at once. In fact his writings and sketches show that he was already well acquainted with Leintwardine and judging by this fragment of a poem he wrote in 1812 with the fishing as well:

> *Adieu sweet river – wandering Teme!*
>
> *No longer by thy crystal stream*
>
> *My days as bright and softly glide*
>
> *As silver grayling thro' thy tide,*
>
> *And trout, in all their speckled pride.*

The General moved into Leintwardine House with his wife Susan and his extremely large collection of war trophies of the American War of Independence, a war in which the General had gained some notoriety but not the rewards that he felt were his due. He was eventually awarded a Baronetcy in 1816 after a great deal of pestering those at Court. His strong friendship with the Prince of Wales, developed on his return from the war, was to have further benefits. Banastre was made Knight Grand Cross of the Order of Bath in the coronation honours list of George IV in 1820. It is from the correspondence arising from this friendship that we find out that not only was George IV aware of the fishing at Leintwardine but had even eaten the grayling caught there which had been sent to him by Tarleton. In a letter copied from the book *The Green Dragoon* we see that the secretary to King George, W Ruppel, had written from the Royal Lodge on 19 September 1820:

"My Dear Tarleton

Your six grayling......arrived in very good condition, and were dressed on Sunday. The King eat (sic) his share, and thought them excellent; You must not however, imagine that we gave you all the praise of having caught them, knowing Lady Tarleton to be an Excellent Angler – I claimed, and obtained for her, half the credit.....The King desires his best regards to you."

We can also see from this letter written to TA Knight at Downton Castle that Tarleton was extremely keen on his fishing and we might surmise that his whole purpose in taking the house was for its connection to the fishery.

"10 Jun 1824

> *My dear Sir,*
>
> *An expression which fell from you (,) a casual one it might be, gives you the trouble of reading this note.*
>
> *You said it was under contemplation to grant the fish in the Teme a jubilee <u>for two years</u>.*
>
> *I acknowledge with truth and gratitude that I have experienced from your uncle and the whole family the greatest liberality and indulgence in rod fishing upon the beautiful stream which flows through Leintwardine.*
>
> *But an abstinence from fly fishing, now my only exercise, at my time of life, would oblige me to take a decisive step, with respect to the house I hold, and my further abode at this place.*
>
> *I pray you, therefore, my dear sir, to give me a definitive notion of the intended jubilee, as the next Lady Day finishes and perhaps will finally terminate my contract with Mr Edwards. I have hitherto enjoyed my diversion in a singular way: no space nor time having precluded my sport, am I therefore (in case of the Jubilee) to consider myself gifted with privilege, or is the interdiction to be general?*
>
> *Yours my dear sir,*

Very sincerely,

Banastre Tarleton"

Tarleton annotated this letter copy with this postscript:
*"The answer was that neither space nor time should interfere
with my sporting in the Teme."*

The letter would seem to indicate that at this stage fishing was still a privilege that was being granted to individuals rather than as a consequence of belonging to a fishing club. Banastre Tarleton also clearly believed the fishing was owned by the Knights. Having received this generous answer to his query there can be little doubt that he continued to fish until close to his death in 1833.

Tarleton made the sketch below:

The River Teme and the quality of the fishing at Leintwardine continued to receive more praise. A further boost to the Fishery's reputation came from Thomas Wright in his *History of Ludlow*, first published in 1822. He included Leintwardine in his description of the *"localities"* and devoted most of the entry to say, *"It lies near the confluence of the Teme and Clun; and from the quantity of fine fish, particularly Greyling, in the surrounding streams, is much resorted to by company from very distant parts, as a fashionable fishing place"* (author's underlining).

Bowlker, whom we mentioned earlier, died in 1799. His son Charles, along with Procter and Jones of Ludlow, and who coincidentally produced Wright's book, *"corrects, improves and greatly enlarges"* his father's original text (probably in 1824) and re-publishes Bowlker's book in 1826 as *Bowlker's Art of Angling*. We then find in the chapter on *"Greyling"* that the Teme near Ludlow is identified as one of three rivers where the grayling *"abounds"*; a clear attempt at promotion. Procter and Jones go on to write the sentence that has become very familiar: *"The largest greyling ever caught in England was taken at Ludlow; it measured half a yard in length and weighed four pounds eight ounces"*. Thomas Pennant's original wording of *"a very rare instance"* has of course been ignored. A further *"new, revised"* edition was printed in 1854, again in Ludlow, but this time by R Jones of Broad Street, and this gives much the same information but adds a description of the Teme: *"This river is one of the most celebrated in the kingdom for its trout and greyling; at Leintwardine is the far famed stream alluded to by Sir Humphry Davy in his Salmonia, or Days of Fly-fishing."*

This quote brings us to the publication of *Salmonia*. Elizabeth Inglis-Jones in her work *The Knights of Downton Castle* wrote of Sir Humphry Davy, *"this passionately keen fisherman in his zeal to outwit his prey wore a suit of green cloth and a coal-heaver's hat dyed to match and bristling with flies, a costume designed to harmonize with the woods and pastures along the banks of the river. Although, as so often happens, the fish seldom fulfilled his expectations. His visits to Downton and the quiet pools and swirling rapids of the Teme had a tantalizing, recurrent magic of their own that he never forgot though they lay so far behind him. Back in London, on a fine, sunny day as he watched the flies revolving in the air, his longing would become so acute that he would exclaim aloud, 'What such a day would be worth at Downton!' "*

Davy paid some noble tributes to Downton and the River Teme in 1828, just as the end of his life drew near, in the book *Salmonia, or Days of Fly-Fishing*. He invited Mrs Frances Stackhouse Acton, Thomas Andrew Knight's daughter, to contribute three engravings to some later editions of *Salmonia*. The one below is of Downton Castle.

Downton Castle. A sketch by Mrs Stackhouse Acton

Davy also had one character in *Salmonia*, Poietes, describe the situation at Hay Mill, another feature on the Downton Estate, that lay half a mile downstream of Bow Bridge:

26

Poietes. This spot is really very fine; - the fall of the water – the picturesque mill – the abrupt cliff, and the bank covered with noble oaks above the river, compose a scene such as I have rarely beheld in this island.

Halietus. We will wander a little longer through the walks. There you will enter a subterraneous passage in the rock beyond the mossy grotto. Behold the castle or mansion house clothed in beautiful vegetation of which the red creeper is most distinct, rises above on the hill! After we have finished our walk and our fishing, I will, if you please, take you to the house and introduce you to the worthy master, whom to know is to love, and to whom all good anglers should be grateful, and who has a stronger claim to a more extensive gratitude – that of this country – by his scientific researches on vegetable nature, which are not merely curious but useful, and which have already led to great improvements in our fruits and plants, and generally extended the popularity of horticulture.

There would seem little doubt that despite the introduction given by Bowlker's book it was the widely read *Salmonia* and Sir Humphry in 1828 that promoted the Teme at Leintwardine as a premier fishery. From the frequent quotes we can gather there was hardly a fishing author in England who had not read Davy's book and henceforth many authors of fishing books would continue to pick up on the theme that the Teme offered excellent grayling fishing. Thomas Boosey in his book of 1835, *Piscatorial Reminiscences and Gleanings*, quotes *Sporting Magazine* in an article of April 1835, "*Ludlow appears the head quarters [for grayling fishing], before they [gentlemen anglers] set off, in April, for the principality. The public conveyances begin to move to the watering places [spas]. The Terme [sic], the Corve, the Clun, and the Onny are the principal streams in the immediate neighbourhood of Ludlow. The grayling here appears brisk and frolicsome, swimming in the middle of the water. The Terme bears the palm for grayling; the Corve for the most delicious pink trout, and fine eels, chub, etc, etc. The sportsman's localities are everywhere at his command in the vicinity of Oakley Park, through the great liberality of the proprietor, the Hon RH Clive.*"

Edward Jesse in his interesting book, *An Angler's Rambles*, published in 1836, recalls "*scenes and circumstances which took place in my younger days*" and devotes a twelve-page chapter to *Grayling Fishing near Ludlow*. He too picked up the one sentence of Davy's in *Salmonia* with regard to the Teme which seems to strike a lasting resonance with many readers, "*and there is no stream in England more productive of grayling,*" and goes on to say, "*The author of Salmonia has made Leintwardine and the Teme interesting localities to all anglers, and especially to those who have had no previous practice in grayling fishing*". The chapter is not however a description of one of Jesse's own 'circumstances' but rather the account of a person only identified by his initials ER who describes himself as follows: "*Living as I do on the banks of the Team, or Teme, and with a most liberal permission to angle both at Leintwardine and Oakley Park, I am perhaps one of the most determined persecutors of the finny tribe....*" ER set forth his own views on grayling and did not wholly agree with Davy's descriptions, ER thinks he is a "*better philosopher than fisherman*", but these disagreements aside some interesting comments are made that help us understand the circumstances that applied to the Leintwardine Fishery prior to any mention of a club being formed. ER inferred that fishing on the Teme was already a popular activity as he commented that the Leintwardine water is *"so much fished"*. This comment is of course relative. For some fishermen just one other angler in sight would make the water crowded. ER supplies a chart of the fish he caught, or at least the ones he brought home, in the summer of 1833, and the interest here is less the number that he caught but rather how he identifies the waters he fished: Oakly Park, Leintwardine, Downton Castle and Little Teme. He has clearly made the acquaintance of the owners of all three local estates. The Little Teme was a common term for the river above the confluence with the Clun and on the Harley Estate. He describes the flies he used but admits that he did not tie them himself but that *"they were made by a man at Ludlow, well known as 'Jones the fisherman', two shillings a dozen"*. He then goes on to reveal his secret for grayling fishing;

"You will always see any person who is a stranger to grayling fishing, and I may add many who have fished for them all their lives, when the water is very low and clear, immediately betake themselves to the streams and curls, from the idea that the fish will see your line in the dead water. Let them do so; they will perhaps catch a few trout, and some shett grayling. But go yourself to a deep dead part of the river, never mind if there is no wind, or if the sun is hot; use the finest gut you can procure (even if you give a guinea a knot for it), and two flies, and when you have thrown your line as light as gossamer, let it sink for eight or ten inches. You will not see arise, but a slight curl in the water, which by a little practice you will understand quite as well, and when you strike you will have the pleasure of finding a pounder or more tugging away at the end of your line. This is the real secret of grayling fishing…."

A Topographical Dictionary of England, published in 1848, has entries for both Leintwardine and Burrington and both note the fishing. The Leintwardine entry reads *"from the quantity of fine fish, particularly graylings, with which these rivers* (Teme and Clun) *abound, it is much resorted to as a fishing place."*

It would seem very likely that the friends and acquaintances of the Knight family having read such intelligence, and knowing that the Teme flowed through the Downton Estate, could only be encouraged to seek for themselves the 'liberality' of Thomas Andrew Knight. Exactly when the transition took place from gentlemen anglers asking permission to fish on the Downton waters to the payment of subscriptions to a club for the privilege, is not certain. Trying to determine the date for this is our next task and in the absence of documentary evidence this will mean interpreting what we do know.

William (Billy) Jones of Ludlow
Angler and well known maker
of artificial fishing flies.

CHAPTER FOUR

THE ORIGINS OF THE CLUB

The creation of private estates throughout the country as a result of the enclosure of common land from the mid-18th century onwards saw fishing on all rivers become largely controlled by the landowners and their agents. The concept of 'common' water did not exist. A river belonged to someone, as did the fish in it, and to fish without permission of the owner was illegal. Sporting rights were rigorously protected and policed by the gamekeepers and river keepers employed by the estates. Most estate owners were magistrates who made quite sure that the law was upheld. The consequence was that fishing became as exclusive to the gentry as once upon a time deer-hunting had been to Royalty. Friends and house guests of the estate owners would naturally be offered every access to their rivers. The only way for others to access the water was to obtain permission from the owner or his agent. So you had to know who they were, and they in their turn were unlikely to consent until they were satisfied they knew you were going to prove an 'acceptable' individual. In other words connections and introductions needed to be made and effected, and then hopefully you would be invited to fish or granted access to do so.

At first permission would have been largely restricted to those friends, and friends of friends, in the local area, say, within a day's horseback ride. As roads improved and inns catered for 'discerning folk' it became practical to travel half way across the country even by horse and carriage for short visits to a chosen fishery. The same discerning folk had become used to making excursions to see 'picturesque sights', or to go on 'sketching expeditions', or 'take the waters' and presumably it was not too difficult for the male members of the family to arrange with friends or acquaintances some fishing along the way.

Richard Payne Knight's guests at Downton Castle included Sir William Hamilton, a known fisherman, who is documented as visiting Downton on at least two occasions, the last being in 1802. It would be difficult to conceive that he would have been unable to resist a few casts on the Downton waters. As the pursuit became more popular estates would have had to formalise arrangements as it must have been time-consuming to deal with a myriad of requests. Richard Payne Knight was away from Downton so often that permission to fish would almost certainly have been given by his agent or servants.

Thomas Andrew, who succeeded his brother at Downton, seems to have dealt with the matter straightforwardly and every report praises his liberality in granting his personal permission. Guests, such as Sir Humphry Davy, used the full extent of the Downton water which we know at that time extended upstream from Tin Mill, near Forge Bridge, then ran in front of Downton Castle, through the gorge and past Bow Bridge and up to Black Bridge.   We know the upstream extent because of the deed of exchange[1] between Harley and Knight in 1741 as mentioned earlier.   This deed settled the fishing rights between the two estates: *"Edward Earl of Oxford and Earl Mortimer…..presents, bargained, sold and conveyed unto the said Richard Knight…..that the Fishery and Right of Fishing…..from a place upon the said river called Criffin (sic) **down** the said river…..through the parishes of…..Burrington and Downton.   …..Richard Knight…..granted, bargained, sold, released and confirmed…..unto Edward…..all that Fishery and right of fishing…..from…..Criffin Ford **up** the said river..."*

Thomas Andrew Knight was a well-liked and generous man, and it is the author's impression that it is unlikely he would have wished to organise fishing in any other way than to grant permission to those guests or friends that requested it. Davy's reference to Thomas Andrew in *Salmonia* *"to whom all good anglers should be grateful"* seems to support this. There is no evidence either that his neighbours, Harley, above the Downton Waters, or Clive, below at Oakly Park, did other than grant permission to fish on request.

Circumstances changed in 1838 when Thomas Andrew died and left no surviving male

heir. His widow Frances continued to live at Downton Castle but the Downton Estate was run by Sir William Rouse Boughton, resident at Downton <u>Hall</u>, and held in trust for his second son Andrew who by the terms of the 'male-entailed' will made earlier by Richard Payne Knight was to inherit the Castle. One might presume that the arrangements in place for the management of the Downton Castle Estate continued for a while. There is no sign in a Downton Castle ledger, 1841-1851, of any payments for labour or materials connected with fishing, whereas for game there are numerous entries.   The only reference to fishing is for expenses paid in 1842 to the agent, J Corbett, for attendance at the magistrates' court at Wigmore in order to

Sir William Rouse Boughton, 1788-1856

prosecute Jones of Ludlow for fishing illegally; unfortunately the court records no longer exist and we cannot make any further inference from this other than that it was normal for any land-owner to prosecute poachers. The Downton Hall accounts for that period are not complete and no reference has been found to support the idea that a club had been formed at this time.

In the absence of any contemporary document stating when the Leintwardine Fishing Club (LFC) was founded we can only cast around for clues. The angling literature of the day provides an excellent source. In 1848 Edward Jesse published a second book, *The British Angler's Manual*, firstly written by Thomas Hofland, but rewritten and enlarged by Jesse who dates the preface 1847. In this book, on page 111, he adds an editor's note: "*The Teme is decidedly the best river in England for grayling, and the river runs through some of the most beautiful scenery in it.*" It would seem that on this occasion, unlike the author of the original publication, he may have been to the area as in another note he recommends flies to use on the Teme in August and September, and comments that Jones of Ludlow makes a large brown fly called the Seg-Fly and comments, "*a killing fly it is*". (This is the same Billy Jones we noted earlier and may be the same Jones who was prosecuted.) The essential point for our narrative is that Jesse still does not mention that any club had control of the water.

Hewett Wheatley in January 1849 describes in his book *Rod and Line* how "*a fine trout was lying close to the stonework of a weir, at Leintwardine, on the Teme*"… He also mentions that he "*killed several dishes of very fine grayling*", and in the next paragraph comments in regard to the use of the grasshopper "*that a most remarkable regulation has lately been made by a Club in possession of one of the best pieces of Grayling water in England*". He goes on to disparage the allowing of grasshopper fishing (see Appendix Three) between 1st October and 1st February and calls the rule "*a most curious regulation for a Club of Grayling fishers*". Whilst he does not directly connect the club with Leintwardine, it is probably fair to conclude that he is referring to the Leintwardine Fishing Club and that this is the first oblique reference to the Club in literary circles.

That the establishment of a club was permitted probably results from the fact that from 1838 to 1856 the close ties of ownership found at Oakly or Brampton Bryan were not present at Downton due to the estate being held in trust. To speculate further, in all probability it was to the mutual benefit of both landowner and keen anglers that fishing at Downton was formalised. After all the water was not exactly lapping the doorstep and the landlord was unlikely to be disturbed. Indeed the distance between Castle and river may have made it more acceptable to allow this 'experimental adventure' into commerce as we must note that neither of the other two estates ever took up such a project.

The earliest direct evidence found so far which formally documents the existence of the Club is the agreement[1] in 1855 between The Right Honourable Jane Elizabeth Harley, Lady Langdale and James Ackers, Treasurer of the Leintwardine Fishing Club. The agreement sets out the terms for the Club to rent that portion of the fishery on the River Teme, belonging to Lady Langdale, between Leintwardine Bridge and Black Bridge, and that the Club, "*their friends agents and servants had the liberty to fish with rods and lines but not with nets, nightlines or spears, and to take and kill fish in a fair, proper and sportsmanlike*" *manner at all proper and seasonable times of the year".* The agreement was for the term of one year, computed from August and from year to year until six months' notice was given to terminate the agreement. This agreement is also the first time that we see the use of the words The Leintwardine Fishing Club. Was the Club formed in or around 1855?

Anecdotally Club members and past Presidents have always thought that the Club was formed in 1811, but offered no evidence in support of the claim. The first person to be associated with the Club, other than Lady Langdale, is James Ackers. Is it possible that *he* formed the Club perhaps earlier than 1855, using solely the Downton water? Investigating Ackers would seem to offer a worthwhile line of inquiry. Who was he? Where did he come from? How did he get involved with the Leintwardine Fishery? Did he have the opportunity to start a fishing club?

The Club knows no more than his name. Much of the mystery, or lack of information, stems from the fact that he was born in Manchester to one James Coops on 4 August 1811 and was given the same name as his father. He was educated at Manchester Grammar School and then at Marlborough before going on to Trinity College, Cambridge. It is from the Cambridge biographies of graduates, *Alumni Cantabrigienses*, that we learn that *"He (Coops) assumed by 'sign manual' the surname of Ackers, in lieu of Coops, on succeeding by will to a large fortune from James Ackers Esq., of Larkhill Saltford, 1827".* On 9th January 1833 he married Mary Anne (née Williams), of a Cheshire family, and took up residence at a house called The Heath, near Clee St Margaret, Shropshire. He would have been 22 years old.

The Heath, now called Heath House, is situated in the hamlet called Heath, and is close by the site of an abandoned medieval village in a delightful rural spot with extensive views over Corvedale. It may be that it was the proximity to both nature and an historic site that prompted James Ackers to become an early member of the Ludlow Natural History Society, the forerunner to the Ludlow Museum. This society was formed in 1833, and by 1834 had 59 subscribers. Interestingly the subscribers' list included Sir William Rouse Boughton, Thomas Andrew Knight, and the Reverend John Rocke, who was to become a long-standing member of the LFC. In the minutes of the second annual meeting of the Society in 1836 Ackers is thanked, amongst many others, for donating to the society's nascent collection; he gave a stuffed pine marten.

As James Ackers was a relatively new arrival in the area we could be forgiven for thinking that he thought a connection with this group of people was an excellent way to socialise with the great and the good of the county. He would certainly have needed their patronage to contemplate standing for Parliament, which seems to have been his intention. At any rate, within a few years he stood as the second member for Ludlow. Beriah Botfield, the first member for Ludlow, was also a subscriber to the same society, and both of them entered Parliament in 1841. Ackers maintained his involvement in the society, and we can see from the minutes that in company with Sir William, and two others, James Ackers was made a Vice-President, possibly, one suspects, in recognition of the £25 donation (approaching £2,000 in today's currency) each gave to the society.

Ackers had other opportunities to make himself known to the gentry in the area and to Sir William in particular. He was a steward at Ludlow Racecourse and was involved with such prestigious events as the Festival of Choirs held in 1835. It may be just coincidence but at this time Sir William's second son Andrew entered Trinity College, Cambridge – the same college Ackers had attended. Sir William had gone to Oxford.

James Ackers left Parliament at the next general election in 1847 and bought Prinknash Park in Gloucestershire which might encourage one to think it unlikely that he would wish to fish in this area. However, he continued his subscription to the Ludlow Natural History Society until 1857 despite living a distance away, so it seems entirely reasonable to expect him to be in a position to be involved with the Leintwardine Fishery.

Around 1846 there is another individual who connects the Natural History Society, Ackers, Downton, Leintwardine and the LFC, and that is Colonel John Colvin. Colonel Colvin moved into Leintwardine House (Tarleton's old home) in the early 1840s after his return from India. He may already have met James Ackers when he first moved to Ludlow and met and married the sister of a fellow soldier, but he certainly would have known him by 1846 when they were both members of the Ludlow Natural History Society. Colonel Colvin's name appears on the first members' list we have of 1863.

We could conclude, therefore, that the foundation of the Club was prior to 1855 and conceivably as early as 1836. By 1836 Ackers may have known both TA Knight and Sir William, and might possibly have been instrumental in setting up a club. However, it seems unlikely. The argument for a later start date for the establishment of the Fishing Club gets stronger as the years go by. Ackers was only 25 years old in 1836 and had only been in the area for three years. Thomas Andrew Knight died in 1838, and we have argued he had no need to form a club, and it was only then that Sir William takes on responsibility for the Downton Estate and its fishing. Ackers entered Parliament in 1841 and left in 1847. His wife Mary died in 1848. The first mention of the Club in any publication is in 1849, with the reference already mentioned in *Rod and Line*. The last angling book that *fails* to include any mention of the LFC is in 1847 in the *British Angler's Manual*. Thus circumstantial evidence makes it reasonable to plump for 1848 as the year that the Leintwardine Fishing Club was founded.

Leintwardine on the Teme, from a sketch by Mrs. Stackhouse Acton.

A further engraving from *Salmonia* showing the Lion Hotel

To the left of the bridge

Lady Langdale,   -1872

CHAPTER FIVE

THE EARLY YEARS 1848 TO 1870

Having made the assumption that the Leintwardine Fishing Club was established in 1848, our next assumption is that Sir William Rouse Boughton, the riparian owner of the Downton Waters, would have been asked by James Ackers to be the President of the Club. It would have been unheard of not to have a president. It certainly would have been the right thing to do as well as being eminently practical to build a relationship with the landowner. Thus Sir William became the Club's first President, with Ackers as his Treasurer and probably Secretary as well.

There is no real documentary evidence available for the first two years of this new Club except for one scrap which may just be co-incidental: in the following year, 1849, some Downton Castle accounts[3] show that two sums of money were spent on expenses for the prosecution at Wigmore of two individuals for poaching fish (again, a man called Jones in August, and Elisha Fisher in October). Frustratingly, no further details are known but this entry could indicate a new regime is in place.

In 1850 Frances Knight, Thomas Andrew Knight's wife, who had been living at Downton Castle, died. Andrew Rouse Boughton, now aged 24, prepared to take up his inheritance by moving into the Castle, in anticipation also of his marriage to Eliza Severne. There is plenty of evidence that the Rouse Boughton family are now actively refurbishing and rebuilding parts of Downton Castle. A new entrance and tower, a ballroom and a chapel are just some of the innovations. A visiting American, Anna Fay, in January 1852 provides a good description of the house. It must have been a busy time, and one could speculate that fishing matters at Downton were not a priority; it is reasonable to presume that Andrew Rouse Boughton, who does not seem to have any history as a sportsman, was only too happy to continue with the arrangement his father had set up with James Ackers.

We have little information as to how the Club was managed at this time but a letter written some 45 years later by Andrew Rouse Boughton Knight, which we shall see in due course, does suggest that at the start of the Club's existence it was Ackers himself who decided who might become a member rather than, as would be expected, the members themselves. The water they fished would have been that owned by the Downton Estate and was probably only the stretch from Bow Bridge to Black Bridge.

A little later in 1853 Alfred Harley, 6th Earl of Oxford, died and Lady Langdale, his sister, inherited the Harley Estate. It is perhaps this event that is the catalyst for the idea to extend the Club water, and which leads to the negotiations that culminate in the agreement in 1855 between Lady Langdale and Ackers mentioned in the last chapter.

The next milestone is the death of the first President on 22nd May 1856. When Sir William died it is very probable that James Ackers took on the roles of both President and Treasurer as is noted later on the 1863 members' list. Andrew Rouse Boughton, although now the owner of the Downton Estate, was probably too busy to be concerned with the management of the fishing and was content to let matters lie. In a very short period of time he was occupied with changing his name, adding by Royal Licence the name *Knight* in 1857, getting married in 1858 and moving into Downton Castle. Proof that the Club continued lies in the record of payments[4] made to Mr Rodney Ward, the Harley Estate agent: £9 was paid first in 1856, and then each half year at Candlemas (February 2nd) and Lammas (August 1st) by Mr Ackers who was noted in the accounts as *"the tenant of the Leintwardine Fishery"*.

It is interesting to note from the Ludlow Natural History Society records that at the time Ackers withdrew from the Society in 1857, Andrew Rouse Boughton Knight joined and paid to become a life member. The coincidence of this fact and the recent death of Sir William makes one think that a change of relationships took place, and one which effected the LFC. This change also supports the premise that James Ackers took over the presidency from this point, 1856/ 1857.

No written record of Acker's tenure as President has survived. There are no minute books or Club member lists. Much later, in 1903, we learn that it was thought that in 1856 there were 25 members, seven of whom were local, who paid £10 a year to fish. The same letter indicates that Ackers had been paying rent for the fishery, first to Sir William some years prior to 1856, and later to Andrew Rouse Boughton Knight. It is not until 1861 that James Ackers' name appears in the Downton Castle accounts books as the tenant of a cottage at Bow Bridge, but there is no mention of any fishery rental. It is probable that previous rental payments were made to Sir William's Downton Hall accounts, and it took until 1861 for Andrew Rouse Boughton Knight to start asserting some control over the Club and to make changes to the arrangements. The first change was probably an increase in the rent.

The next fishing-related entry in the Downton accounts[3] is in 1862, a payment of £90 for the Leintwardine Fishery for a year, and one cottage at Black Bridge for £5. The next year the rent is £100 for the Fishery and two cottages at Black Bridge. Clearly the location of the cottages at Black Bridge is better than Bow for the fishing, but we do not know whether they were used for housing a keeper or as a 'fishing box' for visiting fishermen or both. We do know that Edward Meredith, river keeper, was shown on the census return of 1861 living in one of the cottages and it would seem unlikely that Ackers would wish to live in such close proximity to the Club's employee, or in such modest accommodation. It is more probable that Ackers was renting both cottages for Club servants.

The 1863 Club list, our first and earliest Club record, shows that despite the awakening of interest in the Club by Andrew Rouse Boughton Knight, James Ackers remained the President but acknowledged his landlord by appointing him an Honorary Member. We could presume that this situation continued for the remainder of Acker's tenure as payments for the rental of both fishery and cottages continue for the next six years without change. After Acker's death his son's name, Benjamin St John Ackers, appears in the account books.

As for who else may have belonged to the Club at this time, it is reasonable to assume that the list would have included the three men who appear on the 1863 list: Colonel John Colvin, John Rocke and WH Sitwell, who was another member of the Natural History Society. Another name is that of a self-confessed Club member, Archdeacon William Lea. William Lea provides us with a very particular and graphic picture of fishing on the Club water. He was a contributor to the magazine *The Fishing Gazette*. Later his friends collected together his contributions into a book. This book, *Fishing Reminiscences,* was printed after his death (1889) at Kidderminster in 1892 and includes an article entitled *"A Day at Leintwardine"*. He was not specific with regard to the date of any particular visit and clearly the reminiscence is an amalgamation of many visits over several years. He is not listed as a member of the Club on the 1863 list; he may have fished with the Club in the period 1856 to 1863 whilst holding the position of the Vicar of St Peter's, Droitwich (1849-1887), not too far away from Leintwardine. However, despite not being a member for half a decade he must have kept his ear to the ground as he was able to report, in the same article, and quite accurately, that in 1869 the Club's lease had expired and that the *"proprietor of the river took the water into his own hands"*. The article is reproduced in full at Appendix Five as it provides an excellent description of the water and a unique insight into fishing on the Teme at that time, and yet one that could easily describe fishing on the same water today. One extract:

"It was a heavy dull morning, and thunder was evidently about, and the fish were in the sulks, for I whipped for four hours for three small grayling, going over the loveliest streams which it is possible to imagine and not seeing a fish move in the water though I knew there were cartloads lying somewhere on the bottom."

Lea comments that in the Club water the grayling greatly outnumber the trout and suggests that the keeper's work should be to hatch trout and turn them into the river. He also mentions fishing at the "*Horse-shoe Meadow*" and at "*Temptation Hole*" at the "*great weir hole*", names that echo down the ages but are difficult to pin down to the modern river. The Archdeacon could not only describe the Leintwardine water well, he could also sketch. He made several sketches of the Leintwardine area including the one shown below of Bow Bridge.

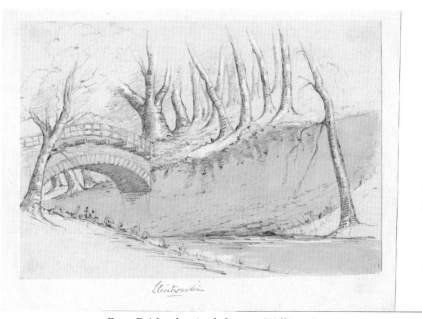

Bow Bridge by Archdeacon William Lea

The keeper at the time, according to Lea, is "*Rufus*", so called because of his florid face or red hair. However, later on he refers to "*old Stock, the keeper*". They may have been the same person. Edward Meredith was witness to the catch Lea made of a trout of 3lbs 4 ounces in one year, and another of just under 3lbs in the following year. Lea records taking the fish to the *"tap room"* (probably of The Lion Hotel in Leintwardine) in order to confound the locals who did not believe that any fish of that size still existed in the river.

Lea suggests that the Leintwardine Fishery may have been becoming over-fished. It is perhaps at this stage in the development of the Club, 1858, a decade after its formation, that James Ackers, who now has full control of the Club, widens the membership from a circle of his friends to include those who apply to join the Club having heard of the Leintwardine Fishery's reputation. This development may have been forced by the times;. Since 1860 magazines such as 'Baily's' (*Baily's Magazine of Sports and Pastimes*) had provided sporting gentlemen with the intelligence necessary to pursue their sport and invariably encouraged the angler to seek out fresher waters than those found in the now-polluted Thames or the over-fished streams closer to cities. The railway network now covered much of the country with several stations close to Leintwardine. Ludlow station opened in April 1852, Kingsland in 1857, Hopton Heath and Bucknell in 1861. We have already noted that many people were actively fishing on the Teme, and it is probably these pressures that force James Ackers to formalise the membership and pro-cedures of the Club.

A closer examination of the 1863 list shows that the 25-strong membership more or less split into three distinct geographic groups. Eight 'locals' living within 10 miles, a further eight from in and around London, and the remainder from places in between. It is un-surprising that fishermen are eager to join the Club from all over the country when the reputation of the fishery is being promoted strongly in magazines and books.

Thus we arrive at the point in 1863 when the Leintwardine Fishing Club is issued with a List of Members and a set of *Rules and Regulations*. These rules are believed to be the earliest known set of rules to be printed and distributed to members of any fishing club existing in the country (a copy is shown at page 83). Both documents show clearly that James Ackers is President *and* Treasurer of the Leintwardine Fishing Club. Unfortunately there is no record of Club activities at this time, and we have to turn back to the fishing literature of the day.

The Fisherman's Magazine, edited briefly by Henry Cholmondeley-Pennell, in an article on grayling informs its readers in 1864 that *"throughout its course, or at all events from Knighton, the Teme is generally pretty strictly preserved, more particularly from Leintwardine to Tenbury, but leave to fish can generally be obtained by gentlemen on application to the proprie-tors. The best grayling fishing is, we believe, at Leintwardine, and from thence to Ludlow, but there is good water all the way to Tenbury, and occasionally to within a few miles of Worcester."*

Edward Hamilton was another fishing author that knew the Teme and the Club waters well during this period. He was probably not a member of the Club, but clearly enjoyed the privilege of fishing Club waters for grayling: *"My chief experience in this delightful sport has been on the Teme at Leintwardine, which I fished every September and October for sixteen*

years, and glorious sport it was".   His charming book *Recollections of Fly Fishing for Salmon,
Trout and Grayling* in an extensive reference to the Club tells us that he fished the full
length of the Club water and also that of Downton and Oakly.   *"The famous places of my
time, may, in all probability, be things of the past. Old friends and fishermen may recall to their
memory the run above the old milking bridge, the upper part o'ershadowed on both sides by
alders.   Ah, what lovely fellows have I inveigled from under their roots! Then the ford below the
Rat Ditch ; General Drummond's Pool ; the Artist's Bathing-place, famous for trout ; Hamilton's
Bath; the Run above the New Weir; Temptation Pool; the Black Bridge, and a host of others"*.

Hamilton had an obvious affection for both the fishing and, as he quotes *Salmonia*, the
scenery around Leintwardine as well.   His advice, as shown in this passage, seems
sound:

*"Patience in grayling fishing always has its reward.   I have seen men change and change their
flies, disgusted at seeing fish rising under their feet and not taking their fly, until they would give
up and go away.   Don't go on whipping over these fish; change the venue; probably at the next
stream or pool the first cast with the fly, useless a few minutes ago, will take a fish, and then
another and another.   Don't be in a hurry to change your flies, and if fish are capricious as in this
way, fish with only one fly. I have killed many a fish in these still pools with one small fly and the
finest of lines, letting the fly drop lightly on the water, and then allow it to sink.   At the slightest
movement in the water, strike very gently, and lo! you are fast into a fish; when you have taken a
fish or two, particularly out of a still pool, leave it for a while, or make a sketch, or eat your lunch
if the time is come, and then fish it again and you will have another or two.   The lower part of the
river at Burrington Bridge affords capital sport, and in a different way to the upper part.   The
river runs through masses of rock with rapid runs and deep pools and high trees.   Wading is
obligatory, and the under cast a necessity.   Big grayling are there, and require nice handling.
Ah! what a river it is, and in what beautiful scenery"*

His choice of flies may still have relevance for some today: *"What fish have I taken out of
the river below, opposite the keeper's cottage and on to the Old Weir! In fact either on the upper
water or on the lower below the Black Bridge, with favourable weather and small flies, light tackle
and patience, you may, or could, fill the biggest creel you can well carry.*

For the Teme, my favourite flies were the following: —

Whirling Blue.	*August Brown.*
Whirling Dun.	*Yellow Dun.*
Blue Dun.	*Iron Blue.*
Silver Twist.	*Claret Spinner.*
Willow Fly.	*Red Tag.*
Orange Tag.	*Pale Evening Blue.*

In August and September: the Duns and August Brown, and Silver Twist and Pale Evening Blue.

End of September, and October; Willow and Wheatley's two flies — Claret Spinner and Red Tag."

Hamilton may also be providing some clues as to the location of the named fishing spots, as not only are they much the same as those that William Lea records, but it would seem from the order in which he names them that they are probably all on the upper water.

One can only admire these gentleman anglers of the past; not only can they fish and write about fishing with great clarity but many, like Hamilton and Lea, are also accomplished artists.   We have already seen Lea's sketch of Bow Bridge, and Hamilton's woodcut of the Teme and Leintwardine Bridge is shown at the front of this book.

All would seem well.   Then in 1868 James Ackers died.

Despite the demise of Ackers, the payments originally agreed in 1855 continued at the same value to the Harley accounts, reasonably regularly, despite some arrears, until February 1870.   Although there is no evidence to say who then acted as President, his son had been a member of the Club since 1863 and he almost certainly assumed his father's mantle.   He took on the payment of the rent, as noted earlier, and it is clear the Club continued to exist.

A note in a later document issued from the Downton Estate office indicates that the Club's river keeper had, at sometime in 1870, killed game adjacent to the river and that Andrew Rouse Boughton Knight objected.   Reading between the lines it would seem that management of the Club was such that Andrew Rouse Boughton Knight was increasingly unhappy with arrangements, and the above incident was a catalyst for change.   We can only assume that he did not get much satisfaction from dealing with Acker's son, Benjamin St John, and set out to take the Club into his own hands and renegotiate the terms with Lady Langdale through her agent, Rodney Ward.   The Leintwardine Fishing Club is about to enter the era of the third President, Andrew Rouse Boughton Knight (ARBK).

Downton Castle c 1870

CHAPTER SIX

ANDREW ROUSE BOUGHTON KNIGHT

1870-1909

Andrew Rouse Boughton Knight (who we will now refer to as ARBK) was 44 years old, married with six children and had now been 'Lord of the Manor' for over ten years. He had refurbished the Castle, laid out the gardens in the latest Victorian style and had built the new church of St Giles in Downton. Hitherto he does not appear to have had any known interest in fishing other than being listed as an Honorary Member since 1863. So how is it, we might wonder, that he now takes over the full management of the Club?

We have speculated that ARBK found the Fishing Club in some disarray following the death of James Ackers. Benjamin St John Ackers had apparently taken on responsibility for the Club but as he was working at Lincoln's Inn and also presumably taking up the reins at Prinknash Park he was probably too busy to pay due attention to the fishing. Perhaps members of ARBK's club in London, the United University Club, brought to his attention some sense of disquiet. More likely it was due to the urging of his friends and neighbours at Downton for someone to take the lead. Several members were local: Colonel Colvin at Leintwardine, Willoughby H Sitwell at Ferney Hall and the two Rockes, the Reverend Owen Rocke and Mr John Rocke of Clungunford. ARBK seems to have been a man who liked to do things 'properly', someone who would not like to be associated with anything which others might find less than satisfactory. He refers later to the fact that *"Mr Ackers permit* (ted) *friends of his own choosing to fish on payment of £10 per an."* It may have been this that offended his sense of how a club should be constituted and was the most important issue he wished to put right. It is possible that he, or some member, did not find all of Mr Ackers' friends socially acceptable. He may well have

43

come under pressure from personal friends to give them access to the fishing. The constraint of having Club members, whom perhaps he did not know, taking up positions and thereby denying his friends their opportunity may have been irksome. This is all speculation. Whatever the reasons members gave for wanting a change, the only way to sort it out was for the President of the Club to conduct business in a manner that was beyond reproach. How ARBK arranged the reformation is not known. Did he invite everyone to rejoin at the new rate of subscription or only some? He may have decided to cull some names, perhaps Crawshay, who was a tenant of his, in order to make space for a friend such as the Reverend John Rogers, who like several other members chosen by ARBK was a fellow student at Cambridge. He no doubt had many advisers and probably leaned heavily on John George Rodney Ward, Lady Langdale's agent, for the management of the Harley Estates. Certainly by the end of October 1869 ARBK was writing from Buxton to Rodney Ward on the matter.

From the letter below it would seem that ARBK gave little option to Club members and set out to remove the right to fish on his waters on the old terms, thus effectively ending the connection with the Ackers family. Regrettably, the letter to Ackers cannot be found but it was evidently quite sharp, to the point, and icily polite. ARBK's letter to Rodney Ward[4] in March 1870 indicates that he allowed no argument, had made his plan and was implementing it with some satisfaction:

"My Dear Sir,

I shall be much obliged if you will have prepared the draft lease to me of Lady Langdale's fishing rights in the Teme. It need not be a very lengthy or complicated affair. Mr Ackers, highly indignant, declines to join the club "good riddance etc."

Yours very Truly, AR Boughton Knight"

From August 1870 the Harley Estate account books[4] and a later résumé found in the office provide further confirmation that a new regime was in place. ARBK negotiated through Rodney Ward and had been granted a lease[1] from Lady Langdale for the right to fish between Criftin Ford Bridge and Leintwardine Bridge for the next 14 years. There is a note to the effect that the new sum of £18 was due at Michaelmas from ARBK.

The outcome was the complete reorganisation of the membership. The size of the Club was reduced by 40%, and the subscription doubled to £20 (£1430 in 2008 money[5]). Seven of the original members were invited to re-join but only four of them could be called 'locals'. ARBK infers later that he *invited* the new members to subscribe on the basis of providing a fair distribution of places to those from both near and far. There was a clear concern that a local man would be able to fish more often, and thus have an unfair advantage. The outcome probably reflects his peer group as most were likely to have been personal acquaintances, if not friends, and one suspects there was a deliberate policy to price out the less socially acceptable or at least those who did not know how to behave.   The result was as follows:

1863 Membership	1870 Membership
Honorary Member ARBK	Honorary Member ARBK
	Honorary Member Lady Langdale
J Ackers	
B Ackers	H Allsopp, Worcester
CV Bayley	CV Bayley, London
H Brown	Earl Breadalbane, Aberfeldy
Colonel Colvin	Colonel Colvin, Leintwardine
F Corbett	Reverend Cook, Pershore
H Crawshay, Leintwardine	
General Drummond	The Honourable HB Devereux, Leominster
W Essington	Earl of Dudley, Worcester
C Gordon Forbes	
F Freeman	
F Garnett	
Reverend Ibbotson	Reverend Ibbotson, London
Sir W Millman, Moor Park	
Lord Northwick	Lord Northwick, Tenbury
J Parker	The Honourable D Pennant, Bangor
T Peters	
Doctor Richardson	Reverend J Rogers, Stanage Park
J Rocke	J Rocke, Clungunford
Reverend O Rocke	Reverend O Rocke, Clungunford
WH Sitwell	WH Sitwell, Ferney Hall
Reverend T Short	
G Whitmore	
Major Whitmore	
T Wood	Morgan Vane, Soham

Part of the preparation for the reformed club was to produce the necessary paperwork. ARBK took the trouble to have Members' Lists, Rules and Regulations, Circulars for Elections, and Calling Notices for meetings printed. Each item was headed with the new logo: a woodcut of a grayling. Finally all was ready for the first formal meeting. The following invitation was sent out:

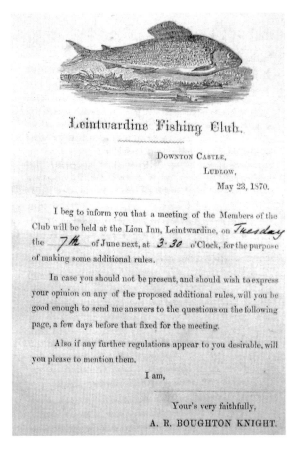

ARBK wrote in the new leather-bound minute book that on March 25th 1870 the Leintwardine Fishing Club had re-formed. He noted that on May 23, 1870 the fifteen paying members were invited to The Lion Inn, Leintwardine, to attend a meeting on the 7th June at 3.30pm to approve the Club Rules and Regulations. Six members in addition to ARBK attended and having taken into consideration the written replies of absent members, the rules set out below were agreed. These have been transcribed exactly as they are not only the first rules properly constituted by the Club, ie voted in, but are also the starting point for many changes over the years.

Leintwardine Fishing Club

JUNE 1870

RULES AND REGULATIONS

I.   *The Club shall consist of Fifteen Members, paying Twenty Pounds each, and of Two Honorary Members, one nominated by Lady Langdale, and one by Mr Boughton Knight.*

II. *Subscriptions are due on the 1st of March in each year, and any Member who has not paid his Subscription by the 1st of April will cease to be a Member of the Club.*

III. *A Member may take one Friend with him to fish, with a fly rod, the whole of the water rented by the Club.   Each Member also, when not present, may give permission to his friends to fish by means of tickets; such tickets to be filled up with the name of the friend, to be dated and signed by the Member: they are not transferable.   For the current year each member shall have 12 tickets, four of which may be used during the Grass-hopper season.*

IV. *Upon a vacancy occurring in the Club, a Member may take the vacant Membership. Should, however, no Member wish to do so, each member shall have a vote in the election of a new Member: in the event of there being an equality of votes, the President shall have the casting vote.   Candidates must be proposed and seconded by Members, and the names of the Candidates, with those of their Proposers and Seconders, sent by post to the President.   Three negative votes shall exclude a Candidate.*

V.   *No keeper, or attendant upon a Member, shall be allowed to fish under any circumstances, with the exception of keepers fishing for Pike.*

VI. *No Trout shall be killed in any way between September 30 and March 1.   No Greyling exceeding 1/2lb. in weight shall be killed between December 1 and August 1.   No Trout or Greyling shall be killed at any time less than 8 inches in length, i.e. 1/4lb. in weight.   No Trolling for Trout shall be allowed during the present season.*

VII. *Members may fish with the Grasshopper from October 1 to the end of the season.*

VIII. *A Member committing a breach of any of the Rules of the Club, or sanctioning any of his friends in doing so, will cease to be a Member of the Club.*

There are two anomalies in the list of members that was issued in March 1870.   Mr JG Rodney Ward is not listed as an honorary member but is noted in the minutes as being one at the request of Lady Langdale.   There is a further and more interesting puzzle concerning Benjamin St John Ackers.   Readers will recall it was to him that ARBK gave *'good riddance'* in his letter to Rodney Ward, and he is not included as a member of the reconstituted Club, and yet the Downton account books clearly have him renting both cottages at Black Bridge for the period 1871 through to 1879 for the sum of £10 per annum. This is far too long a period for it to be a clerical error, and it can only point to the fact that Benjamin was still fishing but not as a member. Perhaps there was still a residue of good fellowship amongst some Club members for the Ackers family. Members did after all have 12 tickets each to dispose of to friends and it would only need one or two to keep Benjamin fishing for as often as he was able.

As the Club accounts for 1870-71 are the earliest available, it is interesting to look at the detail:

LEINTWARDINE FISHING CLUB.

Statement of Accounts for the Year ending March 25th, 1871.

RECEIPTS.	£.	s.	d.	EXPENDITURE.	£.	s.	d.
Subscriptions from 15 Members, £20 each ...	300	0	0	RENT paid to Lady Langdale £20 less Property Tax .. 3s. 4d.	19	16	8
				Paid to Mr. Boughton Knight	120	0	0
				Half costs of Lease, paid to Messrs. Martineau	3	3	0
Summary of Account.				FISHING NET, paid to Mr. Hughes	4	10	0
				BOAT, paid to Mr. Ackers	6	0	0
				WAGES, E. Meredith, 52 weeks and 1 day at			
Receipts...	300	0	0	16s. per week	41	14	8
				T. Picking, 52 weeks and 1 day at			
Expenditure	243	4	1	15s. per week	39	2	6
				Night watching	3	0	0
Balance in the Treasurer's hands				STATIONERY, paid R. Jones	1	13	6
				" " Jarrett	1	0	0
March 25th, 1871, ...	56	15	11	Receipt and Postage Stamps	0	4	0
				SUNDRIES, Powell, 4 days piling 10s. Nails 4s.3d	0	14	3
				Carriage of Net 1s. Boat line 1s.	0	2	0
				Two Men Pike Fishing	0	4	0
				2 Gun Licenses 20s. Powder & Shot 19s. 6d.	1	19	6
					£243	4	1

[VI.]

The next meeting was held at Downton Castle at 12 o'clock on the 30 May, 1871. Reverend James Cook, Mr John Rocke, Reverend John Owen Rocke, Reverend John Rogers, Mr Willoughby Sitwell and Mr Boughton Knight all attended. It was resolved that a committee of management was needed and the two Rocke brothers and Mr Sitwell were appointed for the year. It was further agreed that a member holding two or more memberships should have only one vote. This probably stems from the note in the minute book that up to the year to March 1871 two members, Lord Breadalbane and Colonel Colvin, had died and as no other members were interested in taking up the places, the Earl of Dudley subscribed for both of them. This was not a popular move and the wording in Rule IV was subsequently altered to read *"a member may become a candidate for the vacant membership"* rather than *"may take"* the vacancy. Rule V was changed to allow only the head keeper to fish for pike, and Rule VII was changed to limit the use of the

Grasshopper to members and those friends who had a ticket. Finally a new rule was made, Rule X, that notice of any rule changes was to be given to members. It would be amusing to speculate that with all business done they then sat down to lunch at the circular table in the middle of the very grand Downton Castle dining room, modelled on the Pantheon in Rome by Richard Payne Knight.

Downton Castle dining room.

In due course the rules were printed and dispatched to members with their 12 tickets for friends. The 1871 season clearly went well for the members as the meeting in 1872, again held at Downton Castle, concluded that the subscription could be reduced to £15 and that the only change required to the rules was a correction to the date in Rule VI from December 1 to December 31. The rules were reprinted and dispatched on March 25, 1872. Later that year, on 1 September, Lady Langdale died. Although unrecorded in the minutes, the Club now had a new lessor, Mr Robert William Daker Harley, the 26-year-old son of John Harley of Ross Hall, Salop. The accounts, however, noted that rent was paid in the following year to both Lady Langdale and Mr Harley.

The accounts for the year ending March 1873 show that repairs were done to the footbridges and that a dog was now employed by the keepers. The accounts also show that 2000 trout fry were introduced to the water at a cost of £6 per 1000; including transport from Whitchurch and keep for the fish, this restocking exercise cost £13 3s.0d. This is the first indication of stocking trout in Club waters and must signal the first shift from being a predominantly grayling water to one offering both species. There were no changes in 1873, or in 1874 when even the meeting was dispensed with.

The Club minute book also includes a record of candidates for membership. This list had been restarted in 1871 with seven candidates. The first three names, Brown, Parker and Crawshay, had all been members previously and were present on the 1863 list. The first vacancy occurred in 1875 when the Reverend C Ibbotson resigned; unfortunately Brown had died, so Parker was duly nominated. However, the result of the ballot, examined at Clungunford House, was such that he was not elected. Ballot papers for Crawshay were now sent out and the returned papers were examined at the annual meeting held at Downton on March 13th 1875. Again the result was negative, and Crawshay was *"not elected"*. Crawshay was immediately re-proposed by the same proposers, Willoughby Sitwell and John Rocke. The meeting also considered several proposals to amend the rules but all of these with one exception were either withdrawn or seem to have fallen by the wayside. The exception, that the President should have a casting vote, was carried. In fact this rule was already in place and in the end no rule changes were issued although the subscription reverted to £20.

It is interesting to speculate on Crawshay's non-election. He had already been a long-standing member of the Club under the first President but he was then left off the list, presumably drawn up by ARBK, for the reformed club. Perhaps that was just bad luck as ARBK wanted to widen the membership base. The fact that he is again rejected at the next opportunity, after a further two years, seems a little unfair. He does not get elected for a further eight years despite being proposed by two of the principal members of the Club, both of whom knew him well as they all lived locally. Perhaps that was the problem. He was a local, and could therefore fish whenever he liked; those further away might consider that there were already enough locals on the list. Then again it may have been a question of class. Crawshay was a farmer and, despite living at Stormer Hall, may not yet have been considered enough of a 'gentleman' by some. It would have been sufficient for just three of the members to object to debar him.

At the next balloting occasion, in preparation for the 1876 annual meeting, ARBK decided to speed matters up a little and despite the fact that there was only one vacancy, ballot papers were sent to all members for the next *two* on the list, the new Earl Breadalbane and Major Clowes. Always mindful of doing things 'properly', ARBK went over to Hindlip Hall to examine the returned papers in the presence of Mr Allsopp. The result was that both candidates received sufficient votes, but Major Clowes, who had been proposed just five days after the Earl, would still have to wait for a vacancy to occur.

Lord Dudley now proposed that the Club stop issuing fishing tickets, and Reverend Cook suggested that Grasshopper fishing started earlier in the season. Despite this radical proposal by Lord Dudley no member felt inclined, or was able, to attend the meeting called for 29 March 1876 at Downton. ARBK taking into account the letters he received concluded that Lord Dudley's proposal should not be accepted. Grasshopper fishing however was now to start on September 15th in preference to October 1st. The accounts for the past year showed that a considerable sum had been expended on pilings at Trippleton (£49 - £3430 in 2008 money[5]), but that still left £48 unspent and the subscription was reduced again to £15.

The publication of the *Fishing Gazette*[11] had been produced weekly since 1865. One regular feature was the *Angling Reports* column sent in by various people from around the country. A snapshot of the reportage shows that reports on the state of fishing on the Teme appeared on eight occasions in 1877. In most cases the reports concerned the Teme either at Tenbury or at Ludlow. The Club waters had little mention as they were *"strictly preserved"* and were therefore of less interest to most anglers. Correspondents however, could not resist reporting the odd item of gossip. The report for October 26th by 'T' stated: *"I am told that in the preserved parts of the river the fish are larger than usual this year, as they might well be, seeing that there has really been little or no good grayling fishing for two or three seasons, owing to unfavourable weather or water. Should there be no further disturbance of the weather the river will be fit again in its upper portions by next week. The grasshopper fishing on the Leintwardine water was very successful; one member of the Club, a Rev gentleman, took in four days ninety grayling, all fine fish."*

No meeting was called in 1877. Mr Sitwell examined the accounts and despite Rule II (members who do not pay subscriptions by 1st April will cease to be members) chose not to mention that five members were now in arrears with their subscriptions.   Later, in March, C Villiers Bayley died and, after a six-year wait, Major Clowes became a member. In May the members were consulted with the proposal that *"in consequence of the scarcity of small trout in the Leintwardine Club waters.... trolling for trout shall* (only) *be allowed from 15 June to 30 September"*. This amendment was subsequently accepted for the present year. One other change was agreed: an increase in wages for the two keepers. Meredith and Picking would each now receive 2 shillings more per week, a 10% rise! Before we marvel at this generosity, we should take into account that they had been on the same pay for the last five years.

Only a very few letters to the President from this period (1879-1909) appear to have survived, but fortunately most estates now made use of a method to duplicate outgoing mail, and Downton was no exception. Using the Ellams Diaphragm Duplicator, flimsy and delicate paper copies of hand-written letters were retained within bound, hard covers, usually called letter-books. One book[3] from Downton survives for the period June 1875 to October 1884.   We could conclude that ARBK was not kept too busy with Club matters in this decade as there are only six copies of responses pertaining to the Club in that particular letter-book. However these duplicates are enough to shed some light on the Club and its members.

One letter[3] written by ARBK to Mr Clay in 1877 provides telling insight into what the President, and perhaps the members as well, saw as the ethos of a club such as theirs. Before reading the letter it perhaps helps to put oneself into the shoes of the President in order to imagine the right tone of voice. You are 51 years old; your father held the titles of the 10th Baronet Boughton and 2nd Baronet Rouse Boughton of Rouse Lench; you were educated at Eton and Trinity College, Cambridge; you are happily married and have now completed all the domestic arrangements to turn your castle into a comfortable and impressive residence; you have already served as High Sheriff for the county; and your seven children, including two sons, give you the assurance that your lineage will continue.

Now imagine yourself in your oak-panelled study walking the ten paces across the rug-strewn floor to the ceiling-high, oak-shuttered window. You pull on the cast-brass knob, the sun streams in and you look out onto a glorious view of a valley with a river running through it. Your eyes look up and beyond to the parkland slopes of Bringewood on which your prize-winning Hereford cattle are contentedly grazing amongst the scattered oak trees. The view never fails to gladden your heart as does the knowledge that here and thereabouts is another six thousand acres of prime Herefordshire land that is yours. Your Queen has just been declared Empress of India, and you too feel master of all you survey, including the right to allow or deny fishing on that river below. This reminds you that Mr Clay, a local chap, who really does not understand how things are done, needs an answer to his letter. He *actually* asked if he could be allowed to fish - occasionally - the Leintwardine Fishing Club water on repayment of a few pounds! You write.

"In answer to your letter received this morning inquiring as to the possibility of your being admitted as an occasional member of the Leintwardine Fishing Club, I would say that although I am President and Hon member, I retain no more power in my own hands than any other member of the club has. Either I should have to send copies of your letter to 14 other members of the club and ask them to write me their opinions on your proposal or to summon a special meeting, which few would attend; and at which I could not be present as I am leaving home after next week for two months.

I think it is quite useless taking either of these steps, for I feel sure the members would not accept your proposal for the following reasons: it is against the principles of a club to allow, for a money payment, outsiders to share its privileges; the members are much opposed to any increase in the numbers of Fishermen, and rather unwilling to admit as member anyone living in the immediate neighbourhood: lastly as the income of the club is £300, £2 or £3 additional would not have much weight; and you ask for the privilege of fishing for perhaps 35 days during the best 4 months fly fishing in the year, although you only propose two days a week, no member would average two days a week probably during those months. If anyone was admitted as an occasional member, for a money payment, there would be no just reason for refusing to sell any one a fishing ticket at 1/6d a day. Believe me, yours very truly, AR Boughton Knight".

One can almost see the steam of indignation coming off the page.

On June 1st 1877 Lord Coventry became a member of the Leintwardine Fishing Club. One might suppose that a man of his social standing found it easier to become a member. The 9th Earl was a well-known sportsman and racehorse owner, with a large estate just south of Worcester at Croome. He had a family that could trace its origins back to an association with the City of London and in particular to Richard (or Dick) Whittington (1393-1423). It is apparent that he knew several of the members not least because he played cricket with them. Men such as Allsopp, Curtler, Clowes and Berkeley were all in the Gentlemen of Worcestershire team. It is clear, however, that no special favours were meted out; he too had to wait six years before taking the place of W Morgan Vane who had died. His election was to become significant in the Club's development if only because he was responsible for proposing over 20 members during the period 1881 to 1908, at least nine of whom belonged to the peerage of Great Britain. We shall go on to look further into his influence a little later in the narrative.

Edward Meredith is still shown as the keeper in 1878; however, the under-keeper changed from Picking to E Langslow. Both no doubt were soon occupied with re-stocking the trout, as 4500 were introduced to the water that season, and also repairing, yet again, the footbridge by Graham's Cottage. No meeting was called that year but members were issued with a new members' list, the summary of accounts, and a new set of rules reflecting changes already adopted. Regrettably the list was soon out of date as the Reverend John Rogers, Stanage Park, died and Mr Essington was elected in his place. Essington only enjoyed the opportunity to fish for a few months before he too died, and Mr Frederick Whymper, brother of the mountaineer Edward who conquered the Matterhorn in 1865, became a member in March 1879.

The well-connected Reverend James Cook, a member living in Pershore, who had been asked to second the Earl of Coventry, was taking a close interest in the maintenance of the Club's water for at some time in 1879 he wrote to ask ARBK what progress had been made on repairs to a weir. He is provided with the following answer[3] on November 29th 1879:

"My Dear Sir, The weir at Graham's Cottage is not built; stone has been ready for some months, but the water through the summer has been too high; you 'suggest that it should be done at once', it shall be, if you will find 6 or 8 men who will now stand in the water for 8 or 9 hours a day; here they will only undertake this work in warm weather.

I fully agree with you that we are too liberal with tickets. I should not be sorry to hear them wholly abolished: we can discuss this in March next: will you in due time hand me a proposition, re tickets and any other alterations; there has been no meeting of late years, because no member has sent to me by the 15th February any proposal for alteration in rules.

I thought we ought in any case to have a meeting in March next to discuss among other things the mode of payment for the weir which will be a heavy business: it should not be all club affair or all mine; I have no doubt that if the club ceased to exist, I should remove the weir even if now erected: it causes damage to Trippleton, and some benefit to Black Bridge lands, but the damage certainly exceeds the benefit; raising the weir to a less height than before, as you suggest, would deprive me of all the benefit, (as the level of water would be below the Black bridge cut); it would at the same time lessen the damage.

If 'the new cut below Meredith's has taken away quite £20 worth of excellent fishing' you must give the old course credit for having carried away very many £s worth of most excellent land. You look at the weir and the cut more from a sporting point of view, I from an agricultural, and also £.s.d. point of view, for the rent paid by the club would not financially pay for the annual damage and actual loss of land by keeping up the weir: you may see a dozen places between Black bridge and Trippleton where the river is constantly encroaching.

Believe me,

Yours very truly,

AR Boughton Knight"

It is difficult to be sure exactly where this weir was as nothing remains to-day. Today this site lies nearly 30 metres south of the river bank. As no mill has ever been mentioned in this area, and this is before the pipeline bridged the river, the weir was probably a device to allow flood waters to flow across the flatlands of Wigmore 'Lake' to prevent erosion of the banks in the area of Graham's Cottage. The best guess is the promontory below the sluice shown on a map of 1884 (see photo below) over which a footbridge is shown.

In 1880 Lord Dudley resigned his three memberships on Lady Day (March 25th). There is some indication that Lord Dudley had fallen behind with his subscriptions (arrears of some £4,450 in 2008 money); anecdotally it is understood that he was a notoriously bad payer of bills. Others, who were more interested, would of course benefit and Herbert Crawshay, J Hurlestone Leche and Colonel Ponsonby Bagot all became members.

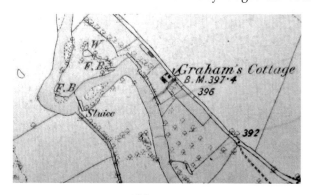

Readers will recall that it was this Crawshay who had been a club member 18 years previously, as shown on the 1863 list, and had been waiting for *ten* years to fish again as a member.

It was in this same year, 1880, that members were asked prior to the Annual Meeting to consider three proposals: if they wished to continue with the practice of issuing tickets, when to allow trolling for trout, and should the weir at Graham's Cottage be rebuilt at the Club's expense.   Mr Sitwell and ARBK examined the written answers at Downton Castle on March 18 and as no one else attended the meeting promulgated the results which were: to stop the ticket system and allow trolling from June 15 to September 30; but the question of rebuilding the weir remained unresolved.   This rule change with regard to tickets probably reflects members' unease at finding people on the water that they did not know and who were not escorted by a member.   Henceforth members could *take* a friend fishing, but could no longer permit a friend to fish alone.

The predicament over rebuilding the weir near Graham's Cottage rumbled on.   It would appear to be Major Clowes who now picked up the problem by writing to the President. The reply, lodged in the letter-book[3], dated 8 May 1880 is as follows:

"Dear Major Clowes,   I am much obliged for your cheque and enclose the formal receipt.

The proposals that there should be no tickets, and that tickets should be allowed are of course carried '(unreadable word probably meaning even)' not counting on either side.

The questions of 'rebuilding the weir' and club contribution thereto (.....are vague and unsettled as ever).

4 out of 17 members are for rebuilding, and contributing to the cost; but until the majority expresses a decided opinion on the two points I do not know that anything can be done.

Perhaps 'dissenting' and 'neutral' members may consider that (as in the letting of a house or farm and buildings) the landlord is bound to keep buildings as they were at the commencement of the taking: if they expressed this much there would be something to argue upon; the poor landlord must then consider whether or not it is worth maintaining a property at a rent of £120 per year, which every few years may require an outlay of £120.

The breach in the weir has considerably widened in the last summer and winter and the cost of rebuilding may now considerably exceed £120, and then is only a temporary job.

The benefit to my property or the contrary by the existence of the weir stands thus: fields below the Black bridge <u>have long</u> benefited by floating (sic): fields above Graham's cottage weir have lately been injured by pounding back the water : floating produces an increased quantity of coarse grass, but involves considerable expense in putting floating gutters in order after cattle have been pas-

tured in the fields; and now that portable artificial manure is readily available, (which produces finer grass) good farmers do not care as much about floating.

My arrangements with the tenants above and below Black Bridge would be the ordinary one; heads tenant wins; tails landlord loses; if the weir be all rebuilt I receive no additional rent for the upper land: if not rebuilt I shall have until a re-letting takes place to compensate the tenant of the lower land. As an estate matter therefore I care very little whether the weir be rebuilt or not.

I think the proposal which you and three others made that the club should pay half the cost or thereabouts or a final sum of £60 would be a fair one.

I am glad you have asked me these questions, as it enables me to deliver myself of a speech which I had intended to loose off at the annual meeting, if more than one member had been present.

Please discuss this matter with any members you may come across and of course make aware of this letter.

There could be time to rebuild the weir this summer if quickly determined upon.

Yours very truly, AR Boughton Knight"

It would seem from the tone of the letter the President felt that he had found a man he could deal with. However, the summer seems to go by and the matter is not resolved. In late autumn the Reverend James Cook wrote again to the President who in reply on October 8th patiently explained what has been going on but also managed to imply that the members could well do with discussing the matter. We can only deduce that the good Reverend has also attempted to give the President some advice on the costs of building the weir and gets for his pains a short lecture on the landlord's point of view of such matters, as we see below:

"My Dear Sir,

I wrote to Major Clowes on May 8. 1880 in answer to a letter from him as to rebuilding the weir at Graham's Cottage and asked him to discuss the subject of my letter with any LFC Members he might come across. –

The heads were shortly this, 4 out of 17 members only desired the weir to be rebuilt and to subscribe towards the cost. – If the Landlord would be expected to keep in repair wholly at his own cost, all erections in existence at the commencement of the taking, it would be for the Landlord to consider whether or not it could be worth maintaining a property which produced a rent of £120 per ann. and (required every 10 or 12 years an expenditure of £120 now perhaps £150) to keep it in repair; (for the restoration now proposed would be only temporary: a mortared stone wall on a curve would be far more costly) –

My farm letting arrangements with tenants are that they keep in repair all buildings in existence at the beginning of the taking, on my allowing materials in the rough and my idea was that the LFC should pay as 2 or 3 proposed half the cost of the new weir.

The benefit to some of my land by the re-establishment of the weir, and the injury to other parts would be about equal.

In May last I said the weir could rebuilt during the summer if quickly determined upon; it would now be impossible do it before winter.

Six men for a fortnight as you suggest, wages perhaps £10, stone raising and hauling another £20 would do next to nothing in rebuilding, and 4 feet high or indeed anything less than the original height would confer no benefit on my land below the weir: the water only just moved along the floating [sic] gutter as it was.

Yours very truly

AR Boughton Knight"[3]

The weir seemed to have become an intractable problem as nothing appears to have been done in the years following this exchange of letters, and it is ten years before we can see from the accounts that some work has been done.   The spring of 1881 saw four changes to the membership: Devereux and W J Rocke had died in the past year, and both Sir Henry Allsopp and Willoughby Sitwell decided to give their membership up.   Subsequently Sir Henry's son Samuel, Herbert Langham, George Smythies and Vere Somerset were all elected members, the latter after only a two-year wait due to the fact that three above him on the list had declined when offered the opportunity to be balloted.   A new membership list was issued in this year and a copy was pasted into the minute book in addition to a statement of accounts[7].

After 1881 ARBK ceases to use the minute book for any form of minutes or even to comment on rule change proposals or any other matter, principally - we should suppose - because there are no Club meetings.   For the next few years he continued to paste in members' lists and accounts' summaries when they are issued but makes no further entry of incidents or events.   The principal use of the book however becomes a truncated record of those who are proposed as members and those that are elected.   (As no meetings are recorded for the next 32 years, 1880 to 1912, it is now a matter of guesswork determining who has resigned to make way for each new member and this lends some uncertainty to the dates listed at Appendix One when members were with the Club. Readers can be certain that those listed were members but some start and end dates may suffer from inaccuracies.)   ARBK is now over 70 years old but despite advancing years he would seem to retain full control of the Club and its management.   There does not appear to be anyone acting as secretary and ARBK deals with any member's correspondence as it arises.   It is noted from the accounts however that a W Landon is paid £1 annually for *"keeping accounts"* so ARBK was getting some help. We can also see that Edward Meredith remained in post as the river keeper.

The following list is a précis of the notes which are now kept in the minute book, the last being in 1887; thereafter the book is used solely to record the list of proposed candidates, the dates they were proposed and by whom. The notes are short and unembellished but they do give some flavour of the turnover within the Club:

1883- W Cook dies, W Pennant resigns, and WA Crawshay postpones his election which allows GE Martin and W Wigram to be elected. Cruxon is now the under-keeper. A new set of rules is sent out with the accounts.

1884- No changes. A copy of the accounts was forwarded to each member and they show that Cruxon is still the under-keeper.

1885- Lord Breadalbane and ER Wigram resign. WA Crawshay, Major Hill, H Gardener and W Earle are asked if they wish to be put up for election. Earle and Gardener declined. Hill was elected, WA Crawshay was not. W King and Colonel Cotton were asked. Cotton postponed, King elected but then declines. Accounts are issued.

1885 is also the year that the series of books is published entitled *The Badminton Library (of Sports and Pastimes)*. Conceived by Henry Somerset, the 8th Duke of Beaufort, and dedicated to the Prince of Wales, *"One of the best and keenest sportsmen of our time,"* the books were certain to be held in very high regard. There were eventually 33 volumes, the first being *Hunting* and the second, *Fishing: Salmon and Trout*. Mr Cholmondeley-Pennel is the author of the fishing volume and he is yet another author who draws attention to the Teme and the Club waters on several pages, thereby further promoting the status of the Fishery to a wide and distinguished audience, for there is little doubt that the series was aimed at the aristocrat, particularly the 250 copies of the blue morocco bound luxury edition.)

1886- Allsopp and Langham resign from the Club. Lord Hardwicke no longer wishes to join, but Colonel Cotton, and Captain Clerke of Seedley House Leintwardine, would like to. Cotton is elected, but Clerke is not. Bullock Webster, now renting Elton Hall, withdraws his application and so Charles Gandolfi Hornyhold is elected in his place. After all these changes a new list of members is issued and accounts are published. It is also worthy of note that the logo on the members list has now changed from that of the grayling to a woodcut of a brown trout.

1887- No proposals were received and no change of members is noted but accounts are published.

LFC logo 1886

The story behind HM Porter's election in March 1889 is told in this interesting, and probably typical, exchange of letters, shown below, illustrating the difficulties and time-consuming bureaucracy surrounding the resignation, balloting and election of members. On May 11 1889 ARBK writes in reply to an unseen letter to Colonel Cotton:

"Dear Col Cotton,

I am sorry you are obliged to leave the Leintwardine Fishing Club. – The Club law is that subscriptions are due on 1st March for the coming year, which means notice of withdrawal should be given by the 1st March in order that the balloting process may be completed and the new member elected by 25th March. The equitable arrangement would be for the new member to pay a portion of the years' subscription, £20 for the current year, - say £15 or £16 if he be elected before may fly fishing begins: If you like I would try to effect an arrangement with the first candidate on the list Francis Alexander Wolryche Whitmore, Kingslee, Chester or possibly you may know him and would do so yourself.

I think I as Treasurer can only look to you for the years' subs £20 but any portion of it which the new member consents to pay; I would remit to your Bankers if you should have left England.

I have 16 candidates on the list, and if I were at liberty to put the vacant place up for auction one or other of the 16 new – hungry to come in – would probably be willing to pay the full £20 but I can only treat with the first on the list, Mr Whitmore: if he no longer desires to become a member of the club I could treat with the second candidate Lord Ducie, but supposing Mr Whitmore should not be willing to pay part of the subscription for part of the years' privileges I am afraid I must consider you as member until Lady Day 1890.

I will write to Mr Whitmore today and sound him. There are 11 candidates on the list before W A Wynne-Corrie, proposed by yourself (Oct 11th 1887) not as yet seconded: 10 on the list before Col P Methuen. Yours very truly, AR Boughton Knight."

The tone of the letter is conciliatory. Probably Colonel Cotton has told ARBK that he is being posted to British Guiana as Inspector General of Police (we know from his biography that he served there for two years) and ARBK must have had every sympathy for him having to live at the ends of the earth in conditions so different from those pertaining in Herefordshire. However, Colonel Cotton responded quickly (unseen) and ARBK wrote back in an obliging way on the 16 May 1889:

"Dear Col Cotton,

Many thanks for your cheque for £20, in payment of your subscription to Leintwardine Fishing Club: I enclose receipt.

I heard yesterday from Mr Whitmore; he says he is going to Norway until October and wishes his position on the candidate list to be put back one peg and let the second candidate be elected now, he remaining eligible for the next vacancy. I have told him this would be against club law, and unfair to a dozen or more candidates below him on the list. That he must (if you now at once create a vacancy) either withdraw his name or accept the vacancy and pay £15 or £16 subs for the current year.

I shall probably hear from him tomorrow: if he withdraws I shall try to treat with Lord Ducie on the same terms and will pay all I can extort, to your credit at Cox & Co, unless you direct me to pay elsewhere.

Of course it is desirable to get the new member started before May Fly time, or we should have to reduce the terms: if therefore you are leaving England shortly, it would be well if you gave me written authority to withdraw your name from the membership, if I think it advisable.

If you had rented fishing from me privately and circumstances like the present prevented your exercising your privileges during any portion of the year, I hope I should not have asked you for any rent, you are good enough to see that as treasurer of the club I can not act as a private individual.

It usually takes about 5 years after proposal to arrive at balloting time; as you say you would like to rejoin the club on returning to England I shall if you so desire be happy to propose you and would arrange for a seconder, say Leche.

Yours very truly,

AR Boughton Knight."

This is not the end of the story. We do not see the next exchange with Whitmore but note that in the minute book he *"temporarily withdraws from election"*. ARBK has now to 'treat' with Lord Ducie, who is at Tortworth Park, Gloucestershire. ARBK's letter to Lord Ducie on 20 May is as follows:

"My *Lord*,

Your name now stands first on the list of candidates for election to Leintwardine Fishing Club. Proposed April 1885 by Lord Coventry, seconded by myself. I should be much obliged if you would let me know if you still desire to join the club and under the following circumstances.

Col Cotton has paid his subscription (£20) for the current year (beginning March 25 1889) and is suddenly called upon to go to Demerara for 4 or 5 years: he would be willing to resign his membership at once: if he does so I have suggested that the incoming member should pay £15 of the years' subscription and Col Cotton £5.

If you should desire to join the club and pay £15 for members' privileges up to March 25th next the process of balloting could be completed in a week after I hear from you.

Would you be good enough to direct to and up to and on Thursday next at

Manor House

Thorpe Mandeville

Banbury

On Friday and after here.

I am, my lord,

Yours faithfully, AR Boughton Knight."

There is no reply available to us, just a note in the minute book stating, "Lord Ducie withdrawn May 1889" and that H M Porter Esq, Birlingham, Pershore was elected. A new members' list was issued. The accounts for the year ending March 1889 show that in 1888 and 1889 a total of £25 was paid to 'Owens' for weir repairs, and that a further £17 was paid to such men as Mellings and Beavan for hauling, timber and labour for the weir. When compared with the estimate given by ARBK earlier that a repair would cost at least £150 it would seem that the Club had decided to make only minor repairs.

Lord Coventry, 1838-1930

LORD COVENTRY

It is at this point in the story that we should make a small diversion from the main narrative to look at the membership of Lord Coventry who was elected in 1877 and remained a member for the next 34 years. Over this period he was actively fishing as well as being engaged to some extent to the management of the Club. He was also one of the members most frequently called upon to propose or second new members and he therefore had a considerable influence on the make-up and tone of the Club. It is very fortunate that during this period in which there is little detail available in the minutes this member kept a journal. Subsequently the journal found its way into the Worcestershire Record Office and a synopsis can be read at Appendix Four.

Lord Coventry, the ninth Earl, lived south of Worcester in the family home of Croome Court. He so enjoyed his fishing that from August 1880 he first rented a house in Leintwardine and then just over ten years later bought the same house in March of 1891. The six bed-roomed house, Warden Cottage (sometimes known as Warden Villa or The Wardens), was promoted as *"an excellent investment for a Gentleman requiring a fishing or shooting box"* and Lord Coventry managed to secure it at auction for £387 10s 0d.

The Wardens

The journal was kept at Warden Cottage. Initially Lady Coventry, and then Lord Coventry himself, recorded in the journal their comings and goings and details of the fish caught. They rarely made a visit for longer than four days and not more than two or three visits a year, but the journal gives a personal dimension to the fishing and an insight into the way a member would weave a day's fishing into the busy life of a Victorian gentleman with many social and administrative obligations.

The journal informs us that both Lord Coventry and Lady Blanche would use their trips to call in at antique shops on their way and buy furniture and small items either for use at Warden Cottage or to take back to Croome. He was almost obsessive in the way he recorded the journey to Leintwardine, noting the method of travel, be it by carriage, train and later automobile, the time taken, and the distance travelled. He noted the fish he and his friends caught, the weather and the state of the river on most of his visits. Often his catch exceeded his capacity to consume the fish and he would dispatch them to friends and relatives as a present. The journal sometimes seems to be less a record of the catch and more a means of instructing the housekeeper, Mrs Castree, as to which address she is to send the fish, for instance "*2 sent to Mr Howlett, Barton Wells, Mildenhall, Suffolk, over 1lb each*". One wonders if a fisherman today would trust either the post or the railways to deliver across country a basket of fish to arrive in a state fit to eat.

Anyone reading his journal will get a clear impression of a thoroughly pleasant individual and sporting gentleman. In her book *The Coventrys of Croome*, Dr Catherine Gordon describes the 9th Earl as: "*Jovial and rather vague, and known to his close friends and family as 'Covey', he posed proudly for photographers alongside his wife, his prize bull or his racehorse, his clothes always a little awry and a benign and a rather bemused smile playing across his face. No county function was complete without his presence, no hunting party nor race meeting seemed so successful in his absence. His popularity amongst his tenants was unprecedented, and he seemed to be regarded with genuine affection wherever he went.*"

His journal helps to confirm and even provide insight into the dynamics of the Club. The Earl notes the visits he makes to friends, and those that visit him. ARBK and his family call at The Wardens and Lady Blanche walks to Downton Castle to repay the visit. Several members of the Club also take lodgings or rent houses in Leintwardine and one presumes some form of social interaction occurred. Lord Coventry has no hesitation in giving his tickets to acquaintances such as the local priest, Reverend Colvin. Lord Coventry often records that he has used the '*grasshopper*' to catch his fish, and there can be little doubt that over the long years that he is a member of the Club he is the person to whom several publications allude in rather derogatory terms for unsporting conduct, namely for over-use of this particular lure. In fact there is so much heated debate in the country around this particular subject that it is worth looking in more detail at the rise and fall of its use amongst the angling fraternity at Appendix Three.

A further diversion to the work of Edward Marston, *Fresh Woods and Pastures New,* published in 1887, will be of interest to those who fish the waters on the Teme above Leintwardine Bridge and both the Lugg and the Arrow. Marston describes in a series of letters that were first published in the Fishing Gazette his holiday in the area in 1886 for the purpose of fishing those rivers. He describes staying in a farmhouse and his letters comment on the people and conditions he finds in the countryside as well as his fishing exploits. Marston's fishing had been granted courtesy of *Squire Harley* and he describes a particularly awkward catch:

"I set up my tackle in a meadow on the Buckton Park Farm. My leading fly was probably a novelty in this water – a small Dun fly with a Red Tag, called by the learned "Yates's Fancy," my second was a fly with a bright green body and light wings, called the "Emerald Dun." At my first throw I rose a fish, and this filled me with courage and hope. I threw again in a rippling stream, and allowed my flies to float gently down over the spot where they had before attracted a rise; and now he comes again! I gave a firm but quick upward movement to the rod, and hooked him. Off he darted up stream till I gradually wound him in; (my trusty and too enthusiastic young friend Chris had gone to the Post Office). I had nearly brought him within reach, when the sight of my net gave him a fresh start, and off he went again. I once more hauled him in, and a beautiful grayling swam into my net, with "Yates's Fancy" firmly hooked in his upper lip. This was encouraging.

Instead of confining myself to the bank, I waded for the most part up the shallow streams, and before Chris arrived I had two more fine grayling in my basket – all victims to the seductiveness of the red Tag on "Yates's Fancy". On we went buoyant with hope; but I fished for an hour without another rise. Luck seemed to desert me when Chris came on the scene; he was too eager, and kept too close behind me. Once I made a beautiful cast intended to captivate a rising fish; luckily it was a gentle throw, for it hooked poor Chris by the chin, and gave him a slight scratch only. Had it been one of my long and vigorous casts, "Yates's Fancy "would certainly have been imbedded in his flesh, and I should have been compelled to perform a severe and doubtless clumsy surgical operation; this incident was a lesson for both of us.

Shortly afterwards I had another rise, and hooked my fish; this time it was a trout that had a fancy for my green-bodied insect, and we got him ashore nicely. Again I fished for half an hour, and I was rewarded with another grayling, and so my fishing ended."

To return to the narrative. At this time there is an indication that some members think some changes are due in the manner in which the Club is conducted. One short letter[4] gives a clue as to the mood of the Club and allows us to re-introduce RWD Harley.

Robert Harley is now a gentleman of some fifty years and an honorary member, listed on the 1891 list. He seems to be the catalyst for change as he is moved to write to a fel-

RWD Harley, 1846-1907

low member, Vale–King, in April:

"I see that you, Major Hill and myself are the committee for the Leintwardine Fishing Club – Do you not think that we ought to have a meeting in order to see if anything is required to be done?"

This is the first clear indication that Robert Harley took an interest in Club matters, but we should not conclude that he had not been actively involved previously. A fishing diary[4] belonging to his son Geoffrey contains a hand-written note pasted to the first page and this details fishing returns for trout *"Caught from Brampton Bryan"* for the period 1890 to 1895. These would indicate that people from Brampton Bryan fished the Club waters quite regularly:

	1890	1891	1892	1893	1894	1895
Teme	643	797	292	361	533	293
Club water	207	53	-	216	145	42
Lugg	103	70	-	81	-	Pond 47

Although, as we have seen, the President may not have had the energy to keep the minute book up-to-date or to encourage meetings from 1886, the accounts of the Club were still published on a regular basis and there are records for the next ten years as well as the reasonably regular publication of members' lists in 1891 and 1894. It would seem that Harley's urgings had some effect and the committee becomes more active. Even as the millennium was being celebrated we can see from a letter[4] to Major Hill from Robert Harley that matters to introduce young trout to the river and alterations to the rules concerning the taking of grayling, of which *"there are far too many"*, are being considered. The millennium is perhaps the catalyst for ARBK, now aged 74 who has been running the Club almost single-handedly for some 30 years, to get the committee to take on more. ARBK writes to Major Hill[3]:

"Our Rules, LFC, say that you, Harley and Vale King, are the Managing "Committee for general management of the affairs of the Club": this was specially inserted in order to put matters of repairs of banks, bridges, restocking of the river etc, etc in your hands, as you three see so much more of the river than I do, and as fishermen know much better what is required.

Matters for some years past have however been referred to me, I can only hand them to Mr Fenn (the current agent for Downton) *and he goes to a Leintwardine Contractor: it would be far more simple if the Managing Committee gave their orders direct to the Contractor.*

As to payments Mr Fenn or I would pay any bills which any two of your Committee sign, as being correct.

Expected receipts for this year would be:

Balance in Hand	23
One year arrears 1899-1900	15
14 Subscriptions 1900-1901	210
1 subscr New Member	<u>20</u>
	<u>368 (sic)</u>

Our standing expenses; Rents, wages, Rates and sundries amount to about £248 leaving £120 for expenditure in the current year on repairs.

You would be quite welcome to over draw £80 in the year ending Lady Day 1901, which would give £200 for repairs in this year.

We want better Engineers than we find at Leintwardine for the repairs of banks, bridges etc; it is grievous to see the sums we have spent in bridges – timber and stones for piling – labour and hauling for ditto – all useless after comparatively few years.

Yours very Truly

AR Boughton Knight"

The above letter is interesting as it confirms an earlier suspicion that ARBK is not actually a fisherman and probably knows little of the detailed requirements for a fishery, beyond the knowledge required of a landlord. It is in his capacity as a landlord, however, that he has already been heavily involved in another matter that affected the Club: the construction of a water pipeline to be built over the Club's water. It is clear from the letter-book[3] that ARBK has been attempting, at least since 1891, to dissuade Birmingham Water Corporation from bringing its aqueduct across the Teme and Downton land. The Corporation, having surveyed the pipeline route, issue their notices to the landowners, and the one shown here was sent to Downton Castle in 1898. In the end neither ARBK

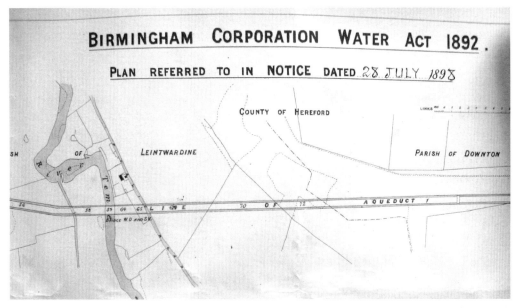

nor the other landlords involved are able to stop or deflect the march of technology and they finally settle for extracting as much money as they can from the Corporation in compensation and rent.

A huge undertaking, the pipeline stretched eastwards from the Elan Valley in Wales for some 73 miles to Birmingham relying entirely on gravity to move the water through the tunnels, pipes and covered brick channels at about 2 miles an hour. The very substantial Downton Bridge, just above the old Bow Bridge, and the pipeline crossing below Graham's Cottage are testament to the engineering effort. The construction and the workers employed would have had a profound effect on every community through which the pipeline passed. There can be little doubt it would have impacted on the Fishery for at least the construction period from about 1898 to the official opening in July 1904. That said, there is nothing in the Club archives that remarks upon the scheme; perhaps the grandeur and inevitability thereof silenced comment. Certainly Club members appear to have fished with equanimity throughout.

Leaving the pipeline aside the pressure over the years from Club members for changes to the rules came to a head. By 1902 ARBK had sought help to amend the rules and he turned to one of his most senior members, then of 25 years standing, and perhaps the one with the most gravitas, Lord Coventry. He wrote[3]:

"Dear Lord Coventry

Many thanks for the sight of Mr Mathews' letter which I now return.

There is a contradiction in the rules as to killing Greyling and this sometimes occurs when words are inserted or taken out of one Rule, and other Rules not sufficiently considered.

I did not desire any changes in the Rules; I however voted for Major (HILL) proposals because common report said that the Greyling were insufficiently killed in winter and were over-coming the trout.

Our Rules perhaps require remodelling before next March, but who is to do this; would you undertake the work, assisted by three or four other members: if so I would send you members' letters on proposed alterations in 1896, 1901 and 1902 which show generally the views of Members.

It is impossible by a circular to get decided answers yes or no to any suggested alterations: Members often accept half the proposal and reject the other half: they often tuck in some other suggestion; e.g. one member suggested an amendment to Major Hill's proposal that fishing tickets should again be issued; another suggested that instead of altering the length of fish from 8 to 10 inches 9 inches should be substituted.

In any alteration I should merely suggest that Rules I, II, IV, V and X be retained: that Rule III should say that the subscriptions are due on April 15, which would give me time to have the accounts made up and circulated and at the same time to [ask] Members whether the subscription should be £15 or £[20]. The Rule [?] notice of resignation to be sent to me by March 15th: or the member [is liable for all next] year's subscription: then the sentence "the Member ceases to be a Member" might be omitted, which [sounds what f......] call "arbitrary".

We might omit Rule IX,

Yours very Truly

AR Boughton Knight" (words within [ ] are illegible)

The result of this appeal would appear to be the new set of draft rules[6] that Lord Coventry has typed up and submitted to the committee and dated 20 September 1902. As might be expected, the draft rules are not acceptable to all and there is plenty to be discussed. In 1903 a number of interesting letters are produced in response.

In February ARBK having reviewed the draft rules and having made some amendments agrees to the draft and writes to Major Hill[3]. It is clear that they have both seen and consulted a set of rules borrowed from the Arrow Fishery. ARBK anticipates that the new rules will not suit everybody and may even provoke resignations! *"Rule 4. - I think is very just in principle: we do not desire that one subscription should free two rods for the whole year, but I expect there will be some rebellion as to the number of tickets to be issued. We must hurry up in deciding upon and circulating the New Rules; there is not much time before March 1 for a Member to send notice of resignation; for* this year *perhaps we might say March 10".*

A little later, on 27 February, ARBK replies[3] to a Colonel Whitmore and again perhaps you should imagine yourself in the oak-panelled study of Downton Castle, rather annoyed and clearly determined to maintain standards. ARBK puts the Colonel firmly in his place:

"Dear Col Whitmore

I duly received your proposal that the LFC should sell *additional tickets to Members at 5/- each. This reached me 10 days too late to be placed before Members this year, but this is not of any consequence, for as soon as possible after such a Rule were carried I should take steps to bring the Club to an end. We might in another year have a proposal that tickets should be sold at the bar of the Lion to an applicant who had paid for a drink,......: This is not my idea of a Club.*

The privilege of taking a friend to fish has been far too liberally used: in Mr Ackers' time, and when I reformed the Club about 1859 (he means 1869); *the intention was that a Member might take a friend* staying in his house, *or occasionally a friend who met him at the river; for some years this privilege was not abused, but later (I forget the year) 12 tickets for friends were given. Later again these were discontinued, as it was found that tickets got into the hands of tradesmen in Leintwardine.*

Now many Members seem to consider that they do not get money's worth, unless they have a friend regularly fishing with them: I have heard of "the friend" staying ten days with the Member and fishing daily: also that two friends of a Member have fished with the Member for two days consecutively: one friend no doubt having a borrowed "hat on".

This is practically equivalent to a subscription of £10 per rod, and I fancy that you do not know any Club fishery in England where over five miles of Trout and Grayling fishing, as good as the Teme, can be had for a £10 subscription: more probably the subscription would be three times this amount: on the Itchen (Hampshire), it is £50 per rod, and very difficult to obtain a Membership.

Rule IV is carried by 9 to 6: I certainly expected a larger majority; names of Members "for" and "against", with new Rules will be sent later.

Yours very Truly

AR Boughton Knight"

The tickets in question are shown below

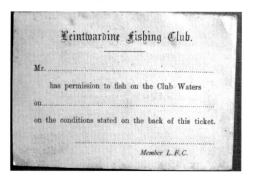
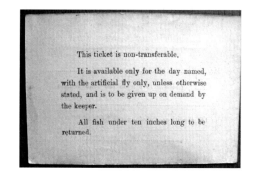

A third letter[3] to Sir Henry Plowden, not a member of the Club, but living in Leintwardine House, not only answers Sir Henry's perceived question about the number of locals permitted to fish but also gives us the best confirmation yet of the origins of the Club. The letter demonstrates again that ARBK was well able to hold his ground and maintain the standards of the Club as he saw them. The letter, written in 1903, is reproduced in full:

"Dear Sir Henry

You were not quite correct in your supposition that 'when the Leintwardine Fishing Club was formed some 40 years ago it was mainly if not exclusively a local club'.

Mr Ackers (living in Gloucestershire) rented the fishery from my father for several years prior to 1856 and from myself from 1856 to 1869; it could then not strictly be called a Club – Mr Ackers permitting friends of his own choosing to fish on payment of £10 per ann.

The lists of Members which I have show that from 1856 to 1869, there were seven local Members (i.e. men living within 10 miles) out of 25 members.

In March 1870 I formed the present club consisting of 15 Members, each paying £20 subscriptions; I named them selecting from the existing list 5 "locals" and 10 "outsider" (i.e. now living in London, Worcestershire, Scotland, and North Wales etc).

Since 1870 all members have been elected, and all alterations in rules made by the members – by voting papers sent to them by me.

The Club has therefore never been 'mainly if not exclusively a local Club'; so far from this being the case I desired to buy your house in 1870 and to form a Clubhouse in order to give good accommodation to distant Members.

I individually (I cannot speak for Mr Harley) have no desire 'to safeguard the interests of local Members', or to alter the constitution of the Club; it seems to me that if the owners of the Fishery reserved the right to nominate Members, with some limit as to the number, it at once destroys all ideas of a 'Club'; I can only say that in every case a candidate proposed or seconded by myself has been elected and I may add that twice I voted for Mr Crawshay's election, and for Mr Clerke and Mr Green.

If a serious alteration in our Rules should be proposed by any Member, to the effect, that Local Members (i.e. men living within 10 or 20 miles from Leintwardine) should pay a double subscription I should be in favour of it.*

I am sorry that the Rules of the Club as they now are should interfere with the selling of your house.

Yours Truly

AR Boughton Knight

Sir H M Plowden KB

Leintwardine

*a common rule in newly formed London Clubs."

The new rules were finally published in March 1903. It is interesting to note that despite the 33 years between the two sets of rules and the perceived unhappiness with the 1870 set, few of the major rules actually change. The main differences can be summed up as follows: 1) a committee for general management is appointed. 2) Members must now accompany friends with tickets. 3) Fishing in June, however, is reserved for members only. 4) Trout are not to be killed between September 30th and March 15th (a two week extension), and no trout under 10 inches at other times (formerly 8 inches). 5) The Club is still to consist of 15 members paying £20 each.

One interesting piece of ephemera found for this period is Lord Coventry's fishing licence[6]. Issued by the Board of Conservators, Severn Fishery District, it cost one shilling

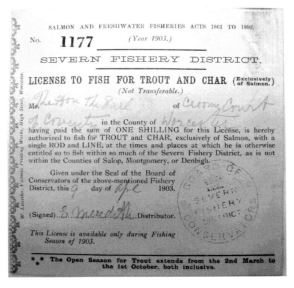

and was sold to the Earl by the river keeper Edward Meredith who is cited as a licence distributor.

Despite the lack of formally recorded detail in the minute book over this period some of the letters and scribbled notes[3] left to us give a reasonable insight into ARBK's continuing and all-encompassing involvement in the management of the Club. New drafts of the rules were written every year from 1903 to 1906, most of which went through ARBK's hands but did not result in any changes being published. Major Hill was probably the catalyst for these proposed changes as ever since his election in 1885 he seems to have become a leading activist.

Another recurring concern was prospective candidates writing to determine how long they might have to wait before being balloted for election. A scribbled note[7] in ARBK's handwriting at about this time states, "*there now being 15 candidates on the list it would take 12 ½ years before a candidate now nominated would be elected*". Major Hill, probably well aware of the waiting list, lost no time in putting forward his friends for membership of the Club. Even in the year of his election he had proposed two new members and ultimately he was to rival Lord Coventry in the number of names he put forward.

In 1904 a personal tragedy hits the President's family hard. His youngest son, Edmund Meysey, died of black-water fever at the age of 28 whilst serving in Kenya. There is no discernible effect on the running of the Club, and no members refer to the tragedy. The death did perhaps made ARBK more aware of his own vulnerability, or maybe he regretted not having a good likeness of his son, for one consequence was that ARBK decided, or was persuaded, to have his own portrait painted. The finished portrait produced in 1906 and shown in the colour section successfully portrays a Victorian gentleman who knows his duty as father, landlord and President and fulfils his responsibilities to the best of his ability. The picture painted by WW Euless RA was shown at the Royal Academy's 138th Exhibition in 1906.

Incidents at this time are not recorded in any of the Club minute books and we have to rely upon diverse sources for information. For instance the log[8] kept by Mr Charnock, the Head of Leintwardine School, can be brought into service. He made the note in 1907, "*31 Oct, Highest flood since May 1886- it was several inches deep in the Lion bar*". This snippet of information is of limited interest but helps explain the comment that Lord Coventry makes in his journal the following January with regard to the size of grayling, namely that although he caught 15, "*the fish are not so big as in former years*". Not surprising, one might think. The fish have been fighting against the elements to stay in place.

On 13 November 1907 Robert William Daker Harley, an honorary member for the past 29 years, died. His influence on the Club was probably low key. He served on the LFC committee and did take the initiative to get the committee working, but he was probably more active behind the scenes wielding influence through members that were his friends and neighbours such as Sir Henry Ripley. It is not clear how much he fished himself. He was succeeded by a keen fisherman, his son Robert George Geoffrey Harley, aged 28, who was to become intimately involved in the LFC and this interest in fishing was to become critical for the future of the Club.

ARBK begins to mention in his letters in 1908 that he feels *"well in himself"* but has trouble standing for any length of time. Earlier references suggest that he has been in poor health for some time and he is possibly suffering from gout. He does manage to record the names and proposers of prospective members in the minute book, but in increasingly very spidery writing. He is not the only one feeling his age and with the new season Major Hill wrote, or in fact dictated the letter to a much younger person[7], in March 1909 to say that he has been ill, but also to report the death of an LFC member, Porter. He reminded ARBK of some agreements they had reached in order to get Mr Clerke into the Club and onto the committee (Drummond had agreed to stand aside). He hopes that ARBK *"got well through the winter, I cannot say that I have for I have been for some weeks and am still in bed"*. It would appear that Major Hill did not recover, as after one more letter in May there is no further mention of him. Clearly, knowing the frailties of those managing the Club, Major Hill is doing his best to ensure a proper succession by recruiting Mr Clerke to the committee.

Amongst the scribble at the end of the *1870 Minute Book* is a younger and firmer hand, probably that of Charles Andrew Rouse Boughton Knight (ARBK's son, known as Andy) to say, *"wrote to all Apr 14th 1909"*, presumably informing the members of his father's illness. But the old man had not given in yet. On 18th April ARBK is still noting those to whom he has written, in this case Hugh Heber Percy. ARBK died 7 weeks later on the 7 June 1909, aged 83.

The following Friday, 11 June, the family cortège left Downton Castle at 2pm and followed the wheeled bier on foot via the private road towards St Giles' Church. At the white gate to the grounds other mourners joined the family to walk the half mile to the church. Several local newspaper reports listed the names of the many friends, relatives and tenants who crammed into the small church anxious to pay their respects. Several of those names were of past and present members of the Leintwardine Fishing Club. ARBK became the first of his family to be buried beside the east wall of the very church that he had funded and had built some forty years earlier. He lies there still in a delightful spot overlooking the Vale of Downton and the River Teme.

Andrew Johnes Rouse Boughton Knight was Leintwardine Fishing Club's President for very nearly 40 years. No other president has had, or is likely to have, such a long and direct association with the Club. Perhaps his legacy lies in the best of the Victorian values and virtues that still resonate within the Club today.

The next minute book we are aware of is the *1912 Minute Book*. It is a ruled and lined exercise book with a black, faux watered silk hard cover, which commences in 1912 with the words *"Leintwardine Fishing Club. This Club was reconstituted in February 1912"*.

What has happened in the meantime?

Before that question is answered, we should look to another individual who, with the President, shared the same dedication to the Club and served for even longer: Mr Edward Meredith, the river keeper.

CHAPTER SEVEN

EDWARD MEREDITH

RIVER KEEPER 1849-1907

"Trusted and Valued"

Edward Meredith's name has been mentioned several times in this narrative and it is appropriate that as he approached retirement, we look to see what is known of this river keeper and try to assess the influence this employee had on the Club. No other man had as long an association with the Club as he.

Edward's father, also called Edward, married Priscilla Davies in Leintwardine in 1832. It would appear that the couple emigrated to Canada via the USA in 1834. On the voyage Edward's brother William was born, and Edward himself was born in Canada in 1835. His mother probably died shortly afterwards, and his father returned to Leintwardine in order that the boy's grandmother, Mary Davies, could help bring up the boys. William is noted on the 1851 census as being crippled, aged 17, and Edward is aged 14 (this age is probably an error, and his age should have been given as 16). The family is shown as living at The Barracks in Leintwardine.

His gravestone (shown at the end of this chapter) records that he was the Club's keeper for 58 years. If tenure is calculated from the year of his retirement in 1907, then he started as keeper at age 14 in 1849. (To be employed as a keeper at this age may seem young by today's standards, but would not have been so unusual then.) For him to have been appointed to a post that not only required skill and knowledge, but also the tact to deal with gentlemen many years his senior, he must have been a young man who was confident in his abilities and of some education. The one picture we have of him shows a tall and well-built man of some presence. It is not surprising that such an individual, and one that has a regular wage, would attract the attention of local girls. Ten years later, aged 24, he has met and married Harriet Goodall. Edward's father was still alive at the time of the marriage, 7th June 1859, and the parish register gives his occupation as labourer. It is probably safe, therefore, to assume that it is the young Edward Meredith that has been the keeper throughout, and not the father.

By the 1861 census Meredith is aged 26, his occupation is given as river keeper and he is living at Criftin Ford Cottage, close by the Black Bridge over the Teme. In 1863 James Ackers is shown renting both the cottages at Black Bridge and it may be that Meredith's conditions of employment included living in one of the cottages. It is probable that Meredith continued to live at Criftin Ford Cottage throughout the period the Ackers were renting the cottages and then moved house sometime before 1870 to Graham's Cottage, which lies half a mile upstream and closer to Leintwardine.

Graham's Cottage was also owned at this time by ARBK and it is noted on his estate map of 1832 as the "*Fishing House*" and it would seem likely that he would have liked to restore the status quo on his estate and have it again occupied by his river keeper. It may have been a welcome move for Harriet for she now had two children to look after. William Rufus was born in 1863, and Ellen in 1866. Graham's Cottage was a small-holding of some 9 acres. We can see from this photograph of the estate map[3] that the land is mostly adjacent to Graham's Cottage and shows the barns, stables and orchard.

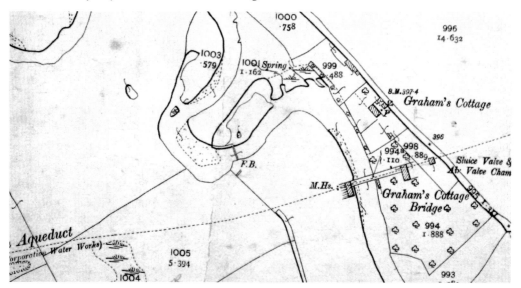

A significant proportion of the land is close to the river and subject to erosion. There is little room for crops other than fruit and so the holding may not have been very productive but perhaps sufficient to have increased Meredith's ability to earn a supplementary wage. As tenant of a small-holding Meredith would have significantly enhanced his status amongst his peers in Leintwardine.

The first Club accounts available are for the same period (1870) and show that Meredith was employed full-time and was paid at the rate of 16/- (shillings) a week. He was assisted by a T Picking at 15/- a week. It is clear that extra money could be made by 'night watching' but it is unclear what the rate of pay was per night, but the total earned in a year came to £3. There are no descriptions of the duties of the river keeper but some Club expenditure indicates functions one would expect. Edward probably kept the keepers' dog and received 1/6d a week for its keep and 5/- a year for the licence. Both men had a shotgun for which the Club paid the licence fee of 10/- a year per gun and various sums for powder, shot and caps (indicating that they were muzzle-loaded weapons). These guns were presumably for keeping predators, of the animal variety, away from the fish: cormorants, heron, otter and even pike were all seen as legitimate targets. Patrolling of the river banks with dog and gun would have taken up considerable time with more than ten miles of bank to patrol, but a regular presence would have been necessary to keep poachers at bay.

The maintenance of the river bank was another task that involved the keeper. The Teme was constantly tearing down its banks, changing course and destroying footbridges. Although contractors were brought in to do piling and repairing, overseeing the work or at least keeping an eye on it and reporting progress, would add to the duties of the keeper. In those years that the Club decided to increase the fish stocks Meredith would be dispatched to a fishery to buy trout fry. These came from various places but in 1872 for instance the fry came from Whitchurch and Meredith received 18/6d expenses for going there and back to buy 2000 trout fry at £6 per 1000. He also received 4/6 for zinc and 'keep' for the fish which might indicate he was growing them on in tanks before releasing them.

In the early days a boat was available to the keeper, as was a net, and we could speculate that they were used to capture unwanted species of fish. This activity seemed to vary over time. In later years, the grayling were considered a nuisance and were thinned out, but in general terms it would seem the net was not over-used. Fishing for pike, however, seemed a regular task and extra money could be earned by either keeper or others from the village.

As far as Club members were concerned, one important duty Meredith would have had was akin to that of the ghillie. Advice to those who travelled some distance to the river and did not know the current conditions would be invaluable, particularly as the river changed by the season and where once a favourite pool lay beckoning, a bank of gravel could have appeared since the angler's last visit. In addition the fisherman needed to know which flies were hatching and which the fish were after. In fact the good keeper fulfilled the role of instructor, advisor and even perhaps sage or saint. He was certainly to be respected and possibly feared a little. It is probably Meredith to whom Archdeacon William Lea is referring in his *Reminiscences*, mentioned earlier, when he recalls:

"I had caught five or six, when I heard a voice behind me, 'You've got enough of them little ones, and they are no use to send away. I should stop now'. It was the voice of Rufus, so called for the same reason as our second Norman king, and in his way equally devoted to sport. He was called 'Keeper'; his better name would have been 'killer', for a deadlier hand never threw a line. Whatever the weather he could always catch fish; and I have a shrewd suspicion that for the heavy baskets which sometimes were brought home, members were partly indebted to his aid."

It has been confirmed by a descendant that many of the Meredith clan were redheads and Edward Meredith may well have been. William Rufus, Meredith's son, would have been too young at the time that the Archdeacon fished.

The census of 1881 tells us that Edward Meredith still lived at Graham's Cottage. Now 46 and probably in the prime of his life the photograph below looks as if it may have been taken at this time. The photograph certainly shows Graham's Cottage and Edward Meredith, looking the archetypal keeper. The photograph has been carefully staged, a woman, perhaps Harriet his wife, can just be made out standing in front of the house. This is a professional photograph designed to record and demonstrate the importance and status of a respected and revered professional.

Edward Meredith fishing below Graham's Cottage.

Lord Coventry in his journal frequently mentions Rufus and Rufus's Cottage, and there seems little doubt that it is to Edward Meredith and Graham's Cottage he refers. Meredith provided a complete service and must have been indispensable to the members; he would have needed his own intelligence network to let him know who and when members were due to arrive. This probably included men like Mellings who drove the wagon that fetched and carried the members from stations, or housekeepers such as Mrs Castree at The Wardens, either of whom could be warned by letter, and later by telegram, of pending arrivals in the village. Lord Coventry reports that Meredith/Rufus called at his fishing 'box' in Leintwardine, Wardens Villa, and *"came to say it might be possible to catch a trout the river (being) much too high for Grayling"* and on another occasion, *"Rufus caught us two eels for dinner."* There is evidence from the angling literature that Meredith would organise a further service for his 'Gentlemen', and ensure that village boys were available to carry the sometimes groaning creels back to The Lion Hotel on payment of a penny. Archdeacon Lea mentions using this service having caught *"33 grayling, 22 of them 'shuck' and 11 larger fish; and 3 trout, one of them weighing a pound. It was now three o'clock. The boy was sent home with the fish; I changed my fly for minnow and set out to fish my way home."*.

Those staying at The Lion Hotel, as many frequently did, would expect the landlord to have been briefed by the keeper on the river conditions and to have sufficient detail to be able to advise on the best places to fish and perhaps to ensure members were not trying to fish the same water. Some years later a scheme was devised to ensure that the rules were adhered to concerning the water between Black Bridge and Leintwardine which stipulated that no more than three rods were permitted at any one time. This scheme involved brass discs that were hung in the bar at The Lion – if none were left hanging, one knew that the water was full and you would have to fish elsewhere.

As is the way of the world when matters are going well little comment is made and little praise recorded. We have no reason to doubt that throughout his career Meredith` gave excellent service but other than receiving increases in pay on several occasions there is nothing actually written to confirm this regard other than on his gravestone. There are however two letters that have been retained that indicated that Meredith's life was not without some problems. The first letter is written by Robert Harley:

"May 20th 1899

Mr Meredith,

I hear there is a great deal of brush cutting going on down the Club Water – I do not know by whose orders –

For the future you had better not have anything in that way done without an order from <u>two</u> of the committee.

The present committee are Major Hill, Mr Vale-King & myself – If wanted I can nearly always meet these Gentlemen or one of them to make any inspection that is required.

Yours faithfully, Robert W D Harley

The letter would seem to indicate that the lines of communication within the Club are not as clear as one might wish. RWD Harley also seems to acknowledge that it is very likely that Meredith is not fully aware of the committee or that he might expect to receive instruction from them and not ARBK. The next letter, some years later, is from ARBK in March 1903 and was filed under *"Notice to Quit"* which sounds rather serious. The subject matter also indicates that a rift is only just avoided, ARBK addressed Edward Meredith:

"Sir

I was informed that your son was at home idle, doing no work anywhere. If he is as you say generally employed by Overtons, at Kinton, Marlow etc. and other places and not concerned (as I was informed) with others in poaching near your house, I can have no objection to his lodging at home.

I was informed, but I should say by an anonymous letter, that game and rabbits were sent off from Hopton Heath Station: the letter did not say by whom: from this side of the estate I know no doubt that hampers have been constantly sent off from Onibury Station.

The estate now, will I have no doubt, be much better looked after by the Keepers of the present shooting tenants, than it has been for some time.

Yours faithfully, AR Boughton Knight"

William Rufus (the son) is shown on the census returns as living at home and working as either a carpenter or gardener, and as Overtons were the local builders in Leintwardine, it does indicate that ARBK was referring to William and not anyone else. What the letter also demonstrates is the power of the landlord over the working man's life. In this case, despite working for his employer for over fifty years and being a tenant for the same period, the landlord was considering a demand for the tenant's son to quit the cottage on the basis of an anonymous letter.

Although in the main narrative we considered the building of the Birmingham Corporation water pipeline appeared to have had little effect on the Club, it would have been quite the opposite for Meredith and Harriet. They would have had to put up with the construction site on their doorstep for several years. The pipeline passes to the south of their cottage by a mere 50 metres; their orchard would largely have been destroyed. Imagine the disruption caused by the men and machines, the dirt and dust in the summer from horses and carts hauling stone and earth to and fro. Hopefully Harriet would have turned the situation to her advantage and sold refreshments to the navvies.

The pipeline was officially opened by George IV in 1904. He did not come anywhere near Graham's Cottage but the ceremony at the Elan Valley would at least have signalled the beginning of a quieter period beside the Teme, for a while at least until the Corporation decided to add some additional piping some decades later. It did not take long for the grass to grow over the large scars across the countryside and even the replanted orchard would have made quick progress.

Meredith was now nearly seventy and Harriet 66, and it is probable that in his advanced years his under-keeper, E Steadman, was taking on more responsibility. It is of interest that Meredith's wages had now been raised to 22/- a week or just over £57 per year (in 2008 money the equivalent of £24,400), not a huge increase on his starting salary of 16/- a week when he started thirty years previously.

The next detail we can find is the fact that Harriet dies on 30 January 1907. After 48 years of married life Harriet's death would have been a blow and it is not surprising that we find in the 1908 statement of Club accounts that a keeper (un-named) has been in receipt of a pension for the past 24 weeks. It would seem that Meredith went into retirement on the 9 October 1907, aged 72.

It is not clear who took over as keeper. The new man may have been E Griffiths who is later confirmed by name as the keeper and as living in Graham's Cottage. How long Meredith is allowed to stay in the cottage after he retires is not known but less than three years later the parish register informs us that on 19 May 1910 Edward Meredith died of chronic bronchitis at Tipton's Row in Leintwardine.

Only eleven months earlier ARBK had died and his son had taken over the Club and it takes another year before the members agree to give their past keeper the recognition he deserves. We can see from the typed circular[6] sent out, and shown below, that Major Wood has taken the initiative to implement the members' desire to produce a headstone with a suitable inscription:

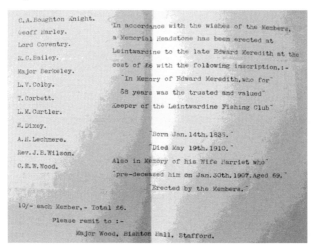

Whilst we can still see the headstone and give respect to this *"trusted and valued keeper"*, it is probably the words of Archdeacon Lea that will endure and ensure that Edward Meredith, or Rufus as he was known, will be remembered as long as the Leintwardine waters are fished *"for a deadlier hand never threw a line"*.

LEINTWARDINE FISHING CLUB.

1863.—4.

Rules and Regulations.

1.—That the Club consist of Twenty-five Members, at Ten Pounds per annum each, to be paid in advance.

2.—That each Member can take one Friend with him to the whole of the water rented by the Club, and such Friend may Angle in the same manner as a Member, with one exception, see Rule 6th.

3—That no Trout be killed in any way from 21st of September to the 1st. of March.

4—That no Grayling exceeding half-pound in weight be taken before the *First of June*; and no Grayling or Trout be killed *at any time of the year* less than Eight inches in length from nose to tail.

5—That no Trolling (**for Trout**) be allowed until the *Fifteenth of June.*

6—That Members *or* their Friends may Angle for Grayling with Grasshopper, or other Ground Bait, during any Six days from the Fifteenth of October to the Thirtieth of November; but a Member *and* his Friend are not to use the Ground Bait on the same day.

N. B. Each day a Friend fishes with the Ground Bait will count as one of the six allowed; (*i. e.* the *combined* number of days that a Member *and* his Friend Angle in the above named manner not to exceed *Six.*)

7—That the months of December, January and February be considered *close* months during which no angling of any kind will be allowed.

8—It is to be distinctly understood that each Subscription be the "*bonâ-fide*" Subscription of one individual.

9—Any Member committing a breach of any of the above Rules, or sanctioning any of his Friends in doing so, will cease to be a Member of the Club.

10—Any Member two years in arrear with his Subscription will lose his priviledge of Angling; and the President will consider him no longer a Member of the Club.

JAMES ACKERS,
President and Treasurer.

UPPER BEAT. ABOVE AND BELOW,THE LEINTWARDINE VILLAGE CONCESSION

UPPER BEAT.   ABOVE, OPPOSITE TRIPPLETON.   BELOW, "WIDE WORLD"

UPPER BEAT.   ABOVE, TOWARDS STANDLEDEAN. BELOW, AQUEDUCT BRIDGE.

UPPER BEAT. ABOVE AND BELOW CRIFTIN FORD or "BLACK" BRIDGE.

MIDDLE BEAT. ABOVE, ABOVE BURRINGTON BR. BELOW, TO BURRINGTON BR.

LOWER BEAT. ABOVE, BELOW BURRINGTON BR. BELOW, BY OWNEY COTTAGE..

LOWER BEAT.   ABOVE, OWNEY MEADOW.   BELOW, OWNEY MEADOW.

LOWER BEAT. ABOVE AND BELOW DOWNTON BRIDGE.

LOWER BEAT. ABOVE, UPSTREAM OF BOW BRIDGE. BELOW, BOW BRIDGE.

ABOVE, GRAHAM'S COTTAGE.   BELOW, CRIFTIN FORD COTTAGES.

ABOVE, TRIPPLETON HOUSE.   BELOW, THE WARDENS

ABOVE, THE LION HOTEL.   BELOW, THE SWAN INN

ABOVE, LEINTWARDINE HOUSE.   BELOW, SIGN ABOVE DOWNTON BRIDGE

ANDREW ROUSE BOUGHTON KNIGHT (1826-1909)   LFC PRESIDENT 1870-1909

DOWNTON CASTLE

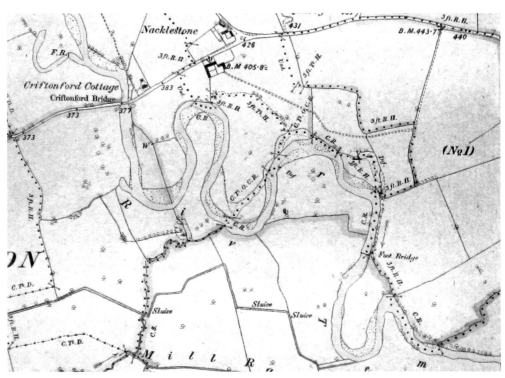

ABOVE, MAP SURVEYED 1885.   BELOW, MAP 1903

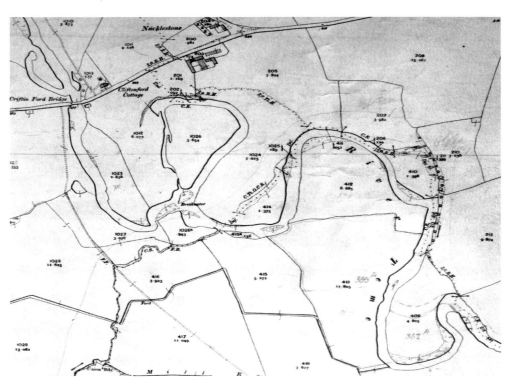

CHAPTER EIGHT

CHARLES ANDREW ROUSE BOUGHTON KNIGHT

1909-1920

"– it is about time their day was ended I think. And I mean to do it."

CABK, or *"Andy"*, as he signs his letters, probably considered that the fates had not treated him kindly. He would seem to have tried to make a career in the military, firstly in the militia, then eventually the Scots Guards, but just at the end of the First Boer War and thus too late to earn any kudos or medals. Only three years later he has resigned from the Army at the age of 26, possibly due to ill health. He rejoined to serve with a reserve formation in 1900 but again it does not work out for him. It would seem that throughout most of his adult life the Downton Estate was not making much money. Agriculture was in the doldrums, and consequently the allowance he received from his father was not as large as he would have liked. He also seems to have developed a poor relationship with his mother, Eliza, a very religious woman. There is little material available concerning CABK, just a few public records and some letters[2] sent to his uncle, Sir Charles Rouse

Charles Andrew Boughton Knight, 1859-1947

Boughton, at Downton Hall to whom he wrote regularly. In these letters he constantly complained about something, usually the dreadful state of Downton Castle, the estate and particularly his parents. His uncle clearly helped him out with generous presents and seems to act almost as a surrogate father as it is from him that he sought advice on which regiment to join, shares to buy etc. When his uncle died in 1906 his confidant then became his cousin, William Rouse Boughton, who has inherited the Downton Hall Estate. Although the correspondence left to us is one-sided – the Boughton-Knight family seem to have kept none of the letters they received – those sent to his uncle do give some idea of the nature of the man.

CABK married Helen Dupré (née Wilson) in 1902, probably against his mother's wishes as his letters reveal that he never felt that she made Helen welcome. The marriage took place in Dublin. CABK consistently complained to his uncle that his mother ignored Helen and refused to visit her. Neither he nor Helen were in good health and required

visits to the *"watering places"*, the health spas of the time, on a regular basis. He underwent quite a severe surgical operation in 1903 and took several months to recover. They had continual battles with tradesmen over poor workmanship or over-charging and found that they cannot afford to live at 9 Norfolk Crescent, their Hyde Park address. He does not appear to have paid employment and presumably he was still living off an allowance from his father. In 1904 they move to rented accommodation in Hinton Admiral in Hampshire, where kind Uncle Charles was still sending them presents,

Helen Boughton Knight, 1868-1926

this time a pony-cart. CABK hoped that his parents would move out of Downton Castle and allow him to get on with running the estate as he believed his father's lack of attention had allowed the agent, Thomas Fenn, and later Fenn's son to get away with considerable mismanagement. Some earlier ideas for him to move to Mary Knoll House situated on Bringewood and owned by the family since Payne Knight's day came to nothing. Later his father and mother also considered moving to Mary Knoll but that idea is dismissed and his parents continued to live at Downton. It is clearly not a happy time for CABK. He does not relish going home at all. Whilst all this turmoil and bitterness is taking place at one end of the estate, at the other none of it seems to affect the LFC activities unduly. It is clear that members continue to take advantage of the privileges due to them as a result of the Club's arrangements with ARBK. The question they had yet to ask themselves was – for how much longer?

Shortly after his father's death, in June 1909, CABK was writing from Pools Farm. He

Pools Farm

may well have moved there as soon as he knew his father was ill. The house is a large red-brick house on the Downton Estate, about a mile west of Downton Castle. We can only suppose that he had not moved into the Castle because his 71-year-old mother was still living there. Finally, at the age of 50, CABK inherited the estate if not the Castle. He was determined to put the estate on a better financial footing and set about removing those people he thought had been feathering their own nests. He wrote to Cousin William, *"I have bitten off a big chunk and now will try and chew it."* William had inherited his estate from Uncle Charles some three years before CABK and had already encountered problems running it and was a source of much advice to CABK. To repay him a little for his guidance it is clear that CABK has invited him to fish and hoped he would *"go often"*. This offer was probably to fish on the Castle waters rather than LFC waters.

So it is from Pools Farm that the new, and presumably unelected, President took on the management of the LFC, or did he? It was more likely that the LFC committee continued to carry on as before for the rest of that year and planned to do so into the 1910 season. This was despite the probable death of Major Hill who had disappeared from the scene. This stalwart of the Club was to be sorely missed. The Club however was fortunate to have another member in the wings ready to take up the reins, Major CE Wood. There are no LFC records for the period 1909-1912 and we rely on the few letters remaining to inform us of LFC activities. The first letter found clearly indicates that CABK is not going to allow the LFC to continue as it is. One wonders why? Presumably it is all part of his plan to make the estate pay its way or is there another motive? Is there a large chip on his shoulder? The letter may also serve to demonstrate a lack of communication between father and son concerning the running of the estate and in particular on anything to do with the Club. In December 1909 CABK writes a letter to Lord Coventry:

"Dear Lord Coventry,

I believe you are the eldest of the members of the Leintwardine Fishing Club and I am writing to tell you I do not feel able to let the Club continue, so far as my water is concerned, at all events under present conditions –

I do not know what notice the members require but as I do not wish to inconvenience them, I propose to let the tenancy continue until one year from now, but not more.

I believe the Club water is 5 ½ miles for which £120 a year is paid –

Considering the rents paid for fishing and the great difficulty in getting any, I consider this a totally inadequate rent.

If the Club desires to continue its tenancy for the year longer that I suggest, I shall be glad to hear as soon as is convenient.

I believe my late Father acted as Secretary to the Club. I do not know whether the Club wish me to do so, but I should be glad if someone else would undertake this --- do you know if there was any written agreement for the Fishery originally made? I can find none at Downton. Yours very truly, C A Boughton Knight."

Lord Coventry writes[6] in response on December 10, 1909:

"Dear Mr Knight,

I am in receipt of your letter of yesterday in which you inform me that you are not disposed to allow the Leintwardine Club to continue under present conditions – I am sure that all the members will regret, as I do, your decision, but, so far as I am personally concerned, I think your proposal fair and I shall be prepared to fall in with your suggestion and to accept notice to give up membership at the close of the season, [oig](sic) Jan 31ˢᵗ 1911 –

I do not know if there was even any agreement other than that contained in the printed rules of the Club – of course I can only speak for myself, but I daresay several members would be glad of the opportunity of joining any Club you may be desirous of forming in the future under fresh conditions –

I do not suppose the secretarial duties, under present conditions, involve much work since I believe these would only include demands for subscriptions in March, and I daresay this business could be undertaken at your estate office, but of this you are the better judge. Believe me, Yours truly, Coventry"

The rumour of closure, no doubt, was rapidly passed around to a deeply concerned membership. Major Wood implores[6] Lord Coventry in March of 1910 to use his influence:

"Dear Lord Coventry

It is very sad to think of there being a probability of the Leintwardine Fishing Club coming to an end. It is quite historical in that it is the oldest fishing Club in the Kingdom it seems a pity it should die without an effort being made. I feel sure Mr Boughton Knight would not willingly do away with it if he knew how much we are all attached to it and its surroundings and past memories.

I also feel sure that if a higher rent is demanded the members would gladly increase their subscriptions.

It will be so kind of you if you would represent this to Mr Boughton Knight as one of the oldest members of the Club and ask him to allow us to continue as before. Yours sincerely, C E W Wood"

Whether Lord Coventry does anything about this request is unclear. In the light of his response three months previously he probably does nothing. Lord Coventry's journal shows that he in fact took advantage of the fishing whilst he was still able. On the 6th January 1910 he reports, *"Went out with the hopper, water high but clear; too wild for fishing. But I caught 4 Grayling, nice fish, and two trout, in beautiful condition, which I returned."* It is very likely that Major Wood is urging other members to write to CABK in an effort to have him change his mind. It is almost certainly these letters to which CABK refers to in the second letter below as offensive "*bombs*".

These next two letters allows us to get a real insight into the desires and motivation behind CABK's plans and his complete ignorance of his father's ideas for the Club. He first writes[3] on April 23 1910 in response to what must have been a quite indignant letter from Geoffrey Harley who had just returned from an extensive big game hunting trip:

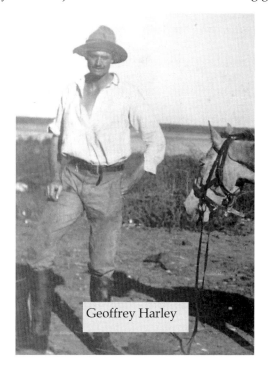
Geoffrey Harley

"*My Dear Harley,*

I have received your letter today. I did not know you were home.

I am sorry the notice to you re. the Fishing Club was accidentally addressed to Admiral Britten who is dead. But whose death I was only told of after the circulars were written.

These will have explained to you that I have given notice to the members of the LFC that the lease of that portion of the water belonging to this estate will cease on April 1 1911.

As I told Major Wood the Club appears to me to be in a thoroughly unbusiness-like state.

I have had a big lot of worry over it since I have come here, and I consider the rent of £120 p.a. quite inadequate for the 6 miles of fishing they have.

The Club was originally organised by my father for the benefit of neighbours and friends living in the neighbourhood.

It seems to me that there are hardly any local members, and that the first object of the Club is thereby defeated – I am only doing what my father would have done had he lived.

I don't think I can say anything more on the subject.

I am very glad you have returned home and hope you are all well. I am living here in a farmhouse near the church and shall be here for some time thanks to Lloyd George and this government.

Yours sincerely, CA Boughton Knight."

It is clear that Geoffrey Harley has found out about the ending of the lease from a third party and CABK is reduced to a barely plausible excuse for failing to write to him. CABK must have realised that his letter was a less than an adequate explanation of his plans and writes a second letter, almost as if he had not written the first, five days later on April 28th:

"My Dear Harley,

I am so glad to hear you are home again safely. I shall be very glad to talk over fishing matters with you when you come down to Brampton Bryan.

I am in a great bother about the affairs of the Leintwardine Club. No one seems to know much. There has been apparently no annual meeting. I have not discovered a committee. There seems no one in authority. The subscriptions are unpaid with few exceptions. What money I have got I have entered in a separate account LF Club in United Counties Bank, Ludlow.

The members are nearly all swearing at losing such fishing for such a subscription and no wonder. I enclose the last and most offensive bomb which has been hurled at me and which I am ignoring of course.

I shall be pleased to talk over your plan with you. And I shall be most pleased in this, as in all matters to fall in with your plans and wishes wherever I can.

I need not say there will be no difficulty in letting the whole or any portion of the fishing at a good rent if I wish to.

I will do nothing until I see you.

I can see no reason however for providing fishing on absurd terms for a lot of strangers.

If you and I formed a little Club for our friends and neighbours then I could see some sense and object in it. But whatever we do we must hold the control and the thing must be run on business lines.

Yours sincerely, CA Boughton Knight"

Nothing appears to happen, there are no further letters, and the season does not seem to be interrupted; we can only assume that members are continuing to fish as entitled. The notice of closure remains and the members arrange to meet towards the end of the year to discuss their position. Their usual meeting place was The Lion, Leintwardine. As the hotel was then owned by the Downton Estate, more neutral ground was selected at Worcester. If any minutes were taken, they have not been discovered but it is very likely that it was Major Wood who called this extraordinary meeting and convened it at Worcester to encourage Lord Coventry to attend. The principal outcome of the meeting was probably to propose that Geoffrey Harley be asked to engage with CABK on the Club's behalf. It would appear that he did so and wrote to CABK passing on the feelings of the Club. This can be deduced from the following letter[3] that CABK sends to Cousin William at Downton Hall on 6 December 1910:

"... As to the fishing Club. Harley wrote some time ago to tell me the members had held a meeting at <u>Worcester</u>!!! This alone shows there is something wrong with the Club, that <u>Worcester</u> should be found the most convenient centre to hold a Club meeting! – That at this meeting it was decided Harley was to ask me to reconsider my decision and allow the Club to go on, although I have <u>repeatedly</u> told several members time after time I would not do so specially Major Wood who has been constantly hanging around here and writing , and worrying me--- When I wrote and told Harley I would gladly see him but that my mind was quite unchangeable he sprung upon me his claim to the 'exclusive right of fishing on both sides of the river from Leintwardine to Black Bridge!' Now in reply to my letter he offers to show me his authority whenever I like. I have looked in the letterbook and find letters more or less unreadable of 1864, and on, relating to agreements with Lord Oxford as to the fishing. That there <u>is</u> something in Harley's claim I have no doubt.

However you shall hear whenever I hear more – also I shall been (be) awfully pleased later to show you all letters, maps etc and talk it over.

The Club blackballed Heber-Percy! And have had, and mean to have, just everything all their own way – it is about time their day was ended I think. And I mean to do it. ..."

This letter gives an insight into the attitude that CABK has towards LFC members. It all rather smacks of the new landlord throwing a petulant tantrum having come under pressure from one or more of the members. Petulant or not, it is clear that CABK wants to make changes. A further indication that he was intending to go his own way was his ordering of books of fishing tickets with receipts. There is no doubt that they were

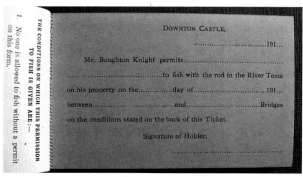

produced for this particular decade as the tickets are printed with the date as 191.. , and the words *"Mr Boughton Knight permits...... to fish with the rod in the River Teme on his property...."* Two of these books[3] have been found so far but none of the tickets are missing, so it might have been an idea that came to nothing. As for the rumour that Heber-Percy was out of favour, it seems to have been just that, a rumour, as nothing has been found to substantiate the claim and furthermore he not only remained a member but was later appointed President.

The weather probably does not help the general sense of unrest. Mr Charnock's Leintwardine School log tells us that the period 6th to the 16th of December 1910 produced serious floods following six inches of rain over that ten-day period and a total of eleven and a half inches in 45 days. It was a very wet end to the year and the pressure to improve the estate and generate income must have been getting to our landlord at Downton because we now come across a letter with which most landlords would be ashamed to be associated.

Readers will recall that Edward Meredith had retired as river keeper and it would appear that E Griffith has taken his place as river keeper for the Club. The letter[4], written in March 1911, is from Geoffrey Harley, an honorary member, to another LFC member, Dr Dixey:

"I daresay you may have heard that Griffiths met with an accident through a fall off his bicycle, and has been dangerously ill – I saw Boughton Knight today, who told me that he had stopped his pay since the day of the accident, as he said that he did not feel that he had authority from the members to spend their money on a man who was unable to work for them. I said I thought the members might wish to continue his wages or a part of them, until he becomes [fit], or for the remainder of the time, necessarily a short one, during which he remains a member of the Club.

At all counts I though it better that the Club should be informed of the circumstances & Boughton Knight has asked me to write to some of the members. Unfortunately I have not a list of members, but have written to Lord Coventry, Major Wood and Mr Bailey - Griffiths is under notice to leave his cottage, but I understand, has received no intimation from the Club that he will no longer be required, & this notice Boughton Knight says he has no authority from the members to give. I do not feel myself able to give an opinion on either of these questions being only an Hon member of the Club but I think they should be settled. I hesitate to trouble you but will you (get some opinion or line) which I can lay before Boughton Knight or else could you write to him direct."

The letter would seem to indicate how difficult it was to deal with CABK. It is fortunate for all of the members, and Mr Griffiths, that Geoffrey Harley was prepared to take up the interests of the Club. There is of course a degree of self-interest as Geoffrey Harley likes to fish and hopes that the Club will continue. The next letter[4] from Geoffrey Harley, written in the same month, is interesting for not only does it confirm that he firmly believes that Boughton Knight will close down the Club but that he also gives us a first indication that fishing on the Leintwardine water is not wholly a male occupation, and that he is very happy to permit ladies to fish on any water that he controls.

"My dear Miss Crawshay

You will recollect that when last we met & talked over the fishing question – I said that owing to change and rumours of change, I should probably have to make different arrangements about my water – but that while matters were in abeyance I hoped that you would fish as before.

Now however that period of abeyance is, or will be, over on April 1st, for it is now definitely settled that the old Club Water then comes to an end.

I am very sorry about it as we are both very fond of fishing & it does not leave very much with the Club Water gone, and all the fishing down to the weir let to my shooting tenants.

We have managed to get a few fish in spite of these cold snowstorms –

Freda had a nice one of 1 1/2 lbs the day before yesterday, and one almost as good two days before.

With all best wishes from us both."

The exact relationship between Miss Crawshay and Herbert Crawshay of Stormer, if any, is unknown. We do know that she lived at Hightree House, Leintwardine, when the 1913 edition of Kelly's Directory was published. It would be interesting to know more of her fishing exploits.

Geoffrey Harley is able to write in such definite terms concerning the demise of the Club as on 25th March 1911 he had received from CABK notice terminating the annual agreement.

Intriguingly the same letter-books in the Harley archives have a series of pages removed. Judging by the index, the letters were written to Mr Beale, a name we have not come across before and at this stage he is not a member of the Club but presumably fishes with Geoffrey Harley on the Harley water. We can only speculate that Geoffrey Harley knows Beale well and is using him as a sounding board with both of them determined not to give up the idea of the continuance of the Club. Perhaps the missing letters discussed matters or opinions that he would rather not have seen exposed in the cold light of day, hence their removal from the letter book.

Despite the notice to terminate there is no indication that the members have stopped fishing. The Harley Estate still received its share of the rent and the Club therefore remained in operation. Thus whilst there is life, there is hope and Geoffrey Harley presumably continued his efforts to galvanise support for the Club. We can see from Geoffrey's fishing diary, a suede-bound volume[4] still in the hands of the family that he went fishing in some far-flung places. In 1910 he was fishing near the source of the Nile at Ripon Falls. In 1911 and again in 1912 he fished the river Figga in Norway taking 18

R.G.G.H.   *fishing at the Source of the Nile*

and 14 salmon respectively. In 1914 he fished Fischells Brook in Newfoundland and took 14 salmon.

However, despite these foreign adventures and owning his own water on the Teme, Geoffrey Harley had an abiding desire to see the Leintwardine Club continue. He was not alone in his endeavours as Major Wood continued his efforts to ensure the continuation of the Club. He wrote from Bishton Hall, Stafford, to the Harley Estates solicitor Mr Martineau in August, *"...it would be a very good thing... to try and get the Club reformed before the autumn."* He went on to explain that the members' consensus was that if the Club is now to pay £250 and be responsible for the river banks and pay a keeper, then Boughton Knight should not have the right to nominate many locals as they *'get all the best of the fishing'*. He clearly feared yet more interference from CABK and went on to state that he thought that the *'old rules of the Club were so excellently thought out that it seems a great pity they should be revised'*. It would appear that the efforts of both Geoffrey Harley and Major Wood had the desired effect for despite CABK's protestations made a year previously another summer of fishing has taken place and there are even indications that he is softening his position.

We find an important comment in Lord Coventry's journal[6] dated 18th October 1911, *"Mr Knight, Mr Harley, and Mr Weyman were, I understand, on the river today discussing plans for the future, and it seems probable they will endeavour to start a Club again, tho' no one, as I understand, has come forward to take the fishing hitherto. The fact is we have been paying a full rent as I always told the members and no one will give more than we have done."*

This is the last comment concerning fishing that Lord Coventry made in his journal. He continued to visit his house in Leintwardine for the next seven years, to attend livestock fairs and sheep sales but, as Catherine Gordon suggests in her book, he probably suffered from rheumatism and gave up fishing. He visited Warden Villa in July 1918 and was clearly disappointed to find that, without consent, two soldiers had been billeted in his house by the local police constable. It is probable that he never set foot in the house again as this is his last entry in the journal.

Geoffrey Harley continued to use all his diplomatic skills through to the close of 1911. The next letter[4] we find is from Geoffrey Harley to CABK clearly in response to a request for advice from CABK:

"Nov: 25th 1911

My Dear Boughton Knight

I am very sorry you had to put off your shoot – but it turned out a bad day so I daresay it was just as well.

I at last send you a list of names. I have put down all I can think of but I hope you know of a good many who will join. Probably one could easily hear of a good many more, but I have mentioned the matter to no one.

Perhaps when you have time you will let me know what you think of it – I hope you will let me know exactly what you would like done, as I have not the slightest feeling about the election of any single name. Yours very sincerely, RG Geoffrey Harley

(On a separate page)

<u>Confidential</u>   (the paragraph numbering is as written)

1.	*H Heber Percy*	*I believe was once elected*
2.	*W H Hurt Sitwell*	*Though a local should probably not be fish-*
3.	*B Sunderland*	*A keen & good fisherman. A busy man*
4.	*P H Martineau*	
5.	*Major Halstead*	*Lives at Dansfield would probably not often*
6.	*A R Beale*	*A keen and very good fisherman but would*
7.	*H Langley?*	
11.	(In pencil) *Sir Henry Ripley?*	
12.	*Major Wood*	*Member of the old Club*
13.	*Major Barclay*	*Member of the old Club*

(Page 3)

14. *L M Cutler*   *Members of the old Club, the first two I do*

15. *F Corbett*

16. *R E Bailey*

17. *John H Starey*   *A friend of R E Bailey's a letter about him*

18. *C Gwyer?*   *Eywood, Titley, Herefordshire*

I have omitted D Dixeys name, as it rather seemed to me that he would require more control than you would probably care to part with but I suppose it is invidious to have any of the old members without them all. Do you propose to ask Lord Coventry to rejoin.

The notes of interrogation, would I think be doubtful but I think satisfactory if they would join."

The response from CABK with his list of names has been lost but we do have the next letter[4] from Geoffrey Harley which was written on December 6:

"My dear Boughton Knight

Many thanks for your letter which I found waiting for me on my return home. I am very sorry to say that I am afraid I shall not be able to shoot with you on 13th or 14th as I am shooting on 15th & expect to have to go to London on 14th. I am very sorry as I should much liked to have come.

With regard to the fishing Club. I cordially agree with the names that you have put down. – eleven - if we include Major Wood & Trevor Corbett.

I would put in a word for RE Bailey who is also a local man living on this side of Hereford, the Club would then still be entirely local in character.

You do not say what you think about -:

Major Halstead [he was not a member of the old Club: he lives at Kington – Frank Hill knows him well]

Tim Sitwell

& A Beale

Curtis the other day at the (Grog?) said something about joining, but was quite (un) certain.

I think we ought to meet & discuss it – as soon as we can....."

CABK's reply of 8 December 1911 is a long one[4]: *"I add a list brought up to date including all your men excepting Beale – add him by all means if you like."* He describes all the expense of river keepers etc that he considers will fall on him and reckons that, *"I should not find much plunder out of £200"*. He goes on to say, however, that he is perfectly content to leave money matters up to the committee provided that Geoffrey Harley was on it and had appointed the other members: *"I wish them all to be thoroughly satisfied with the sub-scription asked. I think you will see I am as anxious as I know you are to have all our rules and conditions approved by all."* He suggests that a committee should go into the detail and suggests that *"a good plan"* would be a committee consisting of *"say Hugo, Tim Sitwell, Mr Martineaux and of course yourself"*.

CABK goes on to inform Geoffrey Harley that he has let The Lion to *"one Burmingham at a low rent of £25 per ann. on condition that he will, 1. Stop drinking by the Leintwardine drinkists. 2. Make the place possible and comfortable for members. 3. I, to help with furniture, and try to make the place known. His wife he assures me is a very tidy cook, he a good waiter and valet, quite able to take in and attend on the members. 4. I, to see to the drinks – I want every-thing to be very good and fair in price. 5. Probably I will help in running a machine to meet members and do a small business. I think we can have a tariff per day for members"*.

Lion Hotel, Leintwardine

How CABK thinks Burmingham will survive under this regime is a mystery. He pre-sumably wants the bar closed to locals and then removes any chance of the landlord making any profit from the sale of drinks to LFC members by purchasing the stock him-self. It would seem that CABK expects his hotel proprietor to make a living servicing the 15 members most of whom now live locally and will not need to stay the night. If CABK has decided to allow the Club to continue because he can see some business advantage to The Lion, he seems to have failed to anticipate the consequences of restricting the clientele to those Club members who live locally or who are not classified '*drinkists*'.

We should note that Geoffrey Harley was still keen to propose Beale although CABK seems less than enthusiastic. CABK now seems to have taken time off for the Christmas festivities and does not seem to understand that the members need a resolution. Again Geoffrey Harley came to the rescue and chivvied matters along with his next letter dated January 22, 1912:

"My Dear Boughton Knight

I wonder if you have received any answers from the prospective Members – Time is getting on - & in another 6 weeks trout fishing will begin – The old Club as you know commenced on March 15th.

Shall you adhere to the old rules – more or less. Not many alterations would be needed. I think.

Taking them (seriatim)

1. *Alterations in the number of members & amount of sub:*

2. *Committee as suggested by you.*

   CA Boughton Knight

   P H Martineau

   H Heber Percy

   R G G Harley

3. *12 "tickets will be issued etc":*

   20 in my copy of the rules is substituted for 12 which I think is right.

4. *Have you decided on the method of replacing the original members.*

The other rules seem alright. Hugo Heber Percy told me that you thought of limiting the fishing days of members -: but this is only hearsay – I enclose you a letter from R E Bailey – with regard to his postscript, I need not say that I was not so presumptuous. I said I would put his friend's name (John H Starey) before you – which I did in Nov: last.

If you have any spare time I should be very glad to see you. I am shooting tomorrow and Wednesday. Otherwise could come & see you. Except Friday – or will you come over here & lunch.

Yours very sincerely, Geoffrey Harley

John H Starey is 60 and (unreadable) *and a very busy man. Unless you have filled your list he sounds alright"*

Both the Club and CABK are very fortunate to have Geoffrey Harley taking so much interest in reforming the Club for whilst Major Wood had worked hard at the problem, it was always unlikely that CABK would have paid much attention to him. Geoffrey Harley clearly recognises CABK's limitations and has led him through the process at every stage. Thankfully all his hard work seems to have done the trick for the next piece of the jigsaw puzzle can be found in the *1912 Minute Book* probably written by AR Beale.

"Leintwardine Fishing Club.

This Club was reconstituted in February 1912. The number of members was limited to 15. Each paying £25 a year. In addition Mr Boughton–Knight and Mr Harley, the lessors, to be Honorary Members without payment but with member's rights.

The first 15 members were invited to join by the lessors.

The following are the names.

RC Bailey Esq. The Pigeon House, Bodenham, Herefordshire.

Major Berkeley. Fieldgate, Kenilworth.

ES Rouse-Boughton Esq. Whitton, Leintwardine.

AR Beale Esq. Seedley, Leintwardine.

ERT Corbett Esq. Radmore, Dorrington, Salop.

HL Heber-Percy Esq. Ferney Hall, Onibury, Salop.

Rowland Kennard Esq. Little Harrow, Christchurch, Hants.

HW Langley Esq. Bedstone Court, Bucknell, Salop.

Sir HWA Ripley Bt. Bedstone, Bucknell, Salop.

WHH Sitwell Esq. The Cottage, Bucknell, Salop.

JH Starey Esq. The Manor, Bodenham, Herefordshire.

Bryan Sunderland Esq. Hope Court, Ludlow, Salop.

HR Sykes Esq. Longnor Hall, Longnor, Shrewsbury.

Ralph Wingfield Esq. Ouslow, Shrewsbury.

Major CE Wood. Bishton Hall, Stafford.

The following Committee was formed. Mr Boughton Knight, Mr RGG Harley, Mr HL Heber-Percy"

The first meeting was held at the Lion Hotel on June 18th 1912. Four members attended with presumably CABK taking the chair: Bailey, Heber-Percy, Starey and Beale. They decided that a formal agreement should be entered into between the lessors and the Club to cover the lease of the water and constitution of the Club, with the lease back-dated to March 1st 1912. They discussed the system for filling vacancies and curiously decided that the first two should be by a ballot of members and *'every third vacancy by the lessors: failing their election, then a new member to be elected by the Club, the intention being that the lessors have every third nomination'*. The minutes do not say who proposed this idea and one can only assume it was CABK: it smacks of his determination to retain influence over the make-up of the Club. It is unclear who held the office of President at this time ; probably, CABK but this is not actually stated. Alternatively it might have been Heber-Percy who took on the role as ex-officio President as it seems that as the only paying member on the management committee, he represents the LFC's interests to the landlords.

The minutes do, however, record that Beale was appointed Honorary Secretary. The handwriting in the minute book would appear to indicate that Beale probably wrote up the first few pages some time after the first two meetings had been held as both the minutes and the preamble are in exactly the same hand. It would also appear that they were produced from notes supplied by CABK. Heber-Percy proposed that friends' tickets be reduced to six per year and that 3,000 six-inch fish should be put in this year and 2,000 each year thereafter. He estimated the cost would be about £22 per 1,000 and should be paid for out of a Fishing Fund. The meeting decided that the members should be asked to subscribe to the Fishing Fund. Mr Bailey then proposed that "*swimming the worm*" be allowed after October 1st in each year, but there is no note as to whether this proposal was adopted.

It is interesting to note that Mr Beale, a new member of just a few months, is voted in as Secretary. We already know that he was proposed as a member by Geoffrey Harley and it looks as if this might have been a diplomatic appointment to balance the presence of Heber-Percy whom we might regard as being a CABK advocate. One wonders how he came to rise to prominence so quickly; he must have had some connections. It was in fact his mother, Mary Dora (née Clerke), who had the connections and it was her family that lived in this area. She was the daughter of the 9th Baronet Hitcham, Lt Colonel Sir William Clerke (who fought at Waterloo) and he had a town house in London and a country house at Bedstone House, Bucknell. Mary Clerke married the Reverend Theodore Beale in 1863 and settled down with him at the vicarage in Hopton Castle.

Their son Arthur Richard Beale was born in 1866 and educated at Radley. Another member of the family, Mary's brother Captain Charles Longueville Clerke, may have lived at

Seedley House in Leintwardine. He gave this as his address when he was proposed as a member in 1882 by RWD Harley. Four years later a note is made in the *1870 Minute Book* to say that he was not elected. He was probably another casualty of the campaign to limit the number of locals.

By 1893 AR Beale was living at The Cottage, Bucknell; there is little surprise that Geoffrey Harley got to know him and his fishing capabilities as he had probably been fishing on Harley's water. By 1912 when AR Beale was being proposed , time had taken its toll on the Clerke family. Sir William, had died and so too had the 10th Baronet, another Sir William; his widow Lady Georgina Clerke continues to live at Bedstone. AR Beale's father had also died and his mother then moved in to live with his bachelor uncle, Uncle Charles at Seedley House. Charles, of course, was still waiting patiently to fish with the Club after his rejection in 1886 despite, as readers will recall, Sir Henry Plowden's letter in 1903 to ARBK. Happily it appears that Uncle Charles did eventually manage to join the Club as although there are no membership lists to prove it, he is listed as proposing two individuals for membership in 1908 which would hardly have been permitted if he was not a member. Unhappily he did not fish for long as he died in June 1910.

Without actually recording whether any of the previously mentioned proposals were passed the next note, as they can hardly be called minutes, informs us that *"an extraordinary General Meeting was held at the Temperance Hotel, Craven Arms on Jan 22nd 1913"*. This time Major Wood and Sykes joined Bailey, Starey and Beale at the meeting, and as Starey took the chair we can only assume that CABK did not attend. The first business was to vote Colonel Twyford into the vacancy created by Sitwell's resignation. The second matter was to agree to turn in 2,000 two-year-old trout bought from the Shropshire Fishery at Cleobury at a cost of £10 per 1,000. Thirdly, the meeting decided to accept CABK's offer to hand over to the Club the £50 per year that he was due to spend on fishing improvements according to the agreement with the Club. No sign of this agreement has been found. The following were then appointed to oversee the expenditure: Heber-Percy, ES Rouse Boughton and Beale, who was now Treasurer.

Major Wood's proposal that no grayling were to be taken out under ten inches was withdrawn.

"Mr Langley and Mr Boughton both wrote suggesting that the present secretary be empowered to give leave in writing to persons not members to fish for pike with live baits".

Major Wood's suggestion that something should be done to repair the bank at the Trippleton footbridge was agreed.

Finally, the meeting felt that a qualified river keeper, controlled by the committee, was required. The Secretary was requested to write to Mr Boughton Knight.

There are two further notes in 1913 which detail the arrival of the fish from the Shropshire Fishery on February 21st and 27th. Two pages of proposed candidates are listed and then a note in 1914 states that Kennard and Langley have retired from the Club and that the lessors have appointed GH Bevan, a tenant of Geoffrey Harley at Brampton Bryan Hall, and the members have appointed Cecil Ackroyd, of Wigmore Hall.

The 1914 annual general meeting was held at The Lion in June and CABK was in the chair. The committee are the only attendees. It is clear that a river keeper, William Bullock, had been hired as it was agreed that he should remain for the following year, and we know from the Downton accounts that he was living in Graham's Cottage, paying 13/6 a week rent. The other resolutions that were provisionally passed subject to other members opinions included:

1. The suggestion that weeds, shrimps and water-snails be introduced to the river.

2. No grayling to be taken out between March 15th and June 15th.

3. Surplus funds after repairs completed should be used for the introduction of more trout.

4. Other matters discussed but deferred until the next meeting: Rule 9 be altered to reduce the catch limit per rod per day from ten brace of trout to five brace, and that the total limit in a year be 150 fish. Friends' tickets should be reduced.

Major Woods then proposed thanks to the President (still CABK) and the Committee. The subsequent report that was circulated was substantial and detailed a considerable amount of progress such as the building of two footbridges: one at Graham's Cottage and another below Black Bridge in Horseshoe Meadow. The milking bridge at Trippleton was also repaired with much of the material being supplied by CABK. At three points bank erosion was repaired with brush, wire rope and piling. It was noted that "*all work has been done with economy, under the daily supervision of resident members, the bailiff..., and frequently the employees of members, without cost to the Club*".

The repair of the river bank was very necessary as there was a real danger that the river would straighten itself out and many yards of fishing would be lost. A Downton Estate map[3] of 1903 (on the next page) showing the Horseshoe Meadow has some pencilled markings indicative of the attempt to keep up with the changes in the river's course. Whilst the Club may well have delayed the inevitable, they were not successful and the whole loop below Knacklestone was lost to an oxbow lake.

A number of angling books at this time have indicated that fishermen could purchase fishing tickets for the Teme if they stayed at the Lion Hotel, Leintwardine. This information has not sat easily with the history and ethos of the Club as we know it. We know the views of ARBK on the subject of selling tickets and it was suspected that the authors

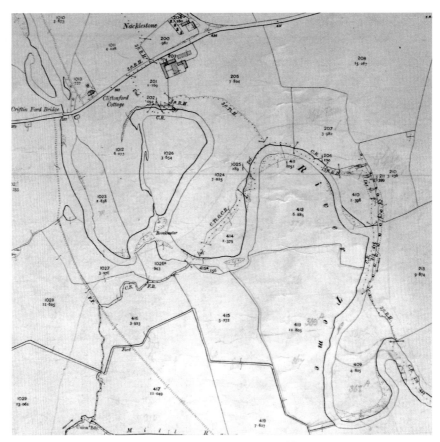

Downton Estate map 1903

had been misinformed. Fortunately a letter in the Harley archives shows that in February 1914 CABK wrote to Geoffrey Harley to let him know that he has given permission for Burmingham, the proprietor at The Lion, to sell tickets for fishing on the Clun. The Downton account books further explain that the water was divided into three stretches, the *"Point of Clun"*, the *"Upper Water"'* and the *"Lower Water"'*. A Mr Cowrie had the Point of Clun water for £25 a year, HW Langley of Bedstone Court (initially an LFC Member) had the Upper Water for £5 a year and Mr HS Burmingham of the Lion Hotel had the Lower Water. Burmingham appeared not to have paid for the lease of the water but sold the tickets and returned the receipts to the estate. The sums were not large and presumably the charges were small, £5 17s.0d was returned in 1915, £3 in 1916 and none in 1917.

The Club must have entered the 1915 season wondering just how the war in France would make its presence felt. Initially there seems to have been little effect but then resignations start to roll in and by March seven members have departed. It is not possible to determine whether this is because members are disenchanted with the Club or whether they are required for military service or other war work. Some may simply have considered it bad form to engage in such recreation at a time of war. In general terms most of those who resigned were beyond the age for active service: Heber-Percy 62, Starey 67, Rouse-Boughton 57, and Major Berkeley 59; others such as Boote, Bailey and Corbett are all unlikely candidates due to their presumed age but they too chose to resign. The Club also lost Sir HWA Ripley Bt temporarily who went into the army, as did Geoffrey Harley who joined the Royal Fusiliers. The war does not seem to have precluded new members from joining as Colonel Twyford, Major Ackroyd and Mr Bevan fill some of the vacant memberships. Military service was the reason given for there being no meeting in 1915.

Despite the war the earlier resolutions of the Club are put into effect and there is a note in the *1912 Minute Book* that 708 trout are added to the river between Trippleton and Black Bridge on March 20th and a further 784 on March 26th between Black Bridge and Burrington. In addition *"4 cans containing water shrimps and moss were put into the river in the second field below Leintwardine Bridge"*. Footbridges at Graham's Cottage and the Horseshoe Meadow were repaired and the bank above Drummond's Hole was strengthened. The above notes are the last in the minute book or the Club archive until the next book is opened in 1935.

Turning to other sources, especially the Harley archives, we can see that Club activities continued throughout the war years. Mr Beale was an efficient Secretary and produced annually an account of *LFC Expenses*, copies of which are kept in the Harley files. These single sheets provide us with the names of subscribing members, of which there were about ten: Hopps, Wood, Beale, Ackroyd, Beavan (sic), Twyford, Heber-Percy, Sykes and Wingfield. Major Lyon joined later. It is clear that the Club had to cut its cloth to suit the reduced subscription and no further fish were introduced, but in general terms fishing is not greatly effected. Geoffrey Harley was of course away serving in France for much of this period which left CABK alone with the *"responsibilities of management"* which never seems to have been his strong point. Then a problem arose.

We can see from the Downton accounts[3] that William Bullock, the river keeper, remained in Graham's Cottage until March 1916 when he *"quits it'* and presumably the job. We learn in a later letter to Geoffrey Harley that CABK *"had to discharge the late keeper"* but he does not say why. CABK also tells Harley that he has engaged Burmingham from The Lion to take on the river tasks. Presumably this is part-time and juggled with his duties running The Lion. This cannot have been entirely satisfactory as one would suspect he had no background in river keeping. The arrangement was not to last. Burmingham was soon shown in the Downton accounts to be in arrears with his rent and a note in purple crayon informs us that he was bankrupt. Thus at one stroke CABK has lost another facet of his estate business, and the Club has lost its keeper, its meeting-place and a convenient hostelry.

The trials and tribulations of management demoralised CABK. When he wrote to Geoffrey Harley earlier in the year about discharging Bullock he gave vent to a long list of complaints. The first was that he had been told that due to the war he would not be able to hire a new keeper – "*goodness knows what will happen*". He bemoans the state of farming – "*everything here is all upside down*". He bemoans the state of the country – "*the future looks bad*". Then, "*I am sick of the Club*", "*what are your views?*" The summer of 1917 does not seem to cheer him up. The situation was further aggravated by the illnesses suffered by his wife Helen which seemed to have confounded several doctors. Fortunately in October he was able to inform Mrs Harley that he was "*thankful to be able to tell you that my wife has made a wonderful recovery*". In December he turned back to resolving his issues with the Club and wrote to Geoffrey Harley to remind him that the Club's lease expired the following year, "*I am not in favour of extending it*" and declared, "*I may let the shoot to some highly satisfactory Birmingham men whom I know. I could probably let the Club water too*". Then again in February 1918 he wrote "*surely we could let to 2 or 3 private people on better terms and save a lot of bother. ...hope you will agree.*" There seems little doubt that yet again the Club is very shortly going to have to fight for its survival.

Meanwhile the members fished on and were probably oblivious to the discussions. Another issue occurred as with The Lion unoccupied, some fish were being taken by local boys fishing from the bank opposite the hotel. CABK wrote to Mrs Harley to ask for a sign to be erected and she speedily complied with the request. Members were probably not enamoured with CABK's next scheme, namely to let The Lion as accommodation for Portuguese labourers for 1918 and for part of the following year. This situation continued until The Lion was sold[4] in August 1919 to a Mr Lloyd, a 'maltster', of Corve Street, Ludlow.

In November 1918 CABK wrote to welcome Geoffrey Harley home from the war but rather brusquely got straight to the main point of his letter[4]: "*The LFC affairs are hung up because chiefly of your absence. Now that fortunately you are home again we can polish this matter off. I some time ago wrote to Wood and told him that so far as I was concerned I would not relet on the same lease... I asked if the present members wished for a renewal? And he said 'Yes'.*" CABK explained that he then got 'flu and so the matter stood unresolved. He continued "*entre nous... I am going to sell land hugely*". In fact he had already informed the Downton trustees of his plans notifying them of his intention to sell a considerable number of outlying properties and land including The Willows and Trippleton. The selling of both of these properties would affect access to the river and the matter needed to be sorted out. CABK promised not to take action without consulting Geoffrey Harley.

Behind the scenes CABK seems finally to have recognised the role that Beale was playing and has talked to him at length of his plans which have now changed from ending the relationship with the Club to one of reaching an accommodation with them. Beale wrote to Harley in December, clearly indicating that he knew him well, *"Dear Geoff"*, and reports his conversation which includes the sentence, *"He said he had enquiries about the water from a former member, whose name he mentioned and I feel pretty sure he would give what BK wanted and it would then become practically a Worcestershire Club again and a case of 'good bye' to all locals."* Beale also goes on to report that he felt, *"BK is anxious to let the water like a farm for a certain sum clear and to be free of any bothers as to looking after it etc. etc. I hope he does not change his mind."*

Beale was happy with the proposals and felt the members would accept the payment of a higher subscription in order to get control of the water. Unfortunately Geoffrey Harley would appear to have misread the letter and believed that CABK meant to eliminate locals from the Club! He was clearly upset and one gets the impression that he is frustrated that he has been away fighting the war to preserve a way of life, only to find on his return that those that haven't been away were planning to change it. Three days later he wrote a long and heartfelt letter which included *"though we may not always see exactly eye to eye – I think it is better, if the Club is to be reorganised, that you should know my views. Nowadays when old institutions, custums (sic), and traditions are like modern thrones tumbling to the ground. It would seem to us, who are 'of the land' (sic) wish to preserve so far as we may – historical fragments, if only as a symbol of a dignified age – now apparently passed.*

Speaking practically I should I should be very sorry to think that so well known and historical a fishing Club had ceased to be: for the Leintwardine Fishing Club, probably the best known of all fishing Clubs. The Badminton Library, which I suppose is our standard book of sport in general – mentions it more than once, & in so unlimited terms of praise. So much for the historical aspect -. With regard to the future subscriptions of the Club might I say that I think it is to be regretted that all local members should be eliminated from the Club - & I rather feel that the man who sees the river flowing past his house should, if a suitable man, have the chance to fish it – and privately I am not sure that there should be an increased subscription – I think that £25 a year is quite what one might expect – I know it is nothing to what some of the well known chalk streams command – but here the characteristics are quite different - I have put my views pretty bluntly in this letter which I think you will not mind –

I think it would be well if we could meet & discuss the subject – I have got a month's leave – Would you suggest a day & come over and lunch.."

CABK wrote back, *"I received your letter...which puzzled me very much... there is no suggestion either that all local members should be eliminated"*. He ended by suggesting that they should meet up once he has heard what the members feel about the proposals. They in fact do not appear to meet but the next letter to Geoffrey Harley sets out what had now been agreed: the Club would rent the water for £200, pay their own rates and taxes and the wages of the keeper, and CABK undertook to erect and maintain certain bridges. There does not seem to be a document, legal or otherwise, which describes any of the terms and conditions of this lease. Perhaps everyone is only too grateful for a resolution and un-willing to risk any further delay by involving lawyers. This lapse however will have its consequences.

We might conclude from a congratulatory letter to Major Wood from Geoffrey Harley that the Club was now wholly responsible for its own administration and that Wood has been elected President: *".....I was very pleased indeed to get your letter… I have the interests of the Leintwardine Fishing Club so very much to heart. I think it is splendid of you taking on the job, and I am sure every member will agree with me..."* He then advises Wood with regard to arranging for a Colonel Westropp to jump the waiting list so that he can be appointed Secretary, requesting him to circulate the proposal to members and get their approval. Wood complied and by October 1919 Colonel Westropp was getting on with the restora-tion of the river banks. Major Wood had been very afraid that the Club would lose a considerable amount of fishing unless the river bank was reinforced in the area of Trip-pleton as a large bend was in danger of being cut off. Colonel Westropp was a Royal Engineer with considerable experience of controlling rivers in India. Furthermore Westropp lived in Leintwardine, at Wheatstone, and was on the spot to oversee any work. The accounts for 1919-20 produced by Colonel Westropp show that he and Major Wood energetically got on with their tasks and bank repairs have been completed (4 wagon-loads of 'scrap' (brush) and 25 larch poles are provided from the Harley Estate).

The members' list in 1919 now looked as follows:

Major CEW Wood , Bishton Hall	Major AO Lyon, Wellington Club, London
Major HC Ackroyd, Wigmore Hall	General LTC Twyford, 56 Hans Place London
HL Heber-Percy, Ferney Hall	AR Beale, Seedley House, Leintwardine
EH Bevan, Brampton Bryan Hall	Sir HWA Ripley, Bedstone House, Bucknell
Major HR Sykes, The Barracks, Bury St Ed-munds	JB Boote, c/o Barclay's Bank, Knighton
Colonel CB Wingfield, Onslow	TW Shaw, Culmington Manor
B Hopps, Thurlaston, Rugby	Dr HE Dixey, Woodgate, Malvern
(From Sep 1919) Colonel FM Westropp, Leintwardine	Captain A Greville RN, Dover

The placing of Major Wood at the top of the list may indicate that he is President at this time, but there is no other proof. It should be noted as well that no honorary members are listed.

There were now 15 paid-up members and Colonel Westropp's arrival boosts that temporarily to 16. Three different keepers followed each other in rapid succession, the last being T James, who was paid rather more than his predecessors and received 40/- a week and a lodging allowance of 5/- a week. Perhaps this was an indication that following the war and promises of a new society the working man was not prepared to work for pre-war wages. Lesson learned.

It would appear that the original terms of the lease, which gave honorary members all the rights and privileges of membership without paying a subscription, had either been forgotten or perhaps ignored. CABK had succeeded in imposing a rent increase, and presumably the members were not in any hurry to remind him that he had the right to join them on the water. Geoffrey Harley who certainly would have wanted to fish, and would have done so anyway, may have been ill. However, apart from the rapid turnover of keepers all would appear to be well again with the Club until we see a letter written to Major Lloyd DSO, the agent for the Harley Estate in March of 1920. Enclosed were the LFC accounts for the attention of the <u>successor</u> of 'poor Captain Harley'.

CHAPTER NINE

TRANSITION 1920-1946

Geoffrey Harley died aged 41. As he said himself "*I have the interests of the Leintwardine Fishing Club so very much to heart*", and his activities on behalf of the Club certainly bore that out. Geoffrey Harley had been the key individual who had persuaded CABK against closing the Club. There can be no doubt that without his continuous support and suggestions as to whom the members might be and how the rules could be written, CABK would certainly not have countenanced the continuation of the Club. CABK would have severed those links between the land, the village and the estates and brought in strangers who would have had little regard for past relationships and loyalties. Geoffrey Harley had recognised it was time that the relationship between landlord and the Club should change. The Club needed to move on from the paternal and patrician style of the Victorian landowner to a more business-like arrangement that permitted the Club to control its own activities in full. This transition was not to be achieved easily or in any one action and, as we have come to expect, it was not done quickly.

Nothing could be more indicative of the transition from the Victorian era than the severing of the Club's and the village's link with one of its foremost members, Lord Coventry. Readers will recall that Lord Coventry had ceased to visit Wardens Villa, his house in Leintwardine, in 1918 but it was several years before he disposed of it. The house was sold at auction at The Lion in July 1921. In August the contents were sold from the villa. First up for sale in the Entrance Hall were Lots 1-7, each *A Capital Fishing Rod and Reel*. Lots 8-9, were *Fishing Basket and Tackle*. Lot 10, *Sundry Fishing Tackle*. Lot 11, consisted of a *Waterproof Cap and Hat and an eel trap*. It was a prosaic conclusion to a prominent and well-liked Club member's fishing career. Perhaps it would be too romantic to speculate that the same fishing tackle continued to be used on the same waters for many years and may even still reside in some Leintwardine attic today?

John Ralph Henry Harley, Geoffrey's younger brother, took over the estate aged 32. He cannot have expected to assume this mantle, and he must have been grateful that Major Lloyd was in place as agent for the Harley Estate. We have an early indication that Major Lloyd was taking an interest in the Club when he informed the Club that Ralph Harley would be away the summer of 1920 and asked to attend the Club's annual meeting in his place. He

R.W.S.H.   +   JRNH.

also raises the issue of the 1/6th of the value of subscriptions that hitherto had been forthcoming from the Club due to the Harley Estate but had not been paid recently. This, like the honorary members' issue, was another matter that had been forgotten in this new arrangement with Downton.

It is not until we see in the Harley archives the typed report and accounts for 1922, written by Colonel Westropp for the LFC and presented at the meeting at the Temperance Arms, Craven Arms, that we can catch up with the Club's activities. The report then surprisingly informs us that Heber-Percy had resigned as President (this was not previously known) and that Major Ackroyd had been voted in (as President) but that due to his absence in Canada, Major Wood is acting for him. Our earlier thoughts that Wood was President are clearly wrong and that he was merely ex-officio President and had probably held that position for the last three years i.e. from the last reorganisation in 1919. Heber-Percy remained a member and on the committee. In the same report the activities of a new keeper, James, are made known. He has clearly been working hard: *"the river keeper has given satisfaction in the performance of his duties. He has killed 68 Pike and 5 Herons, cleared much obstruction from the stream and banks, worked on bank revetment, bridge repair, willow planting, patrolling the river daily, setting trimmers, and other miscellaneous work."* Colonel Westropp also reported that 32 friends of members had fished on the Club water.

The following year the meeting is again held at the Temperance Arms and the report is similar but this time it is reported that 65 Pike and 2 Heron were taken by the keeper and that 42 friends fished for trout and 37 for grayling. There is no mention of any change in the lease. A letter from the Harley archives dated a little later in April 1923 suggests that CABK wanted to increase the rent again much to Ralph Harley's surprise: *"I remember when I lunched with you not long ago you mentioned that you thought the rent paid by the Club was low, but I hardly anticipated your raising the rent to double the present figure with the Club to pay rates and keep up the banks and bridges.'"* Ralph Harley goes on to suggest that although the fishing is good, the river needs managing and if the Club are not prepared to do so due to the increased rent, it is unlikely that he would find others to do as good a job. However Ralph agrees with CABK that the present rent could be increased.

Unfortunately we do not see any resolution of this latest issue but we can infer that a compromise was reached as in 1923 the next set of accounts shows that the rent increased from the previous £200 a year to £350. Once more the Club seems to be on an even keel. There are no minutes to be seen but hand-written accounts were circulated to members by Colonel Westropp. It would appear that business was conducted as normal except for one innovation, namely the creation of a Duck Fund which was allocated a sum averaging £18 each year. This sets the imagination racing. Was the Club introducing ducks? Eventually there is a note to explain that it was a payment to farmers to keep duck off the river! The keeper, and we assume it was still James, as the wages remain the same, continues to "*give satisfaction*". No doubt this was due to the successful cull of pike in the year to March 1924 with the huge figure of 84 recorded as the number taken.

It is sometime since we have found published references to the Club but in 1925 the Great Western Railway Company booklet, *Haunts and Hints for Anglers 1925*, includes the quote, "*The mention of the Teme always sets the angler thinking of pleasant times amongst the grayling for which it is justly famous....needless to say the Teme is either private or preserved (fishing).*"

At this point the paperwork of the Club appears to cease to exist and what little there is becomes hard to follow. The members' lists printed for both 1926 and 1930 show Major Wood as first named and Ackroyd second, without any designation of who was President. Beale is missing altogether in 1930. It is entirely probable that Major Wood is still acting as ex-officio President. If there were any meetings, records have not survived. The members' lists, as a matter of course, show the honorary members as CABK and Ralph Harley but there are no fish returns and no confirmation as to whether they were fishing or not. In fact there has never been any indication that CABK had ever fished.

Fortunately the Harley family still have Ralph Harley's fishing diary and whilst the Club may not have kept fishing returns for this period, Ralph was keeping his own. We can see that although he was fishing on several other waters he was finding time to fish on the Leintwardine water for at least the period 1921 to 1931; 1921 seemed a particularly good year when his total catch was 47 trout and 14 grayling. Two visits in 1921 around Bow Bridge and Black Bridge produced 10 trout. Ralph's last catch was recorded in 1931.

Returning to the narrative. The 1927 LFC meeting was due to be held at Colonel Westropp's house but we do not know if anyone turned up and rather suspect that they did not. Beale signed off the 1928 accounts, which are very straightforward and give no new information but they do indicate that all was well.

After the last rent increase in 1923 CABK seems to have caused the Club little concern. He was clearly happy to have nothing to do with the Club. He also had other concerns as his wife, Helen, died in 1926. They did not have any children and soon after her death CABK moved out of Downton Castle and set up home just outside the Castle grounds at Stonebrook House.

A hand-written page showing a summary of accounts to March 1930 is the last item found for these years. No records or letters have been found for the period up to 1936 and one might wonder if this was due to the Great Depression? Then we find that a new minute book has been started and immediately discover that far from leaving the Club, Mr Beale, absent in 1930, has been *re-elected* President with a Mr Drake *re-elected* as Secretary. It is as if there has been no break in activity and the Club would appear to be thriving. This new, *1935 Minute Book* is no leather-bound volume as once we saw; it is now a buff- coloured, ruled exercise book such as found in any school-room of the time. However, it serves its purpose and ours and records at one end of the book the first minutes we have seen since 1915. At the other end, as if transcribed from another missing book, are listed nine candidates waiting for their chance of election to the Club.

Thus the *1935 Minute Book* records that an AGM was held on March 12th, 1936, back at its traditional location, The Lion Hotel. The attendees: Mr Beale, Colonel Fitton, Colonel

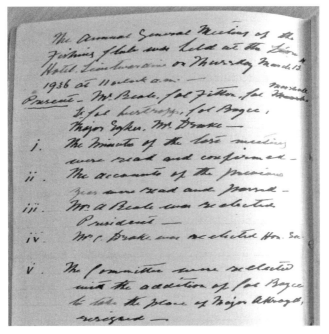

The *1935 Minute Book*

Marshall, Lt Colonel Westropp, Colonel Boyce, Major Sykes and Mr Drake, sound more like a roll-call for some military unit than a fishing club and they are soon down to business. The minutes of the last meeting were read and confirmed, as were the accounts. Mr Beale was then re-elected as President and Mr Drake as Secretary. We learn that Major Ackroyd had resigned from the committee and a Colonel Boyce took his place. We also gather that a river keeper has been employed, but we do not learn his name; as he was awarded a £5 gratuity as before, it is possible it is still T James. Proposals to introduce 1,000 trout and 5,000 snails and shrimps are passed. At this point we learn of a new idea, a proposal to limit the bag to 100 trout per member per season and a daily limit, reduced from twelve to eight trout.

Pencilled notes indicate that another innovation has been introduced. Fish returns are now required and show that in the season 1935-36, 747 trout and 1,585 grayling were taken (in comparison with the 2008 season when the numbers of trout caught are 337).

Noted also are the numbers of predators killed: pike 22, herons 4, and gulls 15. Included in the same list are tench 1, perch 25, roach 8, dace 8, and 427 water hen eggs.

The 1937 meeting, again in March at The Lion, shows that Major CEW Wood was now elected President and AR Beale became Vice-President. Mr Drake remained as Secretary. Why this change of President occurs is not known. If, as we believe, Beale is now 71, it may simply be his wish to let someone else take a turn. In fact in a curious repeat of history Major Wood does not seem to have been present when the election took place, nor does he ever appear to have taken the chair at any of the future meetings. To all intents and purposes AR Beale remained the Club's President.

Unbeknown to the Club negotiations were being undertaken at this time between the solicitors representing the two estates: Mr Weyman for the Downton Estate and Mr Martineau for the Harley Estate. They were in regular communication and trying to ameliorate the adversarial positions being taken by their masters. Simply put, CABK claims to have joint ownership of the fishing rights and Ralph Harley was adamant that he had the sole rights to the upper stretch between Criftin Ford Bridge and Leintwardine. Martineau wrote[4] somewhat wistfully to Weyman, recalling no doubt that same event that Lord Coventry noted in his journal in 1911 that it was *"unfortunate that the proposed settlement in 1913 was never carried through. I remember the lunch and the pleasant afternoon we had on the banks of the River Teme discussing the matter"*.

The Club's management team took matters forward to the March 1939 AGM which again Beale chaired and on this occasion it is noted that Major Wood is created an Honorary Life Member. Even if it has not been clear to us Major Wood has obviously been much appreciated by the Club and although he may not have formally held the role of President the work he accomplished whilst ex-officio President had been enough for him to be given this award.

Another important milestone is noted: the Secretary, Charles Drake, is authorised to negotiate a new lease with the lessors. Both AR Beale and Drake in fact address the task, and by May 1939 are ready to sign. Fortunately a copy of this agreement is available in the Hereford Record Office[1]. We need to remember that this is a copy and not actually signed and there may, therefore, be other versions. However, it is all we have and shows that the lessors, CABK and John Ralph Henry Harley, agreed to let to the Club for an annual rent of £300 that water which the lessors own. This water is described as follows: *"that belonging to Boughton Knight between Black Bridge and Bow Bridge and that which is jointly owned by both Harley and Boughton Knight between Leintwardine Bridge and Bow Bridge"*. This phrasing seems odd as the Harley Estate did not own land below Black Bridge but it prevented an argument of ownership and at least there was now some agreement which allowed the Club to continue fishing. The argument as to who owned the water was put aside yet again for a future occasion

Charles Andrew Boughton Knight always maintained that the water was jointly owned and Ralph Harley maintained that the water was his. Neither side seemed able to prove a position one way or the other but the uncertainty was to cause continuing problems for many years. Ralph was of course being briefed by Philip Martineau and he considered the agreement in 1741 between Lord Oxford and Richard Knight to be quite clear: it gave the fishing to Harley on both banks between Black Bridge and Leintwardine Bridge and since then nothing had been agreed to change that position. CABK disagreed and cited several other agreements made since 1741 but could not produce any proof. At best CABK would allow that Harley had the fishing on the right bank only. Martineau was confident that Harley would win any case taken to court but despite this confidence it is clear that the Harley Estate had no wish to cause a major upset between neighbours and chose not to pursue this through legal channels. Had it done so, it would seem very likely that the Club would have been the loser and whilst CABK may not have cared, Ralph Harley certainly did. Meanwhile as far as the Club was concerned, they were renting the water and could continue fishing whoever owned it. The lessors were also noted in the agreement as being honorary members and therefore able to enjoy all the privileges of the Club.

Shortly after war was declared in September 1939 the committee met at Beale's home, Seedley House, at the end of October, and despite all the hard work to get the latest lease agreed, discussed whether the Club should continue to operate. They decide to write to members to solicit their views and to write to CABK to ask whether the rent would remain the same due to the war. Presumably they hoped there might be a reduction. They decided not to engage a keeper until the following year; possibly the current one had been called up, or was likely to be.

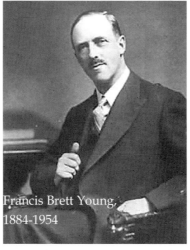

Francis Brett Young,
1884-1954

It is appropriate at this point in the story to mention that one member, Francis Brett Young, a popular and prolific author, had been a member of the Club since about 1936.

He may have been aware of the Club before then as a number of his novels featured the Elan Valley and the pipeline to Birmingham, which crossed the Club's water by Graham's Cottage. We can speculate that when he decided to settle in Fladbury in Worcestershire, having come back from Capri in 1932, he applied to join the LFC. His novel *Mr Lucton's Freedom*, published in 1940, was clearly written during the period he was fishing at Leintwardine. It is a story of a man having a mid-life crisis who tries to drop out of society. During his adventures he describes a fishing party he comes across, supposedly on the Dulas, a tributary of the Usk:

"The company...was entirely composed of trout-fishermen of the leisured class who frequent obscure mountain valleys and lake-sides from early April until the beginning of October, and regard every inn that they patronize as a preserve in which the presence of visitors who do not fish – or even of authentic fishermen unknown to them – must not be encouraged. The members of this particular batch were mostly middle-aged men, accustomed to take plenty of exercise in the open air, to 'do themselves well', and to spend the time which they did not devote to their sport in talking about it. Each entrenched behind a private bottle of whisky on which his initials were scrawled, they continue to describe and discuss the details of their day's fortunes as though these were the only matters of importance in the world. They talked of flies – pheasant tails, Tup's Indespensibles and coch-y-bonddhus; of difficult switch-casts under bushes; of the particular vices prevalent among the trout in the Dulas – the gravest of which was a reasonable 'dourness' in taking an artificial fly. One of their number, a scraggy veteran in a clerical collar who 'knew every stone in the river', having fished it pertinaciously (and jealously, Mr Lucton guessed) for more than forty years, took the head of the table as a sort of self-appointed chairman to whose judgements the younger members tacitly deferred. He had a long, narrow, thin lipped face, with a jutting nose, hooked like that of a bird of prey. A cruel, malicious face, Mr Lucton thought. Another, a stout, rubicund gentleman, with an air of a sulky child, sat gloomily silent, having suffered that day the most crushing misfortune of his life, in the loss of a heavier fish than had ever before been lost in the Dulas. When once they had satisfied themselves... (that none)...were a possible claimant to a beat on the water, they took no more notice..."

Brett Young's hero moves to Chapel Green (Chapel Lawn is the actual name of the hamlet about 10 miles to the west of Leintwardine) and he then frequently goes to the village of *Lesswardine* where he describes at the end of the book, when he is about to return to his old life, how: "He *hung on the bridge that spans the Teme, waiting for the garage to open, and watching the early rise of trout in the shadow under the piers. 'Next year', he thought, 'I shall have to rent some water and tackle this dry-fly business properly. It'll give me an excuse for getting away at weekends. I wonder how much it would cost to take a rod on a river like this?'* "It is amusing to speculate whether Brett Young took some ribbing from his fellow members and whether the Reverend EP Comber, a member at the time, was aware of the description of the cleric. Brett Young resigned in 1946. A little later, and due to ill health, he moved to South Africa where he died in 1954.

The 1940 annual general meeting goes ahead as usual in The Lion with AR Beale taking the chair. The Secretary is authorised to go ahead with the lease which we now know has to be re-affirmed on an annual basis with Mr Boughton Knight. No mention is made of either of the two honorary members either fishing or taking part in the Club's activities despite having the right to do so. The river keeper is again awarded his £5, but does probably leave as the Secretary is authorised to engage another. There seems no question of the Club closing down due to the war and fishing continued. A pencilled note pinned to the following year's minutes gives further confirmation of the Club's continuance in the period 1928 through to 1941 as it lists the amount of trout introduced by the Club each year; this was in most cases 1,000 three- to four-inch trout.

At this point in the LFC history it would be a great error not to introduce a character who although not a member of the Club (it is asserted that he could not afford the subscription) had an intimacy with the Club waters and provided some intriguing insights into the fishing as well as contrasting these with many others on similar rivers in the area. The Reverend Edward Powell, rector of Munslow for 43 years, was a frequent visitor. This fisherman, 1888-1972, was recognised by many contemporaries as a fisherman who had an abiding interest in restoring and maintaining regional traditions of fly fishing in Shropshire and mid Wales. The story of his fishing exploits on the 'Border' rivers is comprehensively told by Christopher Knowles in his book 'Orange Otter'. The book contains many references to both the Teme and the Club's waters and indeed identifies the Leintwardine Teme as the home of Powell's largest trout ever at 2lbs 2oz. Several Club members are mentioned in the book such as Richard Threlfall and George Scott Atkinson, Hopkins is also alluded to. Powell maintained a diary and a typical entry, extracted from 'Orange Otter', in the style of Archdeacon Lea's writing, connects us in a very personal way with the Club water as it was in 1940.

"30th Sept, Leintwardine 10.30-6.30 . Westropp's ticket. Day calm & sunny but cool, water lower than I ever saw it. Began below Cliff. Missed about six fish...first twenty minutes. Met old Sidebotham vicar of Leintwardine fishing downstream wet by the Cliff & saw him land two fish, one a pounder. Fish came well about 12-2 and at one time almost ridiculously so viz at the end of the rough water below Criftin bridge. I had thirteen before lunch viz in three hours, and twenty minutes after lunch had thirteen more. The basket being then full and abominably heavy I walked up to the car which I left at the crossroads, emptied basket and drove back to aqueduct. Found somebody fishing below President's Pool, so went upstream and fished about 1/2 mile above. Met old Sidebotham again who had seventeen and said he was going to cadge some tea and would then fish till dark. Fish came well all day but not in schools. Kept picking up odd ones in likely places like trout and just 1/2 my fish were non-risers brought up against their will by OO. Willow not much good though I used it as bob nearly all day. It would have paid me to put on two OO's. One magnificent trout of a full pound in A1 condition. Lots of fly on, Willow particularly. A wonderful day. Forty-one grayling thirteen trout retd."

The Club was not unaffected by the war and the 1941 minutes reflect this by carrying such resolutions as allowing Sunday fishing for the duration, presumably to allow servicemen on leave to make maximum use of their time and/or to reflect the general shortage of time available for recreation. In addition members were now permitted to apply to the Secretary for four extra grayling tickets and this too may have been to extend the availability of fishing. The Club also resolved that members who had resigned due to the circumstances of the war could, by paying a guinea (£1. 1s. 0d) a year, be allowed priority to rejoin the Club without a ballot.

In 1942 the meeting expressed its regret that Mr Drake had decided to relinquish his role as Secretary and Colonel Marshall had taken over. AR Beale was still chairing the meetings and the Club now decides to employ a keeper again. Three new members were elected in 1942: CS Asbury, S Guy and W Guy. The minute book notes that the 1943 AGM could not be held and that a referendum towards the end of 1942 reduced the member's subscription firstly to £15 and then £12 a year. The note goes on to say that Mr Boughton Knight was thanked for lowering the rent to £100 per annum. Then in a new move for the Club it was recorded that a decision was made to charge new members a one-off joining fee of £20 in addition to their subscription. We are also informed that a Mr Holloway worked as a river keeper for 20 weeks during the year but resigned to take up *other employment*; subsequently he seems to have been either re-engaged or in fact he may never have left.

A fishing return for 1943-44, the only one to record the fishermens' names, allows the first glimpse of a list of members since 1930. It is worth noting that again it seems to omit any mention of honorary members, but does include several names unheard of up to this point:

CS Asbury	WE Guy	Lt Colonel FM Westropp
AR Beale	Lt Colonel DEC Kenny	H White
Reverend EP Comber	Lt Colonel HD Marshall	RF White
JEL England	Dr NJ Rollason	Leslie Wright
S Guy	Major HR Sykes	F Brett Young

The minute book contains no further minutes after the note in 1943, and it may be presumed that Colonel Marshall became ill and died. The same book, however, continued in use for the next 16 years and recorded the names of individuals awaiting election. The final entry was in 1961. The next minute book thankfully is soon put into operation in 1946. Written in a new hand that demonstrates a brisk and workmanlike manner, the *1946 Minute Book* suggests the start of yet another new era in the Club under the direction of a new President.

CHAPTER TEN

HERBERT RUSHTON SYKES

1946-1951

The first entry in the *1946 Minute Book* is the record of the AGM in April 1946 which was held this time at the Swan Hotel, Watling Street, in Leintwardine. Mr Beale was still the

The Swan Hotel

President and took the chair. A new Secretary, Mr CS Asbury, noted early in the proceedings that Mr Beale had indicated that he wished to be relieved of his office due to ill health, and proposed that Major HR Sykes be elected. The new President was elected unanimously by the nine members present. Major Sykes immediately took the chair and thanked Mr Beale for everything that he had done for the Club *"particularly during the war years"*.

HR Sykes first appears in the Club records in 1912 as one of the 15 invited to join the reconstituted Club. His address at this time was Longnor Hall, just south of Shrewsbury; however, by 1919 he was living at Lydham Manor and in 1933 at The Roveries, Church Stoke. He was reasonably active within the Club and attended most meetings often making proposals or seconding those of others. The only record of his fishing is the return of 1943/44 when he took ten trout and 100 grayling in the season. At the time of his election as President he was aged 76 and had just retired from the Shropshire County Council. He was a man of many interests and had a huge capacity for getting involved with local, county and national organisations. This experience combined with 34 years membership of the Club could only mean that he was a natural and very popular choice.

This first meeting under the chairmanship of the new President was characterised by a general tidying-up of Club rules. This included the following points: 1) the fees were set at £30 (a reduction from £40) with a £20 joining fee, 2) the committee was set at three people: Beale, Lovett and Sydney Guy with both President and Secretary as ex-officio committee members, 3) Sunday fishing was to be established as the norm. As always, there was further debate on the issuing of tickets to friends; hitherto none were allowed tickets during the May Fly hatch, now one ticket was allowed. There was also discussion as to where exactly and how far below Leintwardine Bridge members were allowed to fish. Members were already aware that there was an understanding that villagers were allowed to fish in the vicinity of the bridge, but were unconvinced that the villagers knew their limits. It was decided to ask for notice-boards to be erected to mark the boundaries. This is the first indication in any minutes of the existence of any recognition of a 'village water'. No mention of such a privilege is set out in the agreement reached in 1939.

The meeting decided that 1,000 trout should be bought from the Surrey Trout Farm along with some snails and shrimps to increase the feed. For the first time the meeting asks for the use of *'fly-boards'* to be investigated by the committee as it was thought they would be useful towards the *"lower end of the preservation"*. (Fly-boards are tethered wooden boards set on the water to encourage flies to settle and lay eggs. The hope was that this would later produce an increase in flies on the water.) The river keeper, Holloway, was to be retained *"for the time being"* which does not sound like whole heart-ed endorsement by the new committee. Finally we can surmise that the new man on the committee, Sydney Guy, was behind the request to ascertain if heron and black-headed gulls were protected species. We shall see later how keen Sydney Guy was to rid the river of any predator and perhaps this meeting marked the start of his campaign.

The committee met again in July of 1946, or at least Lovett and Asbury did, and reported that the Severn River Catchment Board had been contacted and that the Clerk of the Board and the acting engineer had been taken to see the erosion caused by the river below Trippleton between 'the Black Bridge and the defile'. The Clerk pointed out that it was not the duty of the Board to make the river pursue any particular course but provid-ed the flow of the river was not impeded, the Club could undertake work to strengthen the banks. Mr Lovett and the Clerk arranged to walk the whole length of the preserva-tion the following Wednesday. Mr Asbury also reported on the subject of the village fishing: neither of the agents for the landlords had been able to give the particulars of the boundaries below Leintwardine Bridge and so the committee decided to adjust the rules to read: "*The preservation to extend from a point approximately 200 yards below Leintwardine*

Bridge to Bow Bridge." This left the 200 yards immediately below Leintwardine Bridge available for the villagers.

The committee met again the following April and reported that the river had been well cleaned to Burrington Bridge, the barbed wire had been removed from the vicinity of the aqueduct at Graham's Cottage, and that re-stocking from the Surrey Trout Farm was in hand. Mr Lovett, however, had not been able to do anything about fly–boards due to illness and the weather. A Mr White had asked, by letter, if a map could be prepared giving the traditional names of the various pools. Mr Guy thought such a map existed and would arrange for reproduction. Mr Holloway was now confirmed as a full-time river keeper and we are told that 15 people were on the members' waiting list.

The 1947 AGM was again held at The Swan with five attending and ten sending apologies. Leaving aside the interminable debates on the fishing tickets question, the main points to arise from this meeting and a later committee meeting in November were: 1) that herons were indeed protected; 2) 1,000 fish in good condition were put in to the river; 3) subscriptions were to rise to £45; 4) that the production of a map was proving very difficult as the river had changed so much and identification of names and places was nearly impossible; 5) Mr Beale was ill and asked to resign from the committee; 6) Mr Boughton Knight had died recently and that the new owner was Major William Lennox; 7) the basic petrol ration had been withdrawn and as members could not use the water as much as before the war, the Club should ask Mr Connelly, the Downton agent, for a rent reduction. The Secretary reported that the agent was not hopeful.

The demise of CABK in 1947 hardly raised a comment. Despite what can only be regarded as a general softening of relations between Club and landlord from the 1920s onwards the regard in which Boughton Knight was held clearly did not amount to much. His passing perhaps marked the very end of the 'Transition' period for the Club.

As has now become evident, the death of one of the estate principals seems to be a catalyst for legal activity and in particular for questions concerning the terms of any lease to the LFC. The new owner of Downton, Major Lennox, who was then in Scotland, is naturally keen to understand his position vis-a-vis the Club and he lost no time in directing his legal team, led by a Mr W Patterson in Glasgow, to start asking questions. There was then a flurry of letters between Patterson, Mr D Hudson, the new Downton agent, and Mr RG Gurney, the Harley agent,

Major Billy Lennox, 1892-1969

concerning the question of ownership of the fishing rights below Leintwardine Bridge. It is interesting to note from the Harley archives that it was Ralph Harley who was drafting the letters for Gurney to sign. Ralph Harley makes it very clear that *"there never was any agreement about ownership"* and that this was *"born out by the correspondence"*. He added that it was Boughton Knight who formed the opinion, sometime in 1910, that he owned 5/6ths of the river and although he promised to provide proof, he in fact never did.

The Club members were probably unaware that this interchange was going on, but they were aware that they had no certainty of continuing tenure. At the next committee meeting in March 1948 they discussed the question of rental of the Fishing, the Secretary wrote: *"The lease dated 19th May 1939 was produced. This was for one year only; therefore if the Landlords did not give us notice to terminate it until 25th March instant, the earliest we could be disturbed was 25th March 1950. All members present were unanimously of the opinion that we should continue to pay £300 p.a. and not press for a reduction on account of petrol restrictions. It was felt that if we did so there would be a serious risk of our losing the fishing altogether as there were plenty of wealthy people about who would be ready to take it at £300 p.a. The secretary was accordingly instructed to write to the agent of Major Kincaid-Lennox asking for a lease at £300p.a. for say seven or ten years and to defer sending such letter until after 25th March next."*

Mr Asbury, the Secretary, then reported to the 1948 AGM that *"The Major"* was willing to grant a seven-year lease for an annual rental of £300. The minutes record that the members *"received* (the news) *with considerable satisfaction"*. In fact so delighted were they that they considered inviting the two lessors to take up their Honorary Memberships and *"all the privileges thereof"*. It appears that they did not quite reach a consensus as no action was taken, perhaps partly because members soon learned that reports of the seven-year lease were premature.

The following year, 1949, the members were not quite as happy. The Secretary outlined to the AGM, again held at The Swan, that in an exchange of letters between agents, Major Harley was claiming sole fishing rights from Leintwardine Bridge to Black Bridge. The Downton agent, Mr Hodson, had apparently commented to the Secretary that the position was very involved and that it meant *"going into back records to the extent of 150 years and that litigation might ensue"*. The agent advised that the Club should carry on as at present. Hodson, being privy to the continuing flow of letters from Glasgow asking for copies of deeds and other proofs, knew it was going to take a long time to sort out. Mr Patterson had questioned every aspect of the current arrangement and seemed determined to get to the bottom of it all.

1950 passed relatively uneventfully for the Club. The AGM was held and the minutes written. There was some turnover in Club membership; FG Corser died in February and his loss to both sport and the Club was regretted. Beale and Lovett resigned due to advancing years and three new members: Maslen-Jones, Parkes and Barker were elected. The Secretary was asked to write to Mr Guy to express the Club's hope that he would soon recover from his illness. The members were also told that there was no movement on the fishing rights question. This comment was correct as virtually no work appears to have been carried out by any of the parties throughout 1950.

Sydney Guy obviously did recover from his illness as the AGM minutes for 1951 show that he announced to the meeting that Herbert Sykes wished to resign the presidency on account of his failing health. The members immediately responded and resolved that Sykes should now become an honorary member and they asked Sydney Guy to become their next President. Mr Guy thanked the members for the honour conferred upon him and took the chair at once. One new subject was raised at the meeting and this concerned the sewage plant below Leintwardine Bridge which was being allowed to disgorge effluent into the river *"in a most crude condition"* and rendering the river nearby unfishable. It was resolved to write to the local authority and if that did not have the desired effect then the Angler's Cooperative Association, to which the Club subscribed, would be asked to intervene.

It is apposite at this point to introduce readers to CV Hancock. He was the Literary Editor of the Birmingham Post at this time and a great friend and fishing companion of an LFC member, HA Hopkins. Hancock refers to him as *"the Squire"*. They were both founder members of the Greenwell Club, the story of which is told in Hancock's congenial book *Rod in Hand (1958)*. The book provides clear evidence that Hopkins frequently invited Hancock to fish as demonstrated by an anecdote in his book where he described the impatience of a fellow guest he had seen at the *"celebrated Leintwardine Club on the Teme"*. *"I asked Holloway, the old keeper, how this visitor had fared. 'He had some good baskets,' said Holloway, who rather begrudged him, I think, his exceptional success. Then he added in his very quiet manner: 'He's a very keen gentleman – he runs between pools.'"*

As Literary Editor Hancock is very aware of and quotes much of the literature already mentioned concerning the Teme and the Club water, particularly Archdeacon Lea's contribution. Hancock's lengthy chapter *Grayling Time* has much of interest for those who have fished both the Lugg and the Teme. Hancock was particularly taken with Lea's phrase *"the Mayfly blossom"* as he had not come across it before and because it was clear that Lea was not using the phrase in relation to either the tree in flower or the Mayfly hatch. Lea used it when referring to a scene on the Club water at the head of the Horseshoe Meadow. Lea spotted that in some shallow water grayling were on the rise *"so wading across the stream I began to throw. Yes, it was a shoal on the blossom... Once, twice, thrice; and two fish at least rose each cast at the flies. Sometimes both were landed, sometimes one. After about ten minutes, the blossom as suddenly subsided, and not a fish was to be seen."*

Hancock's recommendations for cooking grayling are noteworthy. The first requisite is that they should be late autumn or winter fish. He likes them grilled with the slight flavouring of mint that is imparted by placing a single small mint-leaf – no more – inside the fish. He goes on to say that he has tried a recipe from *"Downton Castle, above the Teme, that included mustard sauce"*, but cautions that it should be a mild sauce or it will overwhelm the delicate flavour of the grayling. Hancock also provides us with a *"different"* recipe he has found in *The Field Book of Country Questions: "The whole secret is to skin the fish first. Plunge them into boiling water and leave for five minutes. Remove, cut off heads, but do not gut at this stage. Seize the end of the backbone in one finger and thumb and, dipping the other finger and thumb into coarse salt to give a good grip, seize the skin next to the backbone. Pull with each hand in an opposite direction and the skin will come off like a stocking. Now gut and proceed to cook."*

Hancock not only gives us a rare photograph of an LFC member fishing the Club water, his friend, HA Hopkins (the identification was confirmed by Hopkins' grand-daughter), but also provides an excuse to provide a little detail of a Club member in those times. Hopkins was proposed in 1945 by a Birmingham friend, RF White, and is elected relatively quickly three years later in 1948. He would have paid a £20 joining fee and an annual subscription of £45. As one might expect with the company he keeps, Hopkins was a competent fisherman, his LFC fishing returns for 1948/49 and 1949/50 show he caught 46 trout and 133 grayling, and 70 trout and 19 grayling respectively. These figures indicate that he made several visits during the year in both summer and winter. Like most newcomers he attended his first AGM, this time at The Swan, Leintwardine, then sent his apologies for the following years. In 1955 we learn that he has resigned (was he ill?) but he then attended the 1956 meeting at The Lion and was permitted to rejoin. This unusual procedure provokes a note in the minutes: *"It was resolved that in future if a member resigns and then wishes to rejoin he must reapply and go to the bottom of the waiting list."* (The waiting list at that time ran to 26 names which could mean a wait of perhaps eight years. He was a fortunate man.) Hopkins did attend the next AGM in 1957. It was to be his last. At the 1958 meeting the President was minuted as noting the death of HA Hopkins during the previous season and that *"all present expressed their great regret and sympathy with Mrs Hopkins and their family"*. As we see so often in the annals of the Club, Hopkins is one more fisherman who treads the banks of the Teme until the last possible moment and finally surrenders his membership 'with his boots on'.

We return to 1951 to continue the story. While the Club members and their guests fished on, the agents picked up the pace of their correspondence. After several demands by Patterson for sight of more of the old lease agreements, which were never easily found, tetchiness began to show in the letter of 30th July from Patterson to Gurney: *"So far as Major Kincaid Lennox is concerned there will be no more joint letting of the Fishing Rights to the Leintwardine Club, and he would make his own arrangements. Why is it that this matter was never settled during the lifetime of the late Mr Boughton Knight since according to you, there is*

HA Hopkins, 1883-1957, fishing the Teme

no argument in it? In view of the fact that there will be no more joint letting I repeat my question, what are Major Harley's proposals for a settlement?"

Major Harley wrote a draft letter for Gurney to send but it may never have been posted, as towards the end of the year in November 1951 a very similar letter was again prepared in draft. It is shown below in full as it provides a comprehensive summary of the fishing rights question from the Harley point of view. Major Ralph Harley forgot at times that he is drafting a letter for his agent to sign and his use of the first person demonstrates his personal strength of feeling and involvement. This letter did not signal the end of the dispute, that had another four years to run but to use another's phrase, it may have signalled the beginning of the end.

139

"Dear Mr Patterson,

Fishing Rights in the River Teme

Thank you for your letter of the 12th inst: which I was glad to have as at last we seem to have made some progress.

I have taken a few days in answering your letter as I wished to go through my files to refresh my memory and have decided to send you copies of five of the letters that seem to answer some of the points raised by you.

In the whole of the correspondence from 1859 to Dec 1910 between the owners and their solicitors and the owners of this estate and their solicitors I cannot find a single word of dispute or even disagreement until Mr Boughton Knight's letter of Dec 26th 1910 (copy herewith). The letters of April 28th and Nov 18th 1910 do not suggest disagreement between the owners on any apportionment of rights. They do confirm however that Mr Boughton Knight had seriously fallen out with the Club and was determined to push them out but found that he could not do so without Mr Geoffrey Harley's approval and that was not forthcoming. Mr Boughton Knight therefore could not have his own way without reducing Mr Harley's holding on the river which he promptly proposed to do and wrote the letter of Dec 26th 1910. Mr Harley refused to quarrel and asked for a conference which was put off under one pretext or another until 18th Oct 1911.

At the conference I gather that Mr Boughton Knight who was a shrewd business man took charge so that the solicitors although present could not take part (see letter of Nov 18th) and Mr Harley had to conduct his own case, he was not a business man and had not his facts and was hopelessly beaten and glad to accept at that time the terms offered which of course gave Mr Boughton Knight control as the largest landowner. The agreed terms were never confirmed or acted upon.

After the conference the solicitors took counsel's opinion as how best to have the settlement between the "tenants for life" made binding upon their successors and were advised to obtain an order in the Court of Chancery but when all was ready in 1913 Mr Boughton Knight went back on everything arranged and refused to commit his successor.

Mr Harley then gave Mr Boughton Knight notice to terminate all agreements and leases of his portion of the river and called a meeting of his friends to form a Club. Mr Boughton Knight was not asked and took great offence.

Before anything more could be done war broke out and Mr Harley and all his staff joined the Army and it was left for Mrs Harley to renew the old arrangements with Mr Boughton Knight. Mr Boughton Knight then without consulting anyone arbitrarily started paying a rental of 1/6th of the rent paid by the Club. At the conference Mr Boughton Knight seems to have used the following arguments:

1. *That Brampton Bryan estate only had 'rights to a few fields'.*

2. *That Brampton Bryan estate had 'rights on only two fields adjoining Bridge'*

3. *That several deeds of exchange were entered into between 1741 & 1799 besides the two on those dates (Note: These have never been produced).*

4. *That Trippleton was not acquired by Downton Estate until after the deed of 1797 and that the fishing could not therefore have been exchanged and the deed was bad.*

5. *That Downton estate owned the fishing on the right bank between Walford and Leintwardine.*

Mr Boughton Knight was thoroughly conversant with the terms of the deeds of exchange because he had enforced them elsewhere and must have known that his predecessors actually acquired Trippleton by the deeds of exchange from the Brampton Estate and that the deeds reserved the fishing that had belonged to this estate from the 17th Century when the Royal Forest of Bringewood was broken up.

Mr Geoffrey Harley died just after the war and the death of Sir Philip Martineau followed shortly afterwards. Major Harley took over the estate in 1920 and was in the Army again during the 2nd war and I have spent the last 5 years collecting these facts and papers and negotiating with you, which accounts for most of the 40 years mentioned by you.

Major Harley's solicitors have at every opportunity renewed his claim to Messrs Weyman and Mr Boughton Knight just as often found some excuse to cause a postponement.

If I may clear up any other doubt in your mind please let me know but (from) *the last paragraph of your letter it would appear to me to be more appropriately applied to the limit of time to Mr Boughton Knight's claim to the fishing after 250 years than to Major Harley's present claim!!*

Yours sincerely

JRH

WR Patterson Esq.

Estate Office

Campsie Glen

By Glasgow"

(Before we leave this chapter and discover if Ralph Harley's letter had any effect some may feel that insufficient attention has been paid by the Club to Arthur Beale. It was perhaps the presumed absence from the scene following his resignation in 1946 due to ill-health that prevented the Club from formally recognising the debt they owed him for keeping the Club going during some very difficult times over the 26 years that he was either Secretary, Treasurer or President. It can only be that he moved away in his final years before he died. His death was not recorded in any way in any of the Club minutes.)

CHAPTER ELEVEN

SYDNEY SLATER GUY, 1951-1967

Sydney Guy, 1885-1971

Sydney Guy, it will be recalled, was elected President in 1951 due to Herbert Sykes's failing health. Sadly Guy's first duty at the AGM in 1952 was to report the death of Major Sykes, the previous President and a member of the Club for nearly forty years. Major Sykes was much respected as the substantial obituary notice printed in the Shrewsbury Chronicle of 21 March 1952 makes very clear. Sydney Guy offered to have photo-stat copies of the notice prepared and distributed to members. Mr J Ash Garland, the new Secretary, still writing the minutes in pen and ink, but later having them typed up for distribution, noted the "*moving terms*" in which the President referred to Major Sykes. Then the meeting got down to business.

There can be little doubt that Sydney Guy had already brought a more professional attitude to the Club management even before becoming President. It is unsurprising given the size of organisations he was used to managing. A more complete description of his career can be found in Appendix One but in brief Sydney Guy founded GUY MOTORS in 1914. His successful production of a commercial lorry soon led to the Ministry of Munitions taking over the factory for war production and they made several types of vehicles for the military. The Fallings Park factory also became the largest producer of depth-charge firing mechanisms in the country. After the war Guy turned to bus and

Sydney Guy in his tourer

trolley-bus production but by the 1950s he had moved on to heavy goods vehicles The factory gained a reputation for innovative engine design but ran into difficulty when the *Wulfrunian* bus had a series of mechanical failures and Jaguar Cars took over the company in 1961. Guy Motors (Europe) Ltd later became part of British Motor Corporation in 1966. Sydney Guy retired in 1967. The factory production continued but concentrated on the assembly of Scammel Tractors. Production at Fallings Park ceased in 1978 and the works were demolished. All of the Guy trucks sported the distinctive 'Red Indian' logo (this apparently had its origins in an earlier advertising strap line of *"feathers in our cap"*).

It is clear that Sydney Guy had had a long association with the Teme and the Leintwardine area throughout his career as a motor manufacturer. He was already fishing on the Oakly Park waters before joining the LFC in 1942, and a number of references in his after-dinner speeches indicate that he continued to fish at Oakly even whilst in the role of President of the LFC. He is also remembered as a gun on the Harley Shoot. He is listed in the *1935 Minute Book* as number 22 on the waiting list and was proposed by Colonel Marshall and CF Drake. So we presume that he had to wait at least seven years before he was elected. He lost no time in proposing JEL England, from Shifnal, in the same year that he joined.

143

By 1946 he had offered his services to the LFC committee and had been accepted. The committee worked hard and generally met twice a year in addition to the AGM and Sydney Guy attended most of these meetings. It is not surprising that the Club readily chose to elect him President at the first opportunity, as due to the resignations and illness of members and despite only four years on the committee he was probably the only member to have a full working knowledge of the Club's business. The minutes during this era seem to be complete and quite detailed, but remain hand-written until 1960 when they are typed and reproduced. It would be tedious and repetitive to try and follow year by year the various AGM and committee reports for the remaining 15 years of Sydney Guy's time in the chair, and we shall therefore look rather at the progression made under his leadership in the more important subject areas:

<u>Negotiations with Landlords</u> Despite the apparent progress stated in the last letter from Ralph Harley the protracted negotiations continued. The agents advised members to carry on fishing whilst the matter was sorted out. It did not always seem that progress was being made. In May 1953 the Club received a letter from Major Lennox giving the Club notice of one year to quit fishing between Leintwardine and Black Bridge. The Club decided to seek legal advice and then arrange to see the lessors. The Secretary reported in May 1954 that Martineau & Reid, acting for the landlords, had informed the Club they could continue to fish until Lady Day 1955 but that they were now under notice to quit one year from 25th March 1954. Later in November 1954 Major Lennox himself was vexed with the slow progress and wrote to Major Harley at Brampton Bryan[4]:

"Dear Ralph,

Can we come to some definite agreement on the Teme Fishing-the points at issue are:

1. *How many rods we should each have on the Black Bridge – Leintwardine stretch. I would suggest three.*

2. *Do you want to rent my rods and if so what are you prepared to offer me?*

3. *Alternatively do you want to retain your rods and for me to let mine.*

4. *I think any arrangement should be on the basis of an annual let.*

    Yours, Bill"

Of course the Club was unaware of this letter but was also keen to get an agreement drawn up and decided to re-open negotiations on their own account. They authorised the Secretary to offer, if required, a new rent of up to £550 a year. Separately the Secretary was instructed to ask the Downton Estate if they could fish below Bow Bridge but nothing seemed to come of that suggestion and it was not mentioned again. In 1955 the

Secretary reported that terms were agreed (no detail provided) but they had yet to sign any documents.

This time around and largely thanks to Brian Martineau, the son of Sir Philip Martineau, it was in fact the Harley Estate in 1953 which took the initiative to resolve the matter of the Leintwardine Fishery. Brian Martineau first wrote[4] to Ralph Harley and then to his son Christopher, as Christopher had now taken responsibility for the estate, cautioning against litigation regarding the ownership issue for fear of the unpleasantness this would cause between neighbours. In the same letter he then resurrected the solution his father had proposed to CABK in 1908: to have a form of deed whereby each party conveyed to trustees whatever interests each party held in the way of fishing rights thus preventing any interference from either landlord.

With this agreement Mr Christopher C Harley and Major Lennox would retain three rods each on the Leintwardine Black Bridge beat. Major Lennox then leased his rods to the LFC with the limitation that the Club could only fish three rods, at any one time, on that stretch. This would be managed by holding metal discs or 'tallies' at the Lion Hotel which would be issued to those fishing that stretch of water. Mrs Gouldbourn was named as the proprietor of The Lion and gave her permission for the arrangement. She could hardly have done otherwise as it would appear she was already engaged in selling tickets for the Clun as can be seen by this entry in *The Field* magazine booklet produced in 1955 entitled, *Where to Fish 1955-56*. Under the entry for Leintwardine, it asserts: *"Tickets are available from The Lion Hotel for 2 rods on the Clun over a stretch of one mile. 5/- to residents – All fishing on the Teme reserved."*

We learn from the 1955 minutes that although the lease with Downton was on a seven-year basis, that with Harley was on an annual basis. It is of interest that no mention of the continuance of permissions for the village water were included in the lease. The Club, accepted the continuing arrangement, but had to ask for clarification of the boundaries as the LFC had clearly been required by the trustees as a condition of the lease to *"use their best endeavours to preserve the fishing and prevent unauthorised persons from fishing or poaching the waters"*.

In June 1956 the LFC Secretary was able to report that the documents had been signed. When the next re-examination of the lease took place, on the eve of re-negotiating the seven-year lease with Downton in 1960, the Club also agreed a seven-year lease with Mr Christopher Harley. This step forward was reported with satisfaction at the AGM in 1961. The Secretary also showed a copy of the *Village Fishing Agreement* to the meeting (this document has not been traced by the author). At the same meeting it was suggested that the Harley 'rods' be invited to join the Club and thereby remove the restrictions to both banks of the upper waters. Although this last suggestion was not taken up by the time that Sydney Guy eventually gave up the presidency in 1966, the Club's relationship with the landlords had been considerably improved during his tenure and the question of the leases had been largely sorted out even if the issue of ownership had not.

Finally in 1969 the Club agreed with Mr Christopher Harley that he offer the Club his three rods for a yearly rental of £250 and this then allowed the Club unrestricted use of the complete Leintwardine Fishery. The tally system was still in use on the Upper Beat but uplifted to six tallies; members were requested not to fish immediately downstream of Leintwardine Bridge but to start at the Club notice-board, approximately opposite the Fire Station, as the Club – as a gesture to villagers – "*has agreed 'solely at the Club's discretion' to allow local anglers to fish this piece of water[7]*".

Poaching. Following E Holloway's death in 1956, Mr George Morris was taken on as a part-time keeper. He was soon reporting to the Secretary that he was having difficulty with poachers, particularly those fishing from the bridges. Police Constable Stamp was reported as being particularly helpful in obtaining names of motorists who came to fish which allowed the Secretary to write to them. Christopher Harley had agreed to do all he could to "*check this evil*". Unfortunately PC Stamp had moved on but the Club did not forget his efforts and sent him £5 as a token of their appreciation. The new PC, Watkins, was interviewed and promised to do all he could. The *evil* continued into 1959 and PC Watkins attended the meeting that year to inform members of the incidents of recent weeks. He told them that he had, along with Mr Morris, attended at the solicitors, to provide information to prosecute two poachers. The Secretary reported that he was pursuing the matter with the justices. The following year it was reported that the two poachers had been found guilty at Wigmore Magistrates' Court and fined £2 with costs. The Club resolved to erect additional notice-boards along the length of their water with the words "*on both banks*" added and this work was done within the year. Some of these are still in position today although some are being 'eaten' by the trees to which they are attached. A picture of one above Downton Bridge is in the colour section.

Pests, Pike and Pollution. Pike, heron and cormorants have always been a problem to the Club, and as we have seen the keepers always had permission and the means to do what he could to reduce their numbers. It is not, however, until 1960 that the vermin problem was raised on a regular basis at committee meetings. It was Sydney Guy who took the lead on this subject. His first initiative was to send out questionnaires to the members. He then provided an analysis of the fishing and made his recommendations at the 1961 AGM. His first conclusion was that grayling should be more heavily fished. Furthermore he reported that the water had the capacity to take more trout and recommended that more trout, shrimps and snails should be introduced. It was also very clear that he considered that the cormorant had become a "*menace*" and that in addition to the 10/- a bird bounty that the River Board paid for its destruction, further inducements should be offered. Mr Guy announced that Major Lennox had given his approval for Morris to carry a gun.

Heron had been protected for some time and it is resolved to ensure that no action was taken against them. Members were also told that pre-war Club records showed that 20-25 pike were taken out in most years but it was felt there were fewer to be had at this time. Nevertheless two members volunteered to try their hand at pike fishing to ensure that numbers were kept down. As for cormorants, the President persuaded the meeting that he should write to the Severn River Board suggesting they raise the reward for killing them. It was also agreed that appropriate letters be sent to *The Field, Shooting Times, Fishing Gazette* etc encouraging them to deal with this "*menace*". Clearly the Club under the leadership of Sydney Guy was about to launch a campaign against cormorants. Mr Guy then produced a cormorant's skull and a scale drawing of the head, which were

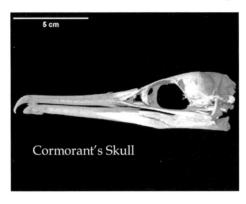

5 cm

Cormorant's Skull

passed around. He pointed out that most of the authorities concerned with the protection of game fishing showed an extraordinary lack of appreciation of the menace of these pests, and he convinced the members that the five or six cormorants which reside most of the winter on the Club water would very quickly devour a larger number of fish than the restocking policy allowed for; he suggested that these pests should be dealt with resolutely when they first appeared from their marine quarters in October and November and that the Club would be well advised to pay £2 per head reward for any bird caught before Christmas and £1 after Christmas. Such was the power of his oratory that this resolution was unanimously carried.

The 1962 AGM minutes reveal that the subject of cormorants was again raised: "*The President, now a widely acknowledged expert on cormorants, gave an interesting survey of the cormorant position in the Severn River Board area. It became clear that the President's battle against cormorants had passed unnoticed by the Severn Fishery Board, when the President reported that the Board's Chief Fishery officer was apparently under the delusion that the cormorant was in the list of protected birds. After considerable discussion it was clear that members were behind the President in trying to bring some pressure on the Severn Fishery Board to face this problem. The President and secretary were given wide powers of discretion to frame a suitable minute for circulation to other fishery Clubs in the Board area with the object of bringing pressure on the Board to make them more aware of this menace.*"

It was resolved that one of the main duties of the keeper was to *"exterminate river pests such as cormorants and pike relentlessly"*. Major Parsons offered to lend a rifle for this purpose and Mr Morris, the river keeper, was instructed to keep a river diary, presumably for recording the kills. Whether the crack and thump of high velocity rounds echoed off

George Morris demonstrating his success with his shotgun

the hills above Leintwardine is unknown, but patently Club members had been imbued with the warrior spirit and were eager for action.

It is of note that Sydney Guy had a full-page article *Cormorants on the Severn* published in the October 1961 edition of *Trout and Salmon*. Later in January 1962 Guy privately reprinted another, and rather longer, article for distribution that again appeared in that month's edition of *Trout and Salmon*, this time entitled *Cormorants and Game Fish*. In both articles Mr Guy had clearly done his homework and produced a convincing argument for the cormorants' reduction. Eventually Mr Guy was able to report that many River Boards had recognised the problem and were actively promoting the destruction of the cormorants and increasing the rewards.

Sydney Guy did a great deal to ensure that the Club had a good relationship with the Severn River Board and other agencies. The accounts show that the Club funded a number of the lunches hosted by Sydney Guy, which no doubt were designed to help promote goodwill and greater understanding of the LFC's problems amongst these officials. The Fishery Officer, Mr Kelsall, became particularly helpful in providing reports on the water. One might suspect he went further than necessary in his desire to oblige by arranging for some trout to be introduced by the Board into the Teme within the boundaries of Club waters. He was also persuaded to fell most of the trees on both banks above Burrington Bridge and some below it. Mr Guy had less success, however, in persuading the various authorities to deal quickly with the pollution in the early 1950s caused by the sewage outlet into the Teme below Leintwardine Bridge. When in 1964 the same problem occurred on the River Redlake, a tributary to the Clun, Mr Guy personally walked the river to assess the discharge and report on the matter to the Clun Rural District Council, but again it took some time for the authorities to act. The picture below shows Sydney Guy, on the right, overseeing operations on the Teme with fellow Club member Scott Atkinson, demonstrating his hands-on approach to his Presidency.

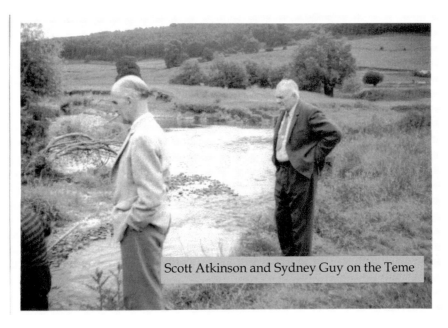

Scott Atkinson and Sydney Guy on the Teme

<u>The Annual Dinner.</u>   Francis Francis, 1867, comments on Club members holding dinners in Leintwardine and of their popularity. Early Club minutes make no mention of organised dinners and judging by the relatively thin attendance at Club meetings over the early years, it seems likely that dinners were not held on a regular basis but were rather *ad hoc* affairs, arranged by members whenever they found themselves fishing together. The minutes before the wars make no reference to an annual dinner either, nor are there any clues amongst the accounts. One suggestion to hold a dinner in the early fifties did not get off the ground, and then in 1959 Mr Mitchell raised the idea *"that another effort should be made to get the members of the Club together for Dinner"*. It was *"finally agreed"* that a dinner should be held at The Lion. The Secretary promised to make the arrangements. It is reported in 1960 that the event did take place at The Lion in 1959, attended by ten members. It was evidently well-received and another was planned for September 1960; the annual dinner has remained a tradition ever since.

Mrs Gouldbourn was still managing The Lion in 1960 and the Club clearly had a good relationship with her. She had already agreed to the use of tallies, and the dinners would seem to have worked well. The AGM in 1963 records that Mrs Gouldbourn was given

149

£20 on her retirement that year in recognition of her past help to the Club. We know that she had been the landlady since at least 1955 and had earned the Club's thanks as it was doubtless she who had the task of passing on the river keeper's advice to resident anglers, amongst her many other duties looking after their comforts. The 1963 accounts also showed that in the previous year two guineas (£2. 2s. 0d) were presented to a Miss G Gouldbourn, the proprietor's daughter, for her 21st birthday.

In later years the dinner moved to October as the preferred month. Members paid for the meal but it became quite usual for some members to provide the wines; typically Mr Guy produced sherry, Mr Mitchell the claret, and Mr White the port. In another year Mr White contributed the beef as well! This is, no doubt, why the cost to each member seemed very reasonable at £1. 3s. 5d. per head that year. In all probability the resurrection of the annual dinners was due to the quiet influence of Sydney Guy as he would appear to have relished the occasions. Members seemed to like the idea as well and the number of attendees rose year on year. They not only enjoyed a good meal and plenty of wine, but also got to hear their President relate his own fishing stories as well as his report on the year past which always contained some amusing incident.

Sydney Guy had tried to stand down as President some years before and he tried again in 1963 stating that "*having held the presidency for 21 years I feel that it is high time that I made way for a younger man*" (Guy is getting a little carried away here. He *joined* the Club 21 years before. He has been President at this time for 11 years only). He also volunteered to resign as a full member in order to allow another to take his place as he admitted only occasionally fishing the Club water as he had a rod on other waters. He did however ask to retain his grayling membership. The members wishing to recognise his long service resolved to make him an honorary full member for life, which he graciously accepted, and then, as before, he was persuaded to continue as President. As it turned out he remained as President for another four years; in 1967 he finally, "*reluctantly*", managed to persuade the Club that Mr AA Mitchell would make a fine successor and he stood down. Mr Guy continued to attend some meetings; his last AGM was in 1970. He died in 1971 aged 87.

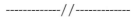

It was never the author's intention to follow the history of the Club through to the present day. It would seem appropriate that we draw to a close before we encounter any current members of the Club. Histories based on living memory are always suspect and prone to bias. It is far better that we conclude this story at the end of an outstanding presidency and at a point which we could fairly consider to be the start of the modern era, and so properly set the scene for a history of the next hundred years to be written by somebody else!

The Club had been set on a course by its President, Sydney Guy, to ensure that it thrived and survived. There perhaps was no-one better qualified so to do for he had many years experience of both the Club, the Teme (he claimed in a 1967 speech to have been acquainted with the Club water for nearly sixty years[7]), and of angling. He had brought the Club to a position heartily supported by its members, and there was a waiting list long enough to replace every one of them nearly twice over. The Club was tackling the problems that affect any fishery with vigour and determination and was planning for the future. Its members were happy with their sport and their Club. Sydney Guy read the fishing literature and kept abreast of references to the Club; he appeared to relish relating the history of the Club and encouraged his fellow members by his example to take the same interest in the LFC's past.

Sadly Sydney Guy's final speech has not yet been found, less for two paragraphs. We are fortunate that the speech made at The Lion in October 1963 was preserved. A typed version was in fact used as Mr Guy's script. It is typical in style to several others he gave over the years, and he clearly thought well of it as he saved it in his personal file on LFC matters[10]. The speech encapsulates much of the content of this book in that it makes clear that the Club appreciated its origins and the efforts its members had made in order to ensure its continuance. Aware of the singularity of the Teme and the peculiarities and delights of its waters, the Club revelled in the recognition that many distinguished fishing authors had given it, and they were gratified by its reputation. Sydney Guy, had he read this book, might have adjusted his speech to a small degree but on the whole it would, with a few changes of name, serve a President of today. Thus we shall leave it to Mr Guy to have this last word on *this* History of the Leintwardine Fishing Club:

"Thanks to the beneficence of Mr Mitchell I should like to take wine with you. I have drunk your health in company, I have drunk your health alone, I have drunk your health so many times I have nearly ruined my own.

The origin of the Club is somewhat obscure but the late Andrew Boughton Knight said he thought it was formed when his father inherited the estate in 1856 but he added it might have been before. No doubt the advent of the railway from London to Ludlow in 1852 had a bearing on the Club's formation, and the list of members in 1863 shows many of whom came from London and the Home counties.

Whilst Sir Humphry Davy in his Salmonia was the first to extol the virtues of the Teme at Leintwardine and many authors have since championed the quality of the Club fishing.

Jesse 'An Angler's Rambles' kindly loaned by Arthur Thompson, records the following catch of grayling in August, September and October 1833 on the Leintwardine, Downton and Oakley Park waters which gives an average of 18 per day, but it is nice to know that from time to time some of our members report a catch not far short of these.

It is also nice to know that the catch of trout has increased during each of the last three seasons, in spite of the fact that some of our older and skilled fishermen do not give an increasing return and indeed two report 'nil'.

Francis Francis in his book 'Angling' mentions that the Leintwardine Fishing Club have an annual dinner at Leintwardine in October and at the same time have a few days grayling fishing, some fishing with the grasshopper and 'the slaughter was positively disgraceful'.

It was said that the annual dinner here 100 years ago became a social affair which probably explains why John Rocke and the Rev Rocke, with a large estate and very nice fishing on the Clun at Clungunford, where both members of the Leintwardine Club a century ago.

Amongst the members there were a number with titles but I do not say any connected with industry.

I know of no river which changes course so much as the Teme between Leintwardine and Burrington bridge and in response to a request of the members I have at last produced a map of the water traced from the Ordnance Survey of 1883 which differs little from the one of 1905, and have superimposed the latest survey of 1952. Comparing the two, I measured that the Club had lost in 85 years approximately 1 1/4 miles of water by the process of erosion and short-circuiting during the floods. In fixing the old place names I have had the benefit of the knowledge of the late Rev Sidebottom who was vicar of Leintwardine years ago, and of our member Westropp, whose father was for some 15 years a prominent member of the Club, and our friend used to accompany the colonel and remembers quite a number of the old names, but alas in spite of the great help of these two gentlemen, some of the places have been lost in the waters of time. (See map on the next page)

Two cormorants were seen yesterday, and we are hoping with the advent of a new Downton Keeper on our beat, who has promised to co-operate with Morris, together with the inducement of our reward of £2 per head before Xmas and £1 thereafter, as well as increased bounties offered by the Wye River Board to £1, will result in at least these voracious birds being relegated to the coast to which they belong.

I regret to say Dr Rollason has given notice of his intention to resign in March owing to ill health, and I am sure you will wish that the secretary should convey to Dr Rollason our best wishes for his recovery and that he may still continue to be amongst our oldest members.

I would again like to pay tribute to Scott Atkinson for the many hours of fishing for trout and grayling he has sacrificed to pursue that fresh water shark the pike with great accuracy, the total caught from all sources last season was 10.

Will you join with me in being upstanding and drinking to the success of our Club and absent friends."

Sydney Slater Guy, 1963

THE END

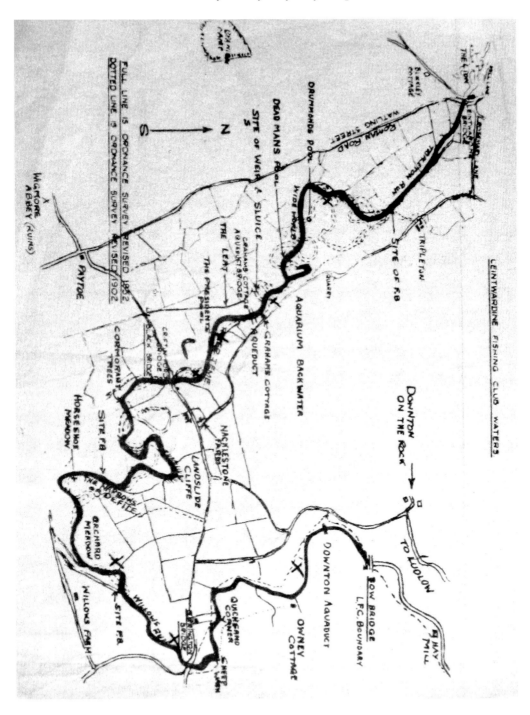

153

CHAPTER 12

POSTSCRIPT 1967-2010

AA Mitchell took over as President from Sydney Guy, and he was assisted by Colonel Watkins as Secretary and WRJ Heatley as Treasurer.

In 1969 there was a significant change at Downton when the Major, Billy or William Mandeville Peareth Kincaid Lennox, died and his grandson Denis Hornell aged 28 inherited Downton and later added Lennox to his name.

Denis Lennox

An interesting anecdote of this time concerning the neighbouring water in Downton is provided by David Houle. As a young man living at the Old Vicarage in Downton and working on the Home Farm for Major Lennox from 1948-50 he was allowed by the Major to fish the Teme from Bow Bridge downstream to Tin Mill but mainly fished upstream from Castle Bridge and reported a regular catch of 3-4 fish in an evening. He recalls that the river appeared well stocked although he was unaware of any stocking programme by the estate. In 1954 Reverend Canon JVC Farquahar and Sir Thomas Lea took the fishing and then Colonel Coldwell in 1955 joined them. They were reported to take 15-20 fish a day during the May Fly time. From 1960 and for the next 20 years David Houle and 6-8 others, which included Philip Miles and Richard Tanner, took the fishing from Castle Bridge upstream to Bow Bridge. He remembers that the fishing had deteriorated by 1960 and few of the syndicate fished more than five times a season taking catches of the order of 1-3 per visit with few trout over the pound. Of grayling he remembers little in the early years but found a few below Bow Bridge in shallow water towards the end of his tenure. David Houle has fond memories of fishing the Teme at Downton and firmly declares that whilst his stretch of the river did not necessarily provide the best fishing in England, it was some of the most beautiful.

By the early 1970s change was taking place at an increasingly hectic pace; the expenses of running the Club waters grew; rates, wages and rents all increased. The Club chose to meet these expenses by dramatically increasing the membership to over double the 15 members of the past rather than raise subscriptions. In 1970 29 members are listed; 31 in 1971; by 1976 there are 5 honorary members and 36 members, each paying £100 subscription per year. New members were asked to pay an additional £30 as a joining fee. Membership of the Club now consisted almost entirely of individuals living in the West Midlands: 50% lived within 20 miles of Birmingham.

We started this history with some accounts, and it is interesting to compare levels of income and expenditure between the first set of accounts available in 1871 and those for 1966 at the end of Sydney Guy's term of office; they are not far apart in value.

1871		1966
Sub £20= total £300	15 Paying Members	Sub £75= total £1125
nil	Grayling Only Members	6 paying £25 = £150
nil	Joining fee	£35
£300 (£20,800 in 2008 money)	Income Total	£1275 (£17,800 in 2008 money)
£140	Rent and rates	£629
£83	Wages	£448
£6 (1873)	1,000 trout	£92
£229	Expenditure Total	£1169

Sadly AA Mitchell died in 1977 and Colonel F Walter James, Vice–President, took the chair at the 1978 AGM and was subsequently elected President. George Morris, the water bailiff for the last 22 years, also retired at the end of that year. His retirement was not complete, however, as he continued to be involved with the Club waters and assisted the new keeper, Fred Banks, for at least the next seven years.

In 1982 the Downton Estate, still owned by Mr Denis Lennox, offered to sell to the Club the Downton Estate's half share of the fishing rights on the water between Leintwardine Bridge and Black Bridge. However, much as the Club would have liked to have taken up the offer, the price asked was too high and Colonel James and his committee began some six years of negotiations. The Downton Estate was finally sold by Denis Lennox in 1986 and became Downton Estates Limited which after a short period was managed by Savills Limited. The question of the fishing rights owned by the Lennox estate remained unresolved, until they were finally sold to the Club in 1989.

Although the Club members came forward to offer assistance with the funding of this new venture, the committee had to increase subscriptions in 1990 to £325 with new members paying an additional £100 joining fee. Given that the subscription in 1871 was £20, with a relative value to 1990 of £815, members were still getting good value for money. The waiting list remained healthy and long.

Sydney Guy was always keen for members to keep a record of their catches and to make a return at the end of the season. This practice continued under subsequent Presidents and the results were made available in AGM reports of the time. The period 1974 to 1994 gave particularly complete coverage. Sadly not all members made returns, and the figures need to be treated with some caution as the number of visits was recorded by some, but not by others. Whilst the statistics are therefore of limited value, they do give an indication of the fishing activities of the Club.

The list shown next has been culled from the AGM reports. It will be seen that in 1988 members were asked not to take grayling for fear of reducing their numbers to a dangerously low level:

LFC Fish Returns 1974-1994

Year	Trout	Grayling
1974	319	463
1975	303	427
1976	292	1183
1977	280	610
1978	277	810
1979	373	408
1980	457	342
1981	488	236
1982	345	140
1983	289	82
1984	301	212
1985	553	103
1986	371	67
1987	362	39
1988	225	-
1989	304	-
1990	294	-
1991	246	-
1992	213	-
1993	240	-
1994	258	-

In 1999, during the period when Alan Henn was President, the Club started to produce a newsletter. It was a good idea but sadly it only ran to some seven issues. Its demise is regretted as from a researcher's point of view it provided contemporary comment not only on Club activities, but also because it gave descriptions of fishing exploits which in modern times seem to have become very rare. Where are those lyrical descriptions such as Lea's and Hamilton's? Fishing diaries, if kept at all, have become bare reports: "21 April, 4 trout, Teme, water low, wind cold". Some articles in the newsletter however came close to the old style. Jack Mawdsley, President from 2002, describes his meeting with an otter on the bottom section of the Club water, opposite Owney Cottage (which he called Cyril's Cottage), in 1998:

"On hearing a small splash, I stopped and crouched to see if it would be repeated and if I could identify exactly where it was. After a few seconds, from immediately below me, an otter swam out from the undergrowth to my complete amazement and delight. I remained motionless but it became aware of me and immediately returned to the bank. Then came the magic moment. The otter re-emerged and, with his rear end still in the water, he planted his forepaws on the riverbank and fixed me with a gaze at a distance of about six feet. We were eyeball to eyeball and I swear he was asking if I meant any sort of trouble for him. Having held me in his gaze for half a minute he obviously decided that I was harmless and quietly went about his business. My disappointment at not catching a fish disappeared and a state of utter wonderment replaced it."

Another article in the Leintwardine Fishing Club Newsletter mourned the death of Fred Banks. Fred Banks had continued as bailiff until he formally retired in 1993. It is clear, however, that Fred continued to keep watch from his bungalow at Nacklestone. The article described Fred as always on the look-out for poachers *"whom he often dealt with in... a summary manner – with much stick waving and shouting"*. The article went on to say that it was his fearless approach which finally brought about his retirement at age 80 as the President and committee became fearful for his safety. The continuing help he gave to the new bailiff, Colin Barr, was recognised by the Club who awarded him an honorarium. Colin Barr, living practically on the river at Trippleton Cottage, took on the mantle of Club Bailiff until 2000 when he became the Club's groundwork contractor and Tony Jones, a qualified Advanced Professional Game Angling Instructor, took up the position for the next nine years.

The Lion Hotel in Leintwardine had been the venue for most Club gatherings throughout the fifties and sixties and this tradition continued until Colonel James became President in 1977; for the next 14 years the AGM was held at The Crown in Munslow. AGMs briefly returned to The Lion in 1994, but members chose to go elsewhere in 1998 when the meeting moved first to The Cookhouse in Bromfield, and later to Old Downton House.

A small but significant change took place in 2002 when it was decided by members that the position of Chairman best suited the Club's purpose and more properly described the role of running the Club rather than that of President. This change allowed the Club the option of selecting individuals for the titular role of President as and when they wished.

In 2011 Daniel McDowell is Chairman, and the post of President is vacant. The Chairman has the final word:

"Nothing changes much in the purpose and operation of a fishing club. Change is not what members seek and the relatively minor changes in the technology of fly-fishing since Isaac Walton's day have done little to undermine the traditional and basic appeal of this ancient sport.

In recent years there have been challenges facing the Club but nothing, as yet, has damaged the goodwill and cooperative spirit which exists between members and between the Club and the local community. The Club has been fortunate in its officers and, in recent years, the role of river-manager has been, and is, carried out with great commitment and energy, involving, as it does, the organisation of working parties and annual stocking.

One problem which first appeared in 2006 was the result of a well-intentioned letter from the Club to Leintwardine Parish Council granting the parishioners the right to fish up to 200 yards below Leintwardine Bridge, while retaining ownership of the fishing to the joint owners, the Club and the Harley Estate. As a consequence, two householders, with gardens running down to the north bank of the Teme, used this development as a weapon in their attempts to prevent other villagers using the footpath running along the bank on the edge of their gardens. A claim was submitted, through lawyers, that the householders owned the fishing abutting their gardens. The Club and the Harley Estate fought this claim and as late as 2010 the claim was dropped but not before substantial legal costs were incurred. However the Club has been extremely fortunate in having as a member and former Chairman and Secretary, Cliff Gammon, a (now) retired solicitor, who took on the task of fighting this claim and in so doing saved the club a great deal of money and much heart-ache.

A major change took place in 2010 when the Club acquired additional fishing some four miles upstream from Leintwardine, initially on a three-year trial period; this fishing, all part of the Harley Estate, cements the long and happy relationship the Club has with the estate and, it must be said, with its owners and employees. The Club's origins and history are closely linked with what we still refer to as the Downton Estate and despite changes in the ownership of the land and of the Castle itself, we are fortunate in having a continuing and co-operative relationship with the owners and their agents

As I write the club has a sound financial basis and a long waiting list; we are blessed in both the quality of fishing and the beautiful and largely unchanged landscape in which it takes place. There will be new challenges and problems but little that an old and well organised club cannot resolve."

The author's end piece

"Rules and cautions; Lastly.   Remember that the wit and invention of man were given for greater purposes than to ensnare silly fish: and that, how delightful so ever Angling may appear, it ceases to be innocent when used otherwise than as mere recreation."

Richard Bowlker, 1766

INDEX OF SOURCES

1. Hereford Record Office, reference series T87/ T74.

2. Shrewsbury Record Office, reference series 6683/4.

3. Private Collection.

4. Edward Harley, Harley Estates.

5. www.measuringworth.com. Website.

6. Worcester Record Office, reference series 778.713/2688.

7. Leintwardine Fishing Club Archives.

8. Leintwardine History Society.

9. David Lovelace.

10. Hugh Hughes.

11. The Flyfishers' Club Library.

LEINTWARDINE FISHING CLUB MEMBERS 1848-1967

The members shown below all joined the club before 1967; their names have been compiled from several sources: available members' lists, notes in the minute books, lists of payments of subscriptions found in some account books and from some fish returns. I gratefully acknowledge the website thepeerage.com for some of the detail.

Abbreviations in frequent use include: JP –Justice of the Peace, DL—Deputy Lieutenant, MP—Member of Parliament.

Benjamin St John Ackers, 1839-1915. LFC Member 1863-1869. Address given as Lincoln's Inn, London. The Rugby School register for 1853 shows Benjamin Ackers, aged 13, son of James Ackers, entering in November that year. He went on to St John's College, Oxford. He was called to the Bar in 1865 at Lincoln's Inn. He married in 1861 Louisa Mary Jane (Hunt, of Bowden Hall, Glos.). He was JP and DL for Gloucestershire and High Sheriff in 1904. Having inherited Prinknash from his father, James Ackers, he is noted as having improved "*the older parts of the house and added a new wing on the south east side*". By 1909 he has moved to Huntley Manor, Gloucestershire. He was President of the Gloucester Literary and Scientific Association and addressed the Association in 1876 on the subject *Deaf not Dumb*; the lecture was published by Longmans the same year. He addressed the Society of Arts on the same subject in 1877. He was a member of the Carlton Club. He sold Prinknash to Thomas Dyer Edwards in 1888.

James Ackers, 1811-1868. LFC Member 1848?-1868. Treasurer 1856, President from 1863 -1868. The Ackers family were originally timber merchants in Salford. The estate papers in the Manchester County Record Office show an assignment dated 1833 recording that James Ackers is the main beneficiary of the will of James Ackers, deceased, "*the lease of Bank Mill together with a corn mill and three properties in Salford*". One of these properties may have been Larks Hill, Salford, which he seems to have retained. His address on the deed of assignment, though, is given as "*The Heath, near Ludlow*". This is probably the principal house at the hamlet of Heath, the site of the abandoned medieval village to the north west of Clee St Margaret, Shropshire. James Ackers was formerly called Coops and was born to James Coops in Manchester 4 August 1811. He was educated at Manchester, Marlborough and Trinity College, Cambridge; he matriculated Christmas 1829 and gained a first in Civil Law Classes in 1831-32. "*He assumed by 'sign manual' the surname of Ackers, in lieu of Coops, on succeeding by will to a large fortune from James Ackers Esq., of Larkhill Saltford, 1827*"(this detail comes from alumni Cantabrigienses). He married Mary Anne Williams on January 9 1833; she died in 1848. In 1834 James Ackers joined the fledgling Ludlow Natural History Society (which became the Ludlow Museum) and quickly became a committee member; by 1846 he is one of four Vice-Presidents, possibly because he had contributed a large cheque. He continued as a member until 1857. James Ackers is noted in Sir Walter Gilbey's book *Racing Cups, 1595-1850*; the entry reads "*a silver cup inscribed 'Ludlow Meeting, 1835, James Ackers Esq., Steward'*". The Ludlow Standard of 1840 listed Ackers as a steward for the Festival of Choirs' performance in September that year. In 1841 he became an MP for Ludlow (2nd member) and remained so until the General Election of 1847. In the same year James Ackers bought the estate and old abbey at Prinknash Park in Gloucestershire, formerly the seat of Abbot Parker who entertained Henry VIII there. Later he was appointed as a JP for Hereford. It is noted that James Ackers "*restored and beautified*" the chapel at Prinknash (see www.prinknashabbey.org for more detail). In the 1863 LFC members' list Prinknash is given as Ackers' address, and he probably remained there until his death September 27 1868, aged 57. He is buried at Upton St Leonard's, Gloucestershire and his son, Benjamin, inherits. He may well have had an elder brother, also James, as the Rugby School register shows a James Ackers, aged 13 joining in 1850. No further detail is known of this child; he may well have died early.

Major H Cecil Ackroyd, 18??-19?? LFC Member 1914-1938. Address given as Wigmore Hall, Kingsland. He was elected President of the LFC in 1922 while he was away in Canada.

William Addiscote, 18??-1947. LFC Member 1946-1947 Address given as Kent. A note in the minute book that HD Marshall met him in The Lion Hotel in 1943.

Sir Henry Allsopp, (Lord Hindlip) 1811-1887. LFC Member 1870-1881. Address given as Hindlip Hall, Worcester. Clubs: Carlton and Windham. Henry Allsopp was the third son of Samuel Allsopp, head of the brewery firm of Samuel Allsopp & Sons of Burton-on-Trent, and his wife Frances Fowler. He succeeded his father in running the family business and also represented East Worcestershire in the House of Commons between 1874 and 1880. Allsopp was created a Baronet, of Hindlip Hall in the County of Worcester, in 1880, and in 1886 he was raised to the peerage as Baron Hindlip, of Hindlip in the County of Worcester and of Alsop-en-le-Dale in the County of Derby. He married Elizabeth, daughter of William Tongue, in 1839. He died in April 1887, aged 76, and was succeeded in his titles by his eldest son Samuel. His son George Higginson Allsopp (1846-1907) was MP for Worcester, 1885-1895, and played cricket for Worcestershire. Another son Herbert Allsopp was also a cricketer and played five first class matches for Cambridge University; he was an army officer. Lady Hindlip died in 1906.

Samuel C Allsopp, MP. 1842-1897. LFC Member 1881-18?? Address given as Marchington, Uttoxeter. Samuel Charles Allsopp, son of Sir Henry (see above). and MP for Taunton 1873-1887. He also represented Staffordshire Eastern. He succeeded to the title of 2nd Baron Hindlip of Hindlip in 1887. He was DL Staffs, and JP.

GS Atkinson, 1899-19?? LFC Member 1959-1971+. Address given as Westwoods Redditch, Worcestershire. George Scott Atkinson was a Birmingham industrialist. He was Chairman of the Greenwell Club and Chairman of the Midland Fly Fishers. He was elected to the LFC committee in 1960. He wrote *A Soldier's Diary* (1923), a personal narrative of the 1914-18 War.

Benjamin St John Attwood-Mathews, MA, DL, JP, 1830-1903. LFC Member 1894-1901. Address given as Pontrilas Court, Herefordshire. High Sheriff of Herefordshire 1891. On August 13, 1857 Attwood-Mathews accompanied by John Frederick Hardy, William Mathews, JCW. Ellis and Edward Shirley Kennedy made the first British ascent of the Finsteraarhorn, Switzerland. The story goes that whilst on the summit they decided to form a club for climbers. Subsequently on December 22, 1857 the Alpine Club, the first mountain sport association in the history of Alpinism, assembled for its inaugural meeting under the chairmanship of Edward Kennedy in London's Ashley's Hotel. He married in 1860 Florence Blakiston.

CS Asbury, 18??-19?? LFC Member 1943-1952. Address given as 7 The Square, Shrewsbury. CS Asbury was the Honorary Secretary from 19??- 1952 when he resigned.

Lt Colonel Ponsonby Bagot, 1845-1921. LFC Member, 1880-1882. Address given as the Guards Club and later Ashstead Park, Epsom. He joined the Scots Guards in 1864 and reached the rank of Lt Colonel by 1875; he retired in 1877 and remained unmarried. His father was Major General Edward Richard Bagot (1808-1874) who was invested as Knight Redeemer of Greece, his mother was Matilda Perkins.

RC Bailey, 18??-19?? LFC Member 1912-1915. Address given as The Pigeon House, Bodenham, Herefordshire. Richard Crawshay Bailey appears in Kelly's Directory for 1913 as a private resident in Bodenham (See Starey below).

William Joseph Barber-Starkey, 1847-1924. LFC Member 1904-19??. Address given as Aldenham Hall, Bridgnorth. Educated at Rugby and Trinity College Cambridge., he was called to the Bar in 1877. Married Margaret Aimée Kinloch in 1873 in Perth. Shortly after his marriage he changed his name from Barber to Barber-Starkey. The couple had 9 children, 5 boys and 4 girls (Aimée Josephine has portrait in National Gallery). One son, William Henry, died of wounds at Le Cateau in 1914.

RG Barker, 19??-19?? LFC Member 1950-1953. Address given as Coton Hill Cottages, Shrewsbury. Robert G Barker was proposed by Guy. He resigned in 1953.

Colonel HJ Bartholomew, 18??-1938. LFC Member 1938. He died a month after joining.

Arthur Richard Beale, 1866-post 1950. LFC Member 1912-1950. Address given as Seed-ley House, Leintwardine, but earlier he lived at The Cottage, Bucknell. In 1926 his address was c/o the Post Office, Leintwardine. In 1937 his address is New House, Leintwardine. He was educated at Radley School. Kelly's Directory of 1913 shows a Mrs Beale living at Seedley House. AR Beale was born at Hopton Castle, son of Rev Theodore Beale and Mary Dora (Clerke). AR Beale was Treasurer in 1912, LFC Secretary in 1915 and then President in 1920. Although he apparently steps down to Vice-President in 1937, he would seem to continue fulfilling the functions of President until 1946. He then continued on the committee until 1947 and resigns in 1950.

Major Berkeley, 1856-19?? LFC Member 1888-1913. Address given as Lypiard Grange, Worcestershire, and later Fieldgate House, Kenilworth. Probably Maurice Henry Berkeley who played cricket for the Gentlemen of Worcestershire 1876-1878. He was noted as being a Captain in the Worcestershire Militia in 1884, (www.cricketarchive.com).

GH Bevan, 18??-19?? LFC Member 1914-1920. Address given as Brampton Bryan Hall.

James B Boote, 18??-19?? LFC Member 1913-1919. Address given as Knighton and c/o Barclay's Bank, Knighton.

MA Boswell, 19??-19?? LFC Member 1962. Address given as Westacre, Finchfield Hill Wolverhampton.

Rev J Bowstead-Wilson, 18??-19?? LFC Member 1905-19?? Address given as Knightwick Rectory, Worcester. A friend of Sir HM Plowden and proposer of Colonel WC Plowden.

Colonel C Boyce, 18??-19?? LFC Member 1936-1937+. Address given as The Manor House, Much Wenlock. He attended 1936 AGM.

The Earl of Breadalbane, 1824-1871. LFC Member 1870-1871. Address given as Taymouth Castle, Aberfeldy. John Alexander Gavin Campbell succeeded to his uncle's estate in 1862. Prior to this he had gained the rank of Captain in the First of Foot, (Ist Royals) and had married Mary Theresa Edwards in 1853. At the same time as becoming 6th Earl of Breadalbane he succeeded to the titles 10th Baronet Campbell of Glenorchy, 6th Lord Glenurchy, and 6th Viscount of Tay and Pentland. He died aged 46 in the Albany, Piccadilly, London.

The Earl of Breadalbane, 1851-1922. LFC Member 1875-1885. Address given as Taymouth Castle, Aberfeldy. Gavin Campbell succeeded his father (above) as the 7th Earl in 1871 and was proposed as a member of the club in the same year by ARBK and The Hon Humphrey Devereux. He was elected in 1875. The Earl held several high positions in the royal household. He was a Lord-in-Waiting from 1873 to 1874, Treasurer of the Household 1880-5, Lord Steward of the Household 1892-5, also ADC to the King and

Lord High Commissioner to the General Assembly of the Church of Scotland in 1893-45. He was created Baron Breadalbane in the peerage of the United Kingdom in 1873, and advanced to the Earldom of Ormelie and Marquessate of Breadalbane in 1885. He was also a Knight of the Garter and a Privy Councillor, and was Keeper of the Privy Seal of Scotland from 1907. He married in 1872 Lady Alma Graham, youngest daughter of the 4th Duke of Montrose. In 1921 he disposed of Taymouth Castle, the town of Aberfeldy, and the lands at the lower end of Loch Tay.

F Brett Young, 1884-1954. LFC Member 1936-1946. No address given, but he lived at Craycombe House, Fladbury, Worcestershire. Francis Brett Young was born in 1884 at Halesowen, Worcestershire, eldest son of Dr Thomas Brett Young. Educated at Iona Cottage High School, Sutton Coldfield and Epsom College, Francis read medicine at Birmingham University before entering general practice at Brixham in 1907. The following year he married Jessie Hankinson whom he had met during his medical studies. She was a singer of some repute, having appeared as a soloist in Henry Wood's Promenade Concerts. Francis set one of his earliest novels *Deep Sea* (1914) in Brixham, but was soon caught up in the Great War. He served in the RAMC in East Africa, and recorded his experiences in *Marching on Tanga*. After the war the couple lived in Capri where a number of novels with African as well as English backgrounds were produced. Popular success came in 1927 when Francis was awarded the James Tait Black Memorial Prize for *Portrait of Clare*. The Brett Youngs returned to England in 1929, staying for a while in the Lake District before settling at Craycombe House in 1932. During this period Francis was at the height of his fame and his annually produced novels were eagerly awaited. During the WWII he laboured on his long poem covering the development of English history from prehistoric times. Entitled *The Island*, it was published in 1944 and was regarded by Francis as his greatest achievement. Following a breakdown in his health, he moved to South Africa where he died in 1954. His ashes were brought back to this country and interred at Worcester Cathedral. (This biography has been taken from the www.fbysociety.co.uk which includes descriptions of all his books and poetry.) In *Mr Lucton's Freedom* Brett Young makes use of his fishing experiences with the Club.)

Admiral Britten, RN, 1843-1910. LFC Member 1899-1910. Address given as Kenswick, Worcester. Admiral Richard Frederic Britten was born in London, the second son of Daniel Britten, of Kenswick, Worcestershire, by his wife Emma, daughter of Mr George Green, of Blackwall. He entered the Navy as a midshipman at the age of 13, and the following year saw service in the China War of 1858, and was present at the bombardment of Nankin, for which he received the China Medal. He served as Lieutenant on board the Royal Yacht, and as Commander and Flag Captain to the Duke of Edinburgh in the Mediterranean. He retired with the rank of Captain in 1892; the year after he was made Rear-Admiral on the retired list. He succeeded to the Kenswick estate and devoted himself thenceforward to county work. In 1890 he married Blanche Cecile, only daughter of the eleventh Baron and first Viscount Colville of Culross, by whom he had three children. He died at Kenswick. He is noted in a Kentucky newspaper for exporting cattle to Kentucky in 1901. He was an amateur painter; one picture *Her Majesty's Royal Yacht Victoria and Albert II in the Solent* was sold at auction in 1990.

J Broad-Bissell, 18??-19?? LFC Member 1901. Address given as Bishopsteington House, North (sic) Devon.

CC Brown, 18??-19?? LFC Member 1928. Address given as East India Club, London.

Henry Brown, 18??-1875? LFC Member 1863. Address given as 4 Douro Villas, Cheltenham. He was proposed as a member of the reformed Club in 1871 by Colonel Colvin and Rev J Rogers but died before a vacancy occurred.

CL Clerke, 1829-1910. LFC Member 1908-11. Address given as Seedley House, Leintwardine. Charles Longueville Clerke was the son of the 9th Baronet Clerke and sister to Mary, AR Beale's mother who later lived at Seedley. He never married. The only indication of his membership is a handwritten note in LFC archives indicating that he replaced Vale-King in 1908. Clerke had been on the waiting list in 1870, number 30, but when put up for ballot in 1886 was not elected.

Major Clowes, 18??-19?? LFC Member 1877-94. Address given as Malvern Wells. Possibly Major Peter Legh Clowes, a magistrate for Herefordshire (Kelly's Directory 1895). Listed in Kelly's 1913 as Lt Colonel Peter Legh Clowes CB DL JP (late 8th Hussars) Burton Court, Eardisland, Leominster, member of the Naval & Military and Arthur's Clubs. His wife was Edith Emily; their son, Lieut. Warren Peter Clowes 8th Bn. King's Royal Irish Hussars, was killed in action (Somme) 30/3/1918, aged 20. (John Clowes, DL, JP, Burton Court, Eardisland was probably father to Peter Clowes).

Lt Colonel Neville Collins, 18??-19?? LFC Member 1946-1948. Address given as Kenton, Wood Lane, Fleet, Hampshire.

Major Colby, 18??-19?? LFC Member 1894-1901. Address given as Rhosygilwen, Rhoshill, RSO. S Wales. Colbys lived at Rhosygilwen from 1697 and for the next seven generations.

Reverend EP Comber, 1868-19-?? LFC Member 1943-1948. Address given as Penn Vicarage, Buckinghamshire. Probably Edward Comber who married in 1902 Jane Frances Hartley. In 1937 Rev EP Comber, vicar of Wrenbury (who played for Aston Cricket Club near Nantwich), presented a silver cup to the Aston club to celebrate the Coronation of King George V1.

Reverend James Cook, 1821-1889. LFC Member 1870-78. Address given as Peopleton Rectory, Pershore. He attended Magdalene College, Cambridge 1847. According to

Crockford's Directory, he also lived at 47 Portland Place, London. From 1855 to 1889 the Rev James Cook was patron and incumbent of the 13th century St Nicholas Church in Peopleton, and his trustees held the advowson until 1892. The manor at that time, Norchard House (now demolished), was owned by Frederick Dineley but by 1869 had passed into the hands of John Parker of Worcester, a solicitor in the firm of Goldingham. Cook is referred to in archives held at Worcester Records Office[6] as giving alms to poor local families in Peopleton in stark contrast to the previous incumbent and lord of the manor, Dineley.

Colonel J Colvin, CB, 1794-1871. LFC Member 1863-1870. Address given as Leintwardine. John Colvin, born 20 August 1794 in Scotland to John and Matilda Colvin. Both his father and a cousin worked for the Bengal Civil Service, and John Colvin followed suit. He joined the Bengal Engineers before he was thirty and advanced rapidly to the rank of Lt Colonel. In 1823 during his time as General Superintendent of Irrigation in Delhi, Lt Colonel Colvin saw through the restoration and extension of the Western Jumna Canal, which was to help greatly with the relief of famine in that area. Colvin left India in 1836. He married Josephine Baker in St Lawrence's Church, Ludlow in 1838 and took up residence in Broad Street for the next few years and produced his first two children. In July 1838, despite being back in England, Colvin was appointed Companion to the Order of the Bath on the occasion of her Majesty Queen Victoria's Coronation, at which time he is still listed as being in the service of the Bengal Engineers, presumably on half pay. At some time in the early 1840s Colvin moved from Ludlow to Leintwardine House and immediately immersed himself in fund-raising for a school which was built in 1847. He became the manager, or governor, of the school, a post he held for the next 22 years. Colvin was also a leading light in the Ludlow Natural History Society from about 1846, acting as both Treasurer and Secretary for many years. As James Ackers also belonged to the same organisation, it is likely that Colvin started fishing with him after this date but long before the publication of the 1863 members' list. Lt Colonel Colvin, CB, was promoted Colonel by brevet on 28 November 1854 and a year later is noted in the Army List and East India Register of 1855 as retired from service. He became a Deputy Lieutenant of Herefordshire on 1 December 1860 (incidentally at the same time as Andrew Johnes Rouse Boughton Knight). He was listed as a member of the Woolhope Society from 1855 and of the Palaeontographical Society in September 1866. Col Colvin died on 27th April 1871 aged 76 and is buried in Leintwardine churchyard. His son, John William Colvin MA (1839-1917), Rugby School 1853, served as vicar of Leintwardine for 32 years. He is listed in Kelly's 1885 as resident at the Vicarage. Rev J Colvin was acquainted with Lord Coventry and visited him at Wardens Cottage, Leintwardine in 1891; he also gave Colvin fishing tickets.

F Connell, 18??-19?? LFC Member 1937-1946+. Address given as Hampton Hall, Worthen, Shropshire.

JSM Connell, 18??-19?? LFC Member 1939-1956. Address given as 4 Carpenter Road, Edgbaston. A pencil note in the minute book has him re-elected in 1943. He resigned in 1956.

Captain Frank Corbett, 1833-18?? LFC Member 1863. Address given as Greenfield, Presteigne. Noted in the list of Old Carthusians as being at Charterhouse in the years 1845-1847, he entered the Army, serving with the 33rd Regiment of Foot, now Duke of Wellington's (West Riding) Regiment.

ERT Corbett, 18??-19?? LFC Member 1912-1915. Address given as Radnor, Dorrington, Salop. Probably Major ER Trevor Corbett .

G Bryan Corser, 18??-19?? LFC Member 1960-1977. Address given as 8 Swan Hill, Shrewsbury.

F G Corser, 18??-1950. LFC Member 1947-1950. Address given as Shrewsbury. He was elected to the committee in 1947.

The Earl of Coventry, 1838-1930. LFC Member 1877-1911. Address given as Croome Court, Severn Stoke, Worcestershire and 106 Piccadilly, London. Lord Coventry, George William, 9th Earl Coventry (1838-1930) lived at the family home at Croome Court. The estate, situated about seven miles south of Worcester, had been in the hands of the family since the late 16th century. He was educated at Eton and Christchurch. As a young man between 1866 and 1886 Lord Coventry played cricket for sides such as the Gentlemen of Worcestershire, the Gentlemen of the MCC, and the Lords and Commons. At least four other cricketers found their way into the LFC through this connection. He was elected president of the MCC in 1859 and in 1869 he chaired a committee to establish the current cricket ground at Worcester. Lord Coventry was an influential member of the Leintwardine Fishing Club. He rented Warden House, Leintwardine, from 1880 and subsequently bought it in 1891. Fishing was certainly the principal reason for his interest in Leintwardine; however, he also bred Hereford cattle having started his herd in 1875 with animals from Mr Tudge, of Adforton. Whilst staying at The Wardens he and his family kept a journal[6] of their visits. The journal mainly records his fishing exploits, but also shows that Lord Coventry appreciated the standard of husbandry in this area for he bought horses bullocks and many sheep to be sent back to Croome. He attended many of the local cattle shows and was often asked to judge horses. He was the owner of two Grand National winners. Amongst many other positions, he became President of the Hereford Herd Book Society and was asked to preside at many luncheons for retiring breeders in and around Leintwardine and found it useful to spend the night before at The Wardens. Much of the journal is written in the third person and was started by his wife, Lady Blanche Coventry, née Craven (1842-1930), third daughter of William Craven, 2nd Earl of Craven, of Coombe Abbey, Warwickshire. Whilst any stay was rarely longer than four or five days, and visits occurred no more than three or four times a year, it is clear from the entries that all the family enjoyed their time at The Wardens The property was sold in 1921, and Lord Coventry died in 1930. Lady Blanche took to her bed one hour after his death and died three days later; they had been married for 67 years.

Herbert Crawshay, 18??-18?? LFC Member 1863-1870 and 18??-1903. Address given as Leintwardine and later as Stormer. Littlebury's Directory and Gazetteer of Hereford-shire for 1876-7 lists Stormer Hall as the seat of Herbert Crawshay Esq., a farmer. A cousin, Alfred Crawshay, Bwlch, was invited to join LFC in 1903 but declined.

LM Curtler, 1857-1912. LFC Member 1911-1912. Not listed in any LFC archives, but sub-scribed to the Meredith headstone, 1911. Lawrence Martin Curtler was born in Droit-wich Spa, Worcestershire. He was educated at Marlborough College and qualified as a solicitor in 1881. He played cricket for the Gentlemen of Worcestershire 1876-79, and later for Llandudno in 1894. When he died in 1912 his address was Shrewsbury House, Church Walks, Llandudno..

WT Curtler, 18??-19?? LFC Member 1926-1930+. Address given as Inchmery, Worcester.

Hon Humphrey Devereux, 1812-1880. LFC Member 1870-1880. Address given as The High Wood, Leominster. Hon. Humphrey Bohun Devereux was the fourth son of Henry Fleming Lea Devereux (1777-1843), 14th Viscount Hereford.   He married Caroline Antrobus, daughter of Sir Edmund Antrobus. Littlebury's Directory of 1876 notes *"The Highwood*, the seat of the Hon. Humphrey de Bohun Devereux, J.P. and D.L., is delight-fully situated on an eminence in this parish (Yarpole), and commands a pleasing and picturesque prospect." He appears in a list of Carthusians 1800-1879, he entered Charter-house in 1824, and is noted as being in the East India Company's service.

Sir Harry E Dixey, DL, MD 1853-1927. LFC Member 1919-1926. Address given as Woodgate, Malvern. Dr Harry Edward Dixey graduated from Aberdeen. He was house surgeon at Preston Royal Infirmary and then practised at Droitwich and Malvern.   He was an alderman of the Worcestershire County Council, Deputy Lieutenant and a Justice of the Peace. He was appointed Sheriff in 1921. He was a commissioned surgeon cap-tain in the 8th Worcester Volunteer Regiment and was chairman of the King Edward VII Memorial Sanatorium Worcestershire. He was knighted in 1926.

Hon George Douglas-Pennant, 1836-1907. LFC Member 1870-1878. Address given as Penrhyn Castle, Bangor. George Douglas-Pennant was educated at Eton College and at Christ Church, Oxford.   In 1860 he became a major commanding the Caernarvonshire Rifle Volunteers, which was affiliated in 1881 to the 4th (Militia) Battalion, Royal Welch Fusiliers; he later became its honorary colonel.   In August 1860 he married Pamela Blanche (1839–1869), daughter of Sir Charles Rushout; they had a son, Edward Sholto

(1864–1927), who succeeded as third Baron Penrhyn. He had six daughters, the youngest of whom was Violet Douglas-Pennant.. Douglas-Pennant's second wife, whom he married in October 1875, was Gertrude Jessy (*d.* 1940), daughter of Henry Glynne, and niece by marriage of WE Gladstone (who was called on to deal with several family disputes); George went on to father an additional eight children, two sons and six daughters. Penrhyn Castle was built by Thomas Hopper (1776–1856) over the years 1820 to 1837 in the revived Norman style. The Pennants' London house was Mortimer House, Halkin Street, Belgravia, and they had country houses at Wicken, Stony Stratford, Betws-y-Coed in Caernarvonshire, and at Cairnton in Banffshire. He was a JP, a county councillor, and the Deputy Lieutenant of Caernarvonshire. In 1866 he was elected unopposed as Conservative MP for Caernarvonshire, but in 1868 he was defeated by the Liberal TLD Jones-Parry. He regained the seat in 1874, but lost it again in 1880 to the Liberal Watkin Williams.   Master of the Grafton Hounds from 1882 to 1891. He became 2nd Baron Penrhyn on the death of his father in 1886. Douglas-Pennant enjoyed horse-racing, shooting, and fishing. (Dictionary of National Biography).

Commander ARC Douton, 18??-19?? LFC Member 1949-19??

CF Drake, 18??-19?? LFC Member ^1936-1946+. Address given as Seedley House, Leintwardine. Charles Flint Drake was re-elected Honorary Secretary in 1936 and remained so until 1942.

General Drummond, 18??-18?? LFC Member 1863. Address given as The Boyce, near Dymock. Slater's 1868 Directory of Newent lists a General John Drummond, JP, of Boyce Court (a Grade 2 listed building originally built in the 17th century but much altered in the 19th).   General John Drummond is also listed as a Fellow of the Royal Geographical Society, and in 1874 as a member of the Grampian Society founded in 1874 by Charles Rogers, a Scottish autho**r,** with the purpose of publishing works illustrative of Scottish literature, history, and antiquities.

The Earl of Dudley, 1817-1885. LFC Member 1870-1878. Address given as Witley Court, Worcester. William Ward, 1st Earl of Dudley (27 March 1817 – 7 May 1885), known as the Lord Ward from 1835 to 1860, was a British peer and benefactor. He was educated at Eton College and Oxford, where he played five first class cricket matches taking 28 wickets. His father who had made a fortune in the iron and coal industry bought Witley Court in 1837; Ward inherited the house in 1833. He married Selina Constance, daughter of Hubert de Burgh, on 24 April 1851. She died on 14 November of the same year, at the age of 22. There were no children from this marriage. In 1860 the earldom held by his kinsman was revived and Ward was created Viscount Ednam, of Ednam in the County of Roxburgh, and Earl of Dudley, of Dudley Castle in the County of Stafford. He married Georgina Elisabeth, daughter of Sir Thomas Moncreiffe and Lady Louisa Hay-

Drummond, on 21 November 1865. They had six sons and one daughter. In the 1850s, the Earl of Dudley engaged the local architect Samuel Daukes to remodel the house in Italianate style using ashlar stone. He also commissioned the garden designer WA Nesfield to transform the gardens. This was Nesfield's 'Monster Work'. (In 1920 Witley Court was sold by the 2nd Earl to Sir Herbert Smith, a Kidderminster carpet manufacturer. The property was sold again following a fire in 1938.) Ward died on 7 May 1885, aged 68, at Dudley House, Park Lane, Mayfair, in London, and was buried in Great Witley, Worcestershire. His remains were later re-interred in Worcester Cathedral. He was succeeded by his eldest son William, who became a prominent Conservative politician and Governor-General of Australia. In 1878 the LFC accounts show that the Earl had three memberships. He has a portrait in the National Gallery.

JEL England, 18??-19?? LFC Member 1943-1980. Address given as Woodlands, Tong, Shifnal. He was the first member Sydney Guy proposed. He resigned in 1954 and again in 1980.

WE Essington, 18??-18??. LFC Member 1863. Address given as Ribbersford House, Bewdley. William Essington Essington.

Colonel Philip Eyton, 1847-19?? LFC Member 1891-94. Address given as Whitton Cottage, Leintwardine. This is probably Lt Colonel Philip Eyton who commanded the Border Regiment. He was the son of the Rev Robert William Eyton, author of *The Antiquities of Shropshire*. A Philip Eyton bought a commission into the 55th Foot, 8th May 1866, and became a Lieutenant by purchase in 1870, and a Captain in 1880. By 1884 the Regiment was known as the Border Regiment and Eyton was promoted Major. Philip Eyton married Ethel Seymour in 1888. His son Robert William went to Mill Mead School, Shrewsbury and was killed in Flanders in 1918.

Colonel GW Fitton, CB, CMG. 18??-19?? LFC Member 1926-1939? Address given as Fairlea, Malvern.

JA Fletcher, 18??-19?? LFC Member 1939-19?? Address given as Mary Knoll, Ludlow.

Francis Freeman, 18??-18?? LFC Member 1863. Address given as 63, Pall Mall, London.

Frederick William Garnett, 1817-1874. LFC Member 1863. Address given as Bonehill House, Tamworth. Garnett is recorded in www.cricinfo.com as playing one match for Oxford University in 1840, scoring a total of 20 runs in two innings and being bowled out by James Cobbett.

MG Garland, 19??-19?? LFC (G) Member 1959-1962 then Full Member 1962-19??. Son of J Ash Garland below.

J Ash Garland, 18??-1960. LFC Member 1945-1960. Address given as Henley in Arden. John Ash Garland later gave his address as Thurlestone, Vicarage Hill, Tamworth-in-Arden, Warwickshire. In 1944 Garland worked for solicitors Lane Clutterbuck & Co. In 1957 Garland was working as a solicitor for Chartered Accountants, Messrs AE Sherry, Garland & Co, 36 Waterloo St, Birmingham. Elected to the committee in 1950, he became Secretary in 1952.

Cosmo-Gordon-Forbes, 1820-1900. LFC Member 1863. Address given as Morrington (sic) Hall, probably Marrington, Chirbury, Shropshire. He married Emily Constable McVickar on 1st June 1859. Slater's Directories of 1868 and 1880 list Forbes as living at Marrington Hall, Chirbury, on the A490 between Church Stoke and Welshpool. The Marrington Hall estate was probably based on one of two manors at Marrington mentioned in the Doomsday Book, the present Hall being a small mid-Victorian Elizabethan style half-timbered country house incorporating a late 16th century timber-framed house. The building is associated with a sundial erected by one Richard Lloyd and originally set within its garden, inscribed *'from dai to dai these shades do flee and so this life passeth awaie'*. By 1878 a Mr Price Davies is living at the Hall. Gordon-Forbes' wife, Emily dies in 1888.

Colonel W Gibbons, OBE, TD, DL, JP.   19??-1972+. LFC (G) Member 1963. Address given as Clare House, Tettenhall, Wolverhampton.

Captain A Greville, RN, 18??-19?? LFC Member 1919-19??. Address given as The Castle, Dover.

Captain Grice-Hutchinson, 1848-1906. LFC Member 1901. Address given as The Boynes, Upton-on-Severn. He gained his captaincy in service with the Scottish Rifles. Captain George William Grice-Hutchinson was returned to Parliament as member for Aston Manor, Birmingham in 1891. He was subsequently re-elected in 1895. Sir John Benjamin Stone painted his portrait in 1897 and this is held in the National Portrait Gallery. His son Lt Colonel Claude Broughton Grice-Hutchinson married into the Coventry family; he went on to win a DSO and served in the Royal Artillery. The Boynes is now a nursing-home.

J Grierson-Clayton, 18??-19?? LFC member 1928. Address given as Brook Hall, Tattenhall, Cheshire.

JMB Guy, 18??-19?? LFC Member 1953-1959.

RS Guy, 18??-19?? LFC Member 1952-1961. Address given as Sauchieleigh, Albrighton, Wolverhampton.

Sydney Slater Guy, 1885-1971. LFC Member 1942– 1971. President 1951-67. Honorary member 1963-1971. Address given as Sauchieleigh, Albrighton, Wolverhampton. Founder of Guy Motors, produced the first British 8-cylinder car engine in 1919. Car production ended in 1925 to concentrate on commercial vehicles. Sydney Guy retired in 1957. In 1961 the company was taken over by Jaguar. Guy production ceased in 1976. Obituary in The Times, Friday, September 24, 1971. A biography can be found at the following web site www.localhistory.scit.wlv.ac.uk/Museum/Transport/Cars/Guy.htm.

TM Guy, 19??-19?? LFC Member 1953. Address given as Sauchieleigh, Albrighton.

WR Ewart Guy, 18??-1953. LFC Member 1942-1953. Addresses given as Keystone?, Badge Heath?, Nr Wolverhampton and Moseley Hall, Fordhouses, Wolverhampton. He served as a Major in the Staffordshire Home Guard, 23 (Wolverhampton) Bn. during WWII.

KRH Habershon, 18??-19?? LFC Honorary Member 1961. Address given as Aston on Clun House, Craven Arms. He was the agent for the Downton Estate.

CC Harley, 1926-1997. LFC Honorary Member 1961-1997. Address given as Stonebrook House, Downton on the Rock, later Brampton Bryan Hall. Christopher Charles Harley second son of JRH Harley inherited the Harley estate from his father in 1953?

JRH Harley, 1888-1960. LFC Honorary Member 1920-1939. Address given as Brampton Bryan. John Ralph Henry Harley married Rachel Gwyer. He was gazetted in 1917, aged 29, as an officer of the Highland Light Infantry for promotion to Acting Captain in the Special Reserve. In 1930 he was Secretary for the Teme Valley Hunt. Again gazetted in December 1939, aged 51, he was promoted to captain whilst serving on the Special List in a National Defence Company. Their eldest son Robert John Mortimer died during WWII at Salerno, so Christopher (see above) inherited the estate. In 1958 Ralph Harley was using the title Major JRH Harley, DL, JP, Bucknell, Salop when representing the Local Councils' Association on the UK's Central Transport Consultative Committee.

RGG Harley, 1879-1920. LFC Hon Member 1907-1920. Address given as Brampton Bryan, Herefordshire. Educated Eton and Magdalene College, Cambridge, Robert George Geoffrey Harley married Annie Winifred (Freda) Ripley. Geoffrey Harley served in WWI with the Royal Fusiliers; he was gazetted in 1918 when he relinquished his commission as a captain on appointment to the RNVR serving with the Royal Air Force.

RWD Harley, 1846-1907. LFC Honorary Member 1878-1907. Address given as Brampton Bryan, Herefordshire. Robert William Daker Harley, Esq, JP, DL was the son of John Harley of Ross Hall, Salop. He was educated at Westminster and Magdalene College,

Cambridge. He succeeded to the Harley estates under the will of Lady Langdale, daughter of Edward Harley, Earl of Oxford, in 1872. He married Hon Patience Anne (Rodney); their children included a daughter, Dorothy, who married LFC member Sir Henry Ripley, and sons RGG and JRH Harley. It is entirely probable that RWD Harley was made an honorary member of the LFC earlier than 1878, *ie* on the death of Lady Langdale in 1872 or shortly after. 1878 is the first reprint of the LFC members' list after Lady Langdale's death.

WRJ Heatley, 18??-19?? LFC Member 1960-1972+. Address given as The Manor House, Albrighton. His membership was accelerated in order to fill the position of Honorary Secretary as there were no other volunteers. He was described by S Guy as aged 47 (in 1960), a Salopian, who was commissioned into the Kings Scottish Light Infantry in WWII, a chartered accountant and a bachelor, living at Albrighton. He was later elected LFC Treasurer.

Hugh Louis Heber-Percy, 1853-1925. LFC Member 1912-1920. Address given as Ferney Hall, Onibury. Known as Hugo, he married Harriet Earp in 1899. His father, Algernon Charles, lived at Hodnet Hall, Shropshire. He was the nephew of the 5th Duke of Northumberland.

Major William C Hill, 18??-19?? LFC Member 1885-1909. Address given as Powyke, Worcestershire, and later The Cottage, Malvern Wells. Hill's name appears on the committee for the production of the Victorian History of Worcestershire; Lord Coventry as Lord Lieutenant of the County was Chairman.

Colonel CAF Hocken, CBE, 18??-19?? LFC Member 1937. Address given as Meadhome, St John's Rd, Eastbourne.

HA Hopkins, 1883-1957. LFC Member 1948-1955, re-admitted 1956-57. Address given as Arden House, Knowle, Warwickshire. Harry Augustus Hopkins, known as Gus, had a factory in Birmingham and manufactured clothing for the retail trade. His wife was called Gladys and they had one child, Philip Augustus. Gus Hopkins was also a member of the Greenwell Club and is mentioned in CV Hancock's book *Rod in Hand*. He was known by Hancock as *'the squire'*.

Bernard Hopps, 18??-1935. LFC Member 1916-20. Address given as Thurlaston, Nr Rugby. A manufacturer of sparkplugs, Hopps is noted as taking delivery of the first 'Derby' Bentley on 2nd March 1934, for which he paid £1,496.6s.6d, approximately 15 times what a new Ford 8hp Saloon of the period cost! The records show that Mr Hopps made a special request for Lodge sparkplugs and also paid for a GB plate to be fitted, doubtless with extended Continental touring in mind. It was not to be: in March 1935 *'Deceased'* appears next to his name in the company's ledgers. This same car came up for sale in 2010 at £85,995 (www.kultkars.net). His son, also Bernard Hopps, was to go on to become Managing Director of Lodge Plugs limited.

JA Hopps, 18??-19?? LFC Member 1926-1930. Address given as Rivington, Knighton Drive, Leicester.

Thomas Charles Gandolfi Hornyold, 1846-1906. LFC Member 1886. Address given as Blackmoor Park, Hanley Castle, Upton-on-Severn, a Jacobean-style mansion built by his father in 1867. In 1873 he exchanged several parcels of land with the Lechmere family (Anthony Lechmere was also an LFC member). In 1880 his house was gutted by fire, rebuilt in 1883. In 1899 he was granted the title of Duke Gandolfi for his services to Catholicism by Pope Leo XIII. Shown as Magistrate for Herefordshire (Kelly's 1895).

J Hurlestone-Leche, 1827-1903. LFC Member 1886-1901. Address given as Carden Park, Chester. The ancient family of Leche once owned Chatsworth and settled in Carden in mid-14th century. Twelve generations of John Leches were superseded in the 19th century by the Hurlestone-Leches. John Hurtlestone-Leche married his second wife, Eleanor Francis, in 1855; he became DL and JP for Cheshire. A person of the same name was admitted to the Cestrian Lodge of Freemasonry in 1850. Carden Hall burnt down in 1912.

Rev C Ibbotson, 1815?-18?? LFC Member 1863-1870. Address given as Oxford and Cambridge Club, London. Charles Ibbotson was educated at Trinity College, Cambridge, 1830-1846. He is listed in the Clergy List 1849-65 but does not appear in Crockford's Directory of 1860 or 1865.

G Jobling, 18??-19?? LFC Member 1928. Address given as St Stephen's Manor, Cheltenham.

Rowland Kennard, 1871-1920. LFC Member 1912-1914. Address given as Little Harrow, Christchurch, Hants. Rowland Stephen Astley Kennard married Winifred Heyworth; they had two children. He was a JP.

Lt Colonel DEC Kenny, 18??-19?? LFC Member 1943-1944+. Appears on a fishing return of 1943-44 but not after.

SM Kent, 18??-19?? LFC Member 1930-1948+. Address given as Shobdon Court, Kingsland, and later Whitton Hall, Westbury, Salop.

AG Ker, JP, 18??-19?? LFC Member 1926-1930. Address given as Leintwardine House, Leintwardine.

The Lady Langdale, 1796- 1872. Honorary Member 1870. Address given as Eywood, Kington. The Lady Jane Elizabeth Harley married Henry Bickersteth, Baron Langdale (1783-1851) in 1835 (portrait National Gallery). He was a Member of the Privy Council and Master of the Rolls in succession to Pepys. She was the eldest daughter of Henry's friend and patron, the Earl of Oxford. Henry died in 1851, Jane Elizabeth survived him, and on the death of her brother Alfred in 1853, 6th and last Earl of Oxford, the Harley estate reverted to her. She died on 1 September 1872.

Herbert Langham, 1840-1909. LFC Member 1881-18??. Address given as Cottesbrook Park, Northamptonshire. Eton, 1st Life Guards 1857-65. Herbert Hay Langham succeeded to the title of 12th Baron Langham in 1893. He hunted with the Pytchley and was Master of Hounds from 1878. He had a daughter, Augusta Frederica, who was later to become Baroness Henley of Chardstock. She died in 1905.

H W Langley, 18??-19?? LFC Member 1912-1914. Address given as Bedstone Court, Bucknell.

Archdeacon William Lea, 1819-1889. LFC Member prior to 1863. According to the biography in the book *The Worthies of Worcester* he was born at Stone House, near Kidderminster. Educated at Rugby and Brasenose College, Oxford; BA, 1842. Vicar of St. Peter's, Droitwich, 1849-87. Archdeacon of Worcester, 1881. As Secretary of the Worcester Board of Education, he zealously promoted intellectual progress. He was also a great authority upon fruit-growing, recommending it especially to cottagers. He established a large experimental garden at *Orchardlea* where he tested the suitability of nearly every variety of apple, pear, and plum to the Worcestershire soil and climate. Carefully tabulated results were kept of every tree, and the results and profits were made known in many village lectures. In addition he wrote: *On the Life of our Lord*; *Sermons on the Prayer Book Preached in Borne*; *Small Farms*; and *Church Plate in the Archdeaconry of Worcester*. He had articles published in the *Fishing Gazette* but of more concern to us is the book published after his death *Fishing Reminiscences of the Late Archdeacon Lea* **(1892)**. Published by Shuttle Office, Kidderminster. '*Published for his most intimate friends and relations. 100 copies printed for private circulation.*' The ten chapters include: *A Day at Leintwardine*.

Anthony Lechmere, 1868-19?? LFC Member 1905-19?? Address given as Kempsey, Worcester, and later Wolverton Hall, Pershore. Anthony Hungerford Lechmere, Esq., was a JP and DL .for Worcestershire. He was a temporary Captain in the Worcestershire Regiment 1914-18. He was awarded the order Knight of Grace of the Order of the Hospital of St John of Jerusalem. His club was the Junior Carlton Club. He married Cecily, née Bridges .in 1920.

H Leigh, 18??-1958. LFC Member 1958. Died in Canada before being able to fish as a member at Leintwardine.

Major E Levett, 18??-19?? LFC Member 1899-18??. Address given as Rowsley, Derbyshire.

Major WMPK Lennox, 1892-1969. LFC Honorary Member 1953-1969. Address given as Downton Castle. Owner and lessor of the Downton Waters on the Teme from 1947-1969. William Mandeville Peareth Kincaid Lennox, Chief of Lennox, came into possession of Downton Castle because Charles Andrew Rouse Boughton Knight had no heir when he died in 1947. CABK's sister Anna Lilly Frances had married William George Peareth Kincaid Lennox and produced a son, WMPKL, who then became next male in line to the Downton Castle estate when CABK died. WMPKL married in 1918, Eva St Clair, and by 1947 already had a daughter, Heather Veronica, who in turn had married Dennis Arthur Hornell in 1940. Heather was widowed in 1941 (Hornell, a Lt Commander RN, was killed during the evacuation of Crete) whilst carrying Hornell's son. WMPKL, the 'Major' as he was known on the estate, signed his letters Bill or Billy and ran the estate for the 22 years. When the Major died in 1969 Dennis Peareth Hornell, aged 28, inherited the Downton Estate, and then added Lennox to his name.

JN Lovett, 18??-19?? LFC Member 1936-1950. Address given as Moorhay, Church Stretton. He is noted in the minute book as being elected in 1936, again in 1940 and again in 1945. He was elected to the committee in 1946. He resigned in 1950.

Major AC Lyon, 18??-19. LFC Member 1918-1920. Address given as Wellington Club, Grosvenor Place, London.

GE Martin, 18??-1905. LFC Member 1886-1894. Address given as Ham Court, Upton-on-Severn. George Edward Martin had become lord of the manor of Upton in 1873 and moved into Ham Court in 1879. He was married to Maria Henrietta and had three children. He was made Sheriff of Worcestershire in 1882, and was also a JP and Deputy Lieutenant for the county. His son Eliot George Bromley-Martin married Katherine Emily (Emmy) in 1899, the second daughter of Andrew Rouse Boughton Knight.

Colonel HD Marshall, CIE, OBE. 18??-19??. LFC Member 1928-1942? Address given as Mary Knoll, Church Stretton. He was elected LFC Honorary Secretary in 1942.

RP Marshall, 18??-19?? LFC Member 1930-1937. Address given as Brockhurst, Church Stretton.

SW Maslen-Jones, 1891-1967. LFC Member 1950-1957. Re-joined as a Grayling Member in 1965. Address given as The Pavings, Wrottesley Rd, Tettenhall, Staffordshire, and later 69 Mill Lane, Tettenhall Wood, Wolverhampton. Doctor Samuel Walter Maslen-Jones MS, FRCS, FRCOG the son of a Baptist missionary, was born in Simla on 6 September 1891, and was educated at Eltham College, and at the Middlesex Hospital, London, where he qualified with the Conjoint diploma in 1914. During the WWI he joined the Royal Army Medical Corps, and saw four years service in Egypt, where he was mentioned in dispatches. In Cairo he met and married Sister Kate Wilde, Queen Alexandra's Imperial Military Nursing Service. After demobilization he graduated MB, BS in 1919, and took the MS and the FRCS in 1920. He went to Wolverhampton to work with Frederick Edge, and in 1921 was appointed to the staff of the Women's Hospital there. During his years in the West Midlands he gained an outstanding reputation, founded not only on his ability and skill as a diagnostician and surgeon, but on the sympathetic understanding and kindliness of approach to all with whom he came into contact. He was a past-President and Honorary Fellow of the Birmingham and Midland Obstetric and Gynaecological Society, a one-time chairman of the South Staffordshire Division of the British Medical Association, and President of the Staffordshire Branch from 1937 to 1940. In his own specialty, he was a founder member of the British College of Obstetricians and Gynaecologists – as it was then called – and in 1931 was elected to the Fellowship. He was elected to the LFC committee in 1955 and resigned in 1957.

Colonel H McMicking, CB, DSO, 18??-19?? LFC Member 1926. Address given as 30 Elvaston Place, London SW7.

E Meade-King, 18??-19?? LFC Member 1928. Address given as Cleeve, Nr Bristol.

Colonel Hon Paul Methuen, CB, 1845-1932. LFC Member 1893. Address given as Corsham Court, Corsham, Wiltshire. Eton and the Scots Guards; he was to become Field Marshall Paul Sanford Methuen. On the death of his father in 1891 he succeeded to the title 3rd Baron Methuen. Proposed in 1887, *ie* before he inherited the title, by Lord Coventry and Colonel Stapleton-Cotton, who had married his sister, Jane. He married firstly Evelyn Hervey-Bathurst in 1878, and secondly Mary Ethel Sanford by whom he had seven children. He commanded Methuen's Horse, Bechuanaland 1885, a Division in South Africa 1899-1902 and GOC Troops South Africa 1908. (National Portrait Gallery).

Sir William Milman, Bart, 1813-1885. LFC Member 1863. Address given as Moor Park, Ludlow. Sir William Milman became the 3rd baronet (in 1857) and married Matilda Francis Pretyman, member of a distinguished family who owned estates near Orford in Suffolk. Her grand-uncle was the Rt Rev Sir George Tomline, DD, Bt., who had been William Pitt's tutor and went on to be Bishop of Lincoln and then of Winchester. Sir William had been a barrister working on the Oxford Circuit. [The Salwey family owned Moor Park until 1874 when the greater part of the estate, including the main house, was sold. In 1861, the then Prince of Wales, later Edward VII, visited Moor Park with a view to buying it as his country estate. He eventually chose Sandringham because of its proximity to London and, it is said, its superior supply of pheasants. In the early 1850s, the house was let for a year to an American family from Boston, and the daughter (Anna

Fay) subsequently wrote an intriguing account of their visit describing Victorian life in Hereford and Shropshire from an outsider's point of view.]

AA Mitchell, 19??-1977. LFC Member 1949-1977. Address given as Devonshire Works, Birmingham 12, and 146 Haunch Lane, Kings Heath, Birmingham. He was proposed by Sydney Guy. He was elected to the committee in 1952 and was elected President in 1967.

Morgan-Vane, 18??-18?? LFC Member 1870-1877. Address given as Chippenham Hall, Soham. This may have been Sir Henry Morgan-Vane (1808-1886), a barrister at law, later secretary to the Charity Commission 1853-1886, and invested as Knight in 1883.

Lt Colonel Mustrapp, 18??-19?? LFC Member 1936-1941. His name first appears as attending the 1936 AGM, but no further references appear after 1942

Dr JC Newbould, 19??-19?? LFC Member 1964-1972+. Address given as 18 Newbridge Crescent, Wolverhampton.

Dr WA Nicholson, 18??-19?? LFC Member 1938-19?? Address given as Kingsland.

The Right Honourable Lord Northwick, 1811-1887. LFC Member 1863-87 Address given as Burford House, near Tenbury. George Rushout-Bowles was born at Burford, the son of Reverend the Hon George Rushout-Bowles, younger son of John Rushout, 1st Baron Northwick. His mother was Lady Caroline, daughter of John Stewart, 7th Earl of Galloway. George was returned to Parliament for Evesham in 1837. In May 1838 he fought a duel with Peter Borthwick, who had been elected alongside George R-B in 1837, but had been unseated on petition in March 1838 following disputed election results. He continued to represent Evesham until 1841, and later sat as Member of Parliament for Worcestershire East between 1847 and 1859. In 1859 he succeeded his uncle to the barony and entered the House of Lords. Lord Northwick married the Hon Elizabeth Augusta, daughter of William Bateman-Hanbury, 1st Baron Bateman and widow of George Warburton, in 1869 at Shobdon. There were no surviving children from the marriage. Lord Northwick died at The Queen's Hotel, Upper Norwood, in November 1887, aged 66. On his death his titles became extinct. Lady Northwick died in May 1912, aged 80. (National Portrait Gallery).

CW Parkes, 18??-19?? LFC Member 1950-1962+. Address given as 34 Danescourt Road, Tettenhall, Staffordshire. Cyril W Parkes was proposed by Sydney Guy. He was elected to the committee in 1952.

John Parker, 18??-18?? LFC Member 1863. Address given as Woodside House, Worcester.

Major WG Parsons, MC, 18??-19?? LFC Member 1956-1972+. Address given as Holles House, Albrighton, Wolverhampton. He was elected to the committee in 1972.

Brigadier-General EC Peebles, CB, CMG, DSO, 18??-19?? LFC Member 1928.

Thomas Peters, 18??-18?? LFC Member 1863. Address given as Knighton.

W Pilkington, 19??-19??   LFC Member 1959-19??   Address given as Spring Cottage, Steventon, Ludlow.

HM Porter, 18??-1909. LFC Member 1889-1909. Address given as Birlingham, Pershore.

Gerald Radcliffe, 18??-19?? LFC Member 1937. Address given as Elton Hall Ludlow.

KG Reid, 18??-19?? LFC Member 1952-1962+.   Address given as Grange Croft, 42 Grange Road, Cambridge.

Dr Richardson, RA 18??-18?? LFC Member 1863. Address given as 6 Mars Terrace Woolwich.

G Ripley, 1881-1959. LFC Member 1926. Address given as Heath House, Aston on Clun. Probably Edward Guy Ripley, a younger brother to Sir Henry, see below. He reached the rank of Lieutenant in the Rifle Brigade and fought in the Boer War, and in WWI became a Captain in the Army Service Corps. He was invested with the OBE in 1919. He was unmarried.

Sir HWA Ripley, Bt, 1879-1956. LFC Member 1912-1915 and 1919-1926. Address given as Bedstone Court, Bucknell. Sir Henry William Alfred Ripley, 3rd Baronet was born on 3 January 1879, the son of Sir Edward Ripley, 2nd Bt and Eugenie Frederica Fulcher Emmott-Rawdon. He married Dorothy Harley, daughter of Robert William Daker Harley and Hon Patience Anne Rodney, on 17 January 1911. He died on 14 December 1956 at age 77. Sir Henry was educated at Eton College. He gained the rank of Captain in the service of the 1st Royal Dragoons and fought in the Boer War between 1900 and 1902. He succeeded to the title of 3rd Baronet Ripley, of Acacia, Rawdon, West Riding of Yorkshire and Bedstone House, Shropshire on 21 November 1903. He fought in WWI and held the office of Justice of the Peace for both Shropshire and Herefordshire. He gained the rank of Major in 1940 in the service of the 7th Battalion, Shropshire Home Guard He had six children, the two eldest sons were killed in WWII and the third, Hugh George Harley Ripley was wounded but went on to a career in the whisky trade. Hugh wrote some amusing memoirs *Whisky for Tea*.

John Rocke, 1817-1881. LFC Member 1863-1881. Address given as Clungunford House. Rocke inherited the house and manor of Clungunford from his father the Rev John Rocke on his death in 1849. His mother was Anne, youngest daughter of Thomas Beale of Heath House. He went to Harrow and Trinity College, Cambridge and became a banker. He was a Lieutenant in the South Shropshire Yeomanry Cavalry. He married Constance

Anne, daughter of Sir Charles Culyer Bart, in 1853. He was a JP and DL for Salop and appointed High Sheriff of Shropshire in 1869. He was an ornithologist of some skill and made a collection of preserved British birds that was of international note. Some of the cases of birds can be seen in the Ludlow Museum.

Reverend TO Rocke, 1822-1892. LFC Member 1863-86. Address given as Clungunford Rectory. Thomas Owen Rocke was born at Clungunford and was the brother of John (see above). He went to school at Bridgnorth and gained a BA in 1845 at Trinity College, Cambridge (Crockford's Directory). He followed in his father's footsteps as rector at Clungunford from 1849-92. He married in 1861 Edith, daughter of Rev TT Lewis of Yatton Court, and again in 1890 (aged 68) Josephine Emily, daughter of Rev A Stonehouse vicar of Walford. One of his sons, William Charles, became the fourth generation of Rockes to be vicar of Clungunford.

Reverend John Rogers, 1817-1878. LFC Member 1870-1878. Address given as Stanage Park, Brampton Bryan. He went to Shrewsbury School and St John's College, Cambridge 1836-44. Rev John Rogers MA of the Home and Stanage Park was formerly Vicar of Aymestrey, 1850-65. Vicar at Stowe 1865-78. JP for Herefordshire and Radnor and Salop. He married in 1851 Charlotte Victoria Newbold; their son, Charles Coltman, assumed by royal licence in 1919 the surname of Coltman (from his maternal grandfather) to become Charles Coltman Coltman-Rogers. His appointments included JP, High Sheriff and MP for Radnor.

Dr NJL Rollason, 1883-1967. LFC Member 1943-1964. Address given as 1 Lythalls Lane, Coventry, and 74 Stoneleigh Avenue, Coventry. Norman John Lancelot was born in Smethwick on 6 May 1883, and educated at Five Ways Grammar School and Birmingham University. After house appointments at Queen's Hospital, Birmingham, he joined Dr John Orton in general practice in Coventry, where he rapidly became a well-loved family doctor. During WWI he served as Surgeon Lieutenant-Commander in the Royal Naval Volunteer Reserve, and from 1914 to 1964 he served continuously on committees concerned with medical administration. He had a distinguished record in the St. John Ambulance Association. He loved Freemasonry and was a past Master of the St John's Lodge of Freemasons and an officer of the Provincial Grand Lodge of Warwickshire. He was an enthusiastic angler; every holiday would be spent fishing in Scotland and later in Leintwardine. In 1908 he married Elizabeth Mary Oakden; she died in 1957. They had no children. He was elected to the LFC committee in 1950 and served until 1955.

Edward Shuckburgh Rouse-Boughton, 1858-1932. LFC Member 1912-1915. Address given as Whitton, Leintwardine. He was still at Whitton in 1913. Second son of Sir Charles Henry Rouse-Boughton of Downton Hall. He never married.

Sir William Rouse-Boughton, 1788-1856. LFC President 1848-1856. Address was Downton Hall, Stanton Lacey, Shropshire. William Edward Rouse Boughton inherited Downton Hall from his father Sir Charles William Rouse Boughton in 1821 and became the 10th Baronet Boughton, of Lawford Parva, Warwickshire and 2nd Baronet Boughton Rouse, of Rouse-Lench, Worcestershire. He graduated from Christ Church, Oxford, was MP for Evesham 1818-1826, and a fellow of the Royal Society. He married Charlotte Knight, daughter of Thomas Andrew Knight of Downton Castle in 1824. They had eight children: Charles Henry, 1825, Andrew Johnes (ARBK), 1826, Algernon Greville, 1828, Catherine Charlotte, 1830, Frances Harriett, 1832, Theresa Louisa Catherine, 1833, Mary Lucy Octavia, 1835, Frederica St John, 1838. Charlotte died in 1842. Sir William held Downton Castle and the Castle Estate in trust for his son ARBK (see next entry) from the death of Thomas Andrew Knight in 1838 until his own death in 1856.

AJ Rouse-Boughton-Knight, 1826-1909. LFC President and Treasurer 1870-1909. Honorary Member, Landowner Downton Castle Estate. Andrew Johnes Rouse-Boughton was born at Henley Hall, near Ludlow on 26 May 1826. He was the second son of Sir William Edward Rouse Boughton and Charlotte (née Knight) of Downton Hall (which was being refurbished at the time). AJRB was educated first at Ludlow, then at a school in East Sheen, and from 1838 at Eton (his elder brother Charles being at Harrow). He went on to Trinity College, Cambridge in 1845. In 1856 his elder brother Charles inherited Downton Hall and Andrew Rouse-Boughton inherited Downton Castle. Andrew was granted the right, by Royal Licence in 1857, to add the name Knight to his name. He then styled himself Andrew Rouse-Boughton-Knight, and signed his letters AR Boughton Knight; ARBK married Eliza Severne (1838-1914) in September 1858 and they went on to produce seven children. Andrew was an honorary member of the LFC from early times until his death in 1909. He was listed as a Magistrate for Herefordshire (Kelly's 1895).

Charles Andrew Rouse-Boughton-Knight, 1859-1947. LFC President 1909-1936, Honorary Member 1909-1947. First born and eldest son of AR Boughton-Knight and Eliza (née Severne). Charles Andrew Rouse-Boughton-Knight was known as 'Andy'. In 1876 he was listed as Sub-Lieutenant in the Hereford Militia and two years later as Lieutenant in the Worcester Militia. By 1881 he is a Lieutenant in the 23rd Foot (Royal Welch Fusiliers) and then in April 1882, age 23, he joins the Scots Guards, but resigns in 1885. By 1896 he was living locally at Lodge Farm, Downton, and then at Overton Grange and is occupied as Chairman of the Ludlow Guardians. He married Helen Dupré (née Wilson) 30 April 1902 in Dublin and moved to London. He became ill in 1903 and underwent surgery. Later he moved to Hinton House, Hinton Admiral, Hampshire. By 1909 he had inherited the Downton Estate and was living at Pools Farm, Downton. He was listed as a Magistrate for Herefordshire (Kelly's 1895). Helen died in 1926. He died 21 October 1947.

TW Shaw, 18??-19?? LFC Member 1919-1928. Address given as Culmington Manor, Craven Arms.

Rev Thomas Short, BD, 1789-1879. LFC Member 1863. Address given as Trinity College, Oxford. Short was born in Manor Cottage, Solihull, Warwickshire on June 24th 1789. He was educated at Solihull School, but he had entered Rugby School by 1803. He took an exhibition from the school in 1807, and matriculated as commoner at Trinity College, Oxford in October. In 1811 he was awarded a Third Class in the Honour School (Classics), and the following year his BA degree. He returned to Rugby as under-master in 1811 and was ordained whilst there. In 1816 Short returned to Trinity as fellow and tutor. He was at one stage a candidate for the headmastership of Rugby School, but Dr Arnold beat him by one vote. He went on to become Vice-President of his college. A book printed in 1909 titled *An Oxford Tutor: The life of the Rev Thomas Short, BD of Trinity College, Oxford* and written by CEH Edwards gives further detail of his life as *'the best tutor of his time'* and of his regard for fishing, but sadly gives no indication that he fished the Teme. He probably did most of his fishing once he had retired back to Manor Cottage. The book can be read on Archive.org. Short never married.

HS Shorthouse, 18??-19?? LFC Member 1939-19?? Address given as Salamo, Wilford on Avon, Stratford on Avon.

WWGH Sitwell, 1828-1909. LFC Member 1863-1881. Address given as Ferney Hall, near Ludlow. Probably William Willoughby George Hurt Sitwell, JP. He was appointed High Sheriff of Shropshire in 1855. He married Harriet Margret in 1853 (died 1855), and then Eliza Harriet in 1858 who died 1888. He was a Lieutenant in the Shropshire Yeomanry. Ferney Hall, Onibury, was built in 1856 on the site of an older house following a fire. Designs for the gardens of the old hall appear in one of Humphrey Repton's Red Books in 1789. The 1881 census shows WWGH (Esq) Sitwell as head of household (b 1828), Eliza Sitwell (b 1831), presumably his second wife, Francis Hurt Sitwell (b. 1860), second son and daughter Elinor (b 1865), who married Sir William Grenville Williams 4th baronet in 1884.

WH Sitwell, 1881-1929+. LFC Member 1912-1913. Address given as The Cottage, Bucknell. Willoughby Hurt Sitwell second son of Hurt Sitwell. Magistrate for Herefordshire (Kelly's 1895).

George Smythies, 18??-19?? LFC Member 1886-1891. Address given as Marlow, Leintwardine. Listed as Magistrate for Herefordshire (Kelly's 1895).

Vere Somerset, 1854-1904+. LFC Member 1886-94. Address given as Prees Hall, near Shrewsbury, Shropshire. Vere Francis John Somerset, educated at Wellington College, married in 1875 Annette Catherine (née Hill). They had two sons.

GE Sparrow, 18??-19?? LFC (G) Member 1959- 1972+. Address given as Cloverfield, Olton, Warwickshire.

Colonel Hon Richard Stapleton-Cotton, 1849-1925. LFC Member 1886. Address given as Combermere Abbey, Whitchurch. His father was Colonel Wellington Stapleton-Cotton, 2nd Viscount Combermere of Bhurtpore, his mother Susan Alice Sitwell. He married the Hon Jane Charlotte Methuen in 1870 and they had six surviving children. (The names Sitwell and Methuen both appear in members' lists). Colonel Hon Richard Southwell George Stapleton-Cotton gained the rank of Colonel in the service of the Scots Guards and later served with the rank of Colonel in the 3rd Battalion, Wiltshire Regiment. He was Inspector-General Police for British Guiana between 1889 and 1891. JP for Cheshire and JP for Shropshire. He held the office of DL of Anglesey, and died at Plas Llown, Llanfair Pg, Angelsey aged 76.

JH Starey, 1848-1928. LFC Member 1912-1915. Address given as The Manor, Bodenham, Herefordshire. This may have been John Helps Starey listed in Kelly's Directory for 1913 as a private resident in Bodenham, living in the Manor. A man of the same name published in 1890 *The Paddy Tax in Ceylon: A Letter Addressed to the Cobden Club*. He was a manager of an agricultural company in Ceylon and resident there for 18 years. The Starey family bought the 590-acre Milton Ernest Hall Estate, Bedfordshire, in 1853 but had to sell it after stock market disasters in 1872. In 1919, having made a second fortune in Ceylon, the family bought back Milton Estate and owned it until 1968. During WWII the Hall became the HQ of the US Eighth Air Force. In July 1944 Glenn Miller played there in the grounds just before his last flight.

Bryan Sunderland, 18??-19?? LFC Member 1912-1914+. Address given as The Bolands, Tenbury, and later as Hope Court, Ludlow.

JL Swanson, 18??-19?? LFC (G) Member 1959–1972+. Address given as The Orchard, Tettenhall Wood, Wolverhampton.

Major HR Sykes, 1870-1952. LFC Member 1912-1951. Address given as Longnor Hall, Shrewsbury, and then Lydham Manor, and from 1933 The Roveries, Churchstoke. Herbert Rushton Sykes, LFC Honorary Secretary 1946, LFC President 1946-1951, was appointed Honorary Member in 1951, having resigned the Presidency due to ill-health. He died in March 1952. Educated at Rugby and Christ Church, Oxford (MA 1897), in 1894 he gained an athletics half-blue against Yale. In 1903 he joined an expedition to Persia and was subsequently elected a Fellow of the Royal Geographical Society. Twice he represented England in a rifle competition, the Elcho Shield, at Bisley. He was commissioned into the 4th Volunteer Battalion Cheshire Regiment and then the Montgomeryshire Yeomanry, TA. He obtained his Majority by 1914. During WWI he commanded an

Army Agricultural Scheme at Bury St Edmunds. He was Mayor of Bishop's Castle twice and High Sheriff of Shropshire in 1928. He was very active throughout his life in county matters. At the age of 73 he was appointed Treasurer of the Royal Salop Infirmary. He married the Hon Constance, daughter of 11th Viscount Masserine and Ferard, in 1905.

SV Thomas, 18??-19?? LFC Member 1926. Address given as Bryngny, Rhayader.

AH Thompson, 18??-19?? LFC Member 1959- 1965+. Arthur Thompson.

RE Threlfall, 1891-19?? LFC Member 1961-1975. Address given as The Quarry, Pedmore, Stourbridge. Richard Evelyn Threlfall was a glass manufacturer, the son of Sir Richard Threlfall (1861-1932), a fellow of the Royal Society. He was noted as a consummate angler and wrote *On a Gentle Art* (1951).

Colonel LTC Twyford, 18??-19?? LTC Member 1913-1919. Address given as Naval & Military Club, 56 Hans Place, London SW. He served in the North Staffordshire Regiment, and was married to Vera. He was gazetted in June 1916 for gallant conduct in the field with rank noted as Temporary Brigadier-General in the Reserve of Officers.

W Vale-King, 18??-19?? LFC Member 1886-1901. Address given as Elton Hall, Ludlow and earlier Woodlands, Pinner, Middlesex. Listed as Magistrate for Herefordshire (Kelly's 1895).

Brigadier-General E Vaughan, CMG, DSO, 18??-19?? LFC Member 1928. Address given as Croftmead, Kingsland.

C Villiers-Bayley, 18??-1877. LFC Member 1863-1877. Address given as Privy Council Office, London.

JG Rodney Ward, 18??-19?? LFC Honorary Member 1870-18?? Address given as Yatton Court, Kingsland which in Littlebury's Directory of 1876 is described as *'a modern stone building, beautifully situated on the banks of the Lugg'*. John George Rodney Ward was agent for the Harley Estate during the time of both Lady Langdale and RWD Harley; he was involved with the LFC and the initial agreements over fishing rights. The local directory lists him as a principal landowner in Aymestrey, a churchwarden and JP. He was a governor of Kington Grammar School. He was Lady Langdale's nomination for honorary membership and attended at least one LFC meeting at Downton Castle in 1872, but his name did not appear on any of the members' lists.

Colonel HB Watkins, OBE, DL, 18??-19?? LFC Member 1961-1973+. Honorary life member from 1971. Address given as Shirley, Knighton. LFC Secretary 1967-73. Colonel Watkins commanded the 1st Battalion Radnor Home Guard and was awarded OBE in 1944.

Lt Colonel FM Westropp, DSO, 18??-19?? LFC Member 1920-1951? Address given as Wheatstone, Leintwardine.

FGM Westropp, 19??-19?? LFC Member 1948-1972. Address given as 19 Church Rd, Hampstead, London, and Greyhound Cottage, Glemsford, Suffolk. Proposed by his father and AR Beale.

Major FA Whitmore, 1845-1927. LFC Member 1863-1901. Address given as 1 Westbourne Park Crescent, London, and later as Larden Hall, Much Wenlock. Francis Alexander Wolryche-Whitmore JP, BA (Oxon), was an Hon Colonel and later Lieutenant Colonel Commanding Salop Militia. He married Alice Mary in 1871. He purchased Larden c. 1897. After he died in 1927, Larden passed to his son John Eric Alexander Wolryche-Whitmore in 1931.

George Whitmore, 1881-1929+. LFC Member 1863. Address given as 28 Oxford Square, London. This is probably Geoffrey Charlton Wolryche-Whitmore, son of FA Whitmore.

H White, 18??-1970. LFC Member 1943-1970. Address given as Ashleigh, Avenue Road, Wolverhampton, and Ridgemead, Lower Penn, Wolverhampton; later at Glen Tower, Avenue Road, Wolverhampton. Harry White was elected to the committee in 1957

RF White, 18??-1949. LFC Member 1943-1949. Address given as Wylde Green, Birmingham, and later 5 Greenhill Road.

Frederick H Whymper, 1838-1901. LFC Member 1886. Address given as Carlton Club, London. Frederic Whymper was an artist as well as an author and mining engineer. He was best known for his watercolour seascapes and survey expedition illustrations, especially of Alaska. He was born in England in 1838. As a young man, he worked with his brother, Edward (of Matterhorn fame), on Alpine books. In the late 1850s he travelled as the official artist with the Waddington Expedition in British Columbia. Between 1862 and 1867 he made numerous visits to San Francisco. He published *The Heroes of the Arctic and their Adventures* in 1889.

ER Wigram, 1860-1929+. LFC Member 1883-1885, and 1892. Address given as Guards Club, London. Possibly Eustace Rochester Wigram, Lieutenant (retd) Coldstream Guards. Married 1889, Mary Grace.

WG Willcocks, 18??-19?? LFC Member 1938-19?? Address given as Ryecroft, Leominster.

Rev TB Wilson,   18??-19?? LFC Member 1928-1937+. Address given as Wolverley Vicarage, Kidderminster.

Colonel CRB Wingfield, 1873-1923. LFC Member 1912-1920. Address given as Onslow, Shrewsbury. Lt Col Charles Ralph Borlase Wingfield. Married to Mary Nesta Williams, they had three children. He was Mayor of Shrewsbury 1912-13, also a JP for the county. In 1908 he was elected President of the Yorkshire Ramblers' Club and their vice president 1919-21.

TS Withington, 18??-19?? LFC Member 1957-1972. Address given as White Lodge, Four Oaks Warwickshire.

Major CEW Wood, 18??-19?? LFC Member 1901-1943+. Address given as Bishton Hall, Stafford. A leading member of the Club and ex-officio President in the period 1922-1930, he appears to have been elected President in 1937 but latterly did not serve in that role, Mr Beale standing in. In 1939 Wood was made an Honorary Member. Bishton is mentioned in the Domesday Book; the Hall is a Grade 2 listed Georgian mansion dating to about 1750. Today (2011) it is a preparatory school and wedding venue.

John Wood,18??-19?? LFC Member 1891-1894. Address given as 43 Upper Brook Street, London, (now the Le Gavroche Restaurant).

Thomas Wood, 18??-18?? LFC Member 1863. Address given as Twyford Abbey, Acton, Middlesex.

Wing Commander RE Woolley, GM, 19??-1978. LFC Member 1964- 1978. Address given as Germany BFPO 40 and later c/o Virginia Cottage, Leintwardine. Wing Commander RE Woolley GM, MRCS, LRCP, DPH was in the RAF Medical Branch and was promoted Group Captain in 1970.

J Leslie Wright, 18??-1956. LFC Member 1943-1955. Address given as Compton Court Farm, Kinver, Worcestershire, and 78 Harborne Road, Edgebaston.

Alfred Wynne-Corrie, 1857-1919. LFC Member 1894-1901. Address given as Park Hall, Oswestry. Park Hall was one of the finest Tudor mansions in England before its destruction by fire in 1918. Prior to that tragedy the Park Hall Estate had passed through various childless marriages until in 1870 it was bought by Mrs Wynne Stapleton Cotton, who later married her second husband, Alfred Wynne Corrie, and become Mrs Wynne Corrie in 1886. She was extremely wealthy, and did a great deal of charity work in and around Oswestry. Alfred was a JP and is noted as opening a new reservoir at Pen-y-gwely, about seven miles distant in Wales in 1893. Alfred was a student at Charterhouse and left in 1872 to be articled to a solicitor.

Mrs P Yates, 19??-19?? LFC Member 1959-19?? Address given as The Wood, Codsall Wood, Staffs.

APPENDIX TWO

BIBLIOGRAPHY FOR *FISHING IN TIME*

(In date order of publication of editions accessed)

1.   The Universal Angler, Or, That Art Improved In All Its Parts, Especially In Fly-Fishing. (1766, possibly as early as 1747)   Author: Richard Bowlker.   Publisher: *"And sold by all the booksellers in town and country"*.

"Rules and cautions; Lastly.   Remember that the wit and invention of man were given for greater purposes than to ensnare silly fish: and that, how delightful so ever Angling may appear, it ceases to be innocent when used otherwise than as mere recreation."

2.   British Zoology: (Illustrated by Plates and Brief Explanations). (1776). Author: Thomas Pennant.   Printed by William Eyres, for Benjamin White, London

Page 272/3 on grayling; *"it is found…..in the Tame near Ludlow….',*   *'The largest we ever heard of was taken near Ludlow, which was above half a yard long, and weighed four pounds six ounces, but this was a very rare instance'"*

3.   Angling In All Its Branches, Reduced To A Complete Science. (1800) Author: Samuel Taylor.   Publisher: TN Longman and O Rees, London.

Page 34:   *"The river Teme , or Temd, which passes by the town of Ludlow in this county, and falls into the Severn near Worcester, abounds with fine trout and grayling, of which kinds I have taken, with a fly, between nine and ten dozen in a days' fishing".*

4.   Rural Sports. (1801).   Author: William Barker Daniel, 1753-1833. Volume 2. Subject: Sports; Hunting; Fishing; Falconry; Fowling.   Publisher: Bunny and Gold, London.

Of the Teme: *"This river abounds with excellent Grayling and Trout".- "Mr Pennant mentions one taken near Ludlow above half a yard long, and weighing four pounds six ounces as a rare instance."*

5.   Art of Angling. (1826).   Author: Charles Bowlker.   Publisher: Procter and Jones. A reworked version of his father's work shown above.

6.   Salmonia; or, Days of Fly Fishing. (1828).   Author, Sir Humphry Davy Bt   Publisher, London, John Murray.

7.   **The Life of Sir Humphry Davy, Bart. LL. D., Late President Of The Royal Society, Foreign Associate Of The Royal Institute Of France, &c ... (1831).** Author: John Ayrton Paris, (1785-1856). Volume: 1. Publisher: Colburn and Bentley, London.

Several passages on the skill or lack of it, re Davy's fishing. His attire (page 295) His temperament whilst fishing (page 297)   Nothing specific to Teme but TA Knight letter (page 321) saying how he (Davy) enjoyed staying with him to fish for Grayling.

8.   **New Sporting Magazine**, May 1832, Volume III, No 13- Baldwin and Craddock, London

"*A word or two on trolling*".   Author: GSW.

9.   **Piscatorial Reminiscences And Gleanings: To Which Is Added A Catalogue Of Books On Angling (1835).**   Authors: Thomas Boosey; Sir Henry Ellis (1777-1869); William Pickering (1796-1854).   Publisher: : William Pickering, London.   Page 64 re grayling: "*Ludlow appears the HQ…..Sporting Magazine April 1835*".

10.   **An Angler's Rambles. (1836).** Author: Edward Jesse. Publisher: John Jan Voorst, London.

11.   **A True Treatise On The Art Of Fly-Fishing, Trolling, etc., As Practised On The Dove, And The Principal Streams Of The Midland Counties; Applicable To Every Trout And Grayling River In The Empire. (1838)**. Author: William Shipley; Edward Fitzgibbon, (1803-1857). Publisher: Simpkin, Marshall and Co, London, .

Refers to Davy's visit to the Teme.

12.   **A Handbook Of Angling: Teaching Fly-Fishing, Trolling, Bottom-Fishing, And Salmon-Fishing; With The Natural History Of River Fish, And The Best Modes Of Catching Them. (1847)**. Author: Edward Fitzgibbon, (1803-1857). Publisher: Longmans, Brown, Green, and Longmans, London,.

Page 332 Long letter from Mr Henry George of Worcester re grayling on the Teme being the best: "*Of all rivers running through 'merry England', I think none produce such fine grayling as the Teme –*"

13   **A Topographical Dictionary of England, (1848).** Edited by Samuel Lewis.

Contains entries for Leintwardine and Burrington with reference to the fishing.

14.   The British Angler's Manual, Or, The Art Of Angling In England, Scotland, Wales, And Ireland. (1848). Author: Edward Jesse. Publisher: HG Bohn, London.

15.   **The Rod And Line Or, Practical Hints And Dainty Devices For The Sure Taking of Trout, Grayling, etc. (1849).** Author: Hewett Wheatley. Publisher: Longmans, London.

— Page 80: *"a fine trout was lying close to the stonework of a weir, at Leintwardine, on the Teme, ..."*

Large section on the Grasshopper and (page 53) *"a most remarkable regulation has lately been made by a club in possession of one of the best pieces of Grayling water in England"*

16.   Bowlker's Art of Angling: Containing Directions For Fly-Fishing, Trolling, Making Artificial Flies, &c.: With A List Of The Most Celebrated Fishing Stations In North Wales. (1854). Author: Charles Bowlker. Printed and sold by R. Jones, Ludlow.

Passing reference to Leintwardine waters where Davy fished, coyly not saying exactly where. A chapter on Grayling, several mentions of the Grasshopper.

17.   The Modern Angler, Containing Instructions In The Art Of Fly-Fishing ... (1864). Author: Otter. Publisher: Alfred & Son, London.

Page 96: *"...and the Teme, especially in the neighbourhood of Ludlow, being famous for its grayling."*   Page 34: *"The best grayling rivers are those of the Midland Counties such as the Dove, Teme, etc.".*

18.   The River's Side: Or, The Trout and Grayling, And How To Take Them. (1866). Author: Randal Howland Roberts. Publisher: H. Cox.

Page 124 has quote re size of grayling on Teme.

19.   Fishing Gossip; Or, Stray Leaves From The Note-Books Of Several Anglers. (1866). Author: Henry Cholmondeley-Pennell (1837-1915). Publisher: A. & C. Black, Edinburgh.

Puff piscartorial, a fume against the grasshopper and the merchants who peddle it.

20.   A Book on Angling: Being a Complete Treatise on the Art of Angling in Every ... (1867). Author: Francis Francis. Publisher: Longmans, Green & Co.

Preface: *"I commenced collecting the matter for the present work nearly twenty years ago".* (ie 1847).

Page 260: *"The Greyling. I have a very fine opinion of this fish. If the trout be the gentleman of the streams, the greyling is certainly the lady, and I think it in some respects little inferior to the trout,…"*

Page 263: various ways of fishing for grayling. Re grasshopper *"I suppose I must give the information, or it would be considered an 'hiatus', though not perhaps 'valde deflendus'. (a 'deficiency') though not perhaps 'to be greatly deplored'*

Page 264: Of the grasshopper; *"At Leintwardine, on the Teme, it was allowed for a short time, and the slaughter made of the greyling was positively dreadful, and it was again prohibited, save for about four days in the year, that is, two days before and two after the annual dinner at Leintwardine, as a sort of bon bouche for those who go down to the dinner. Tremendous bags are made then, but it is found that its use spoils the fly fishing, as does the minnow with trout, and it has been clearly proved there that when it is not used the big greyling rise much more freely to the fly. It is certainly an artificial bait, and that is all that can be said for it; if it be used, some restriction should be placed on it."*

21. A Handbook for Travellers in Gloucestershire, Worcestershire, and Hereford-shire... (1867). Author: John Murray. Publisher,: J. Murray, London.

Page 297: Route 34 Leintwardine to Downton Castle *"The red (sic) lion is a comfortable inn, much praised by anglers who frequent this spot to enjoy trout and grayling fishing. Permission to sport in the preserved water can be obtained from the landlord of the inn, on payment of a small contribution to the club fund."*

22. The Modern Practical Angler. A Complete Guide To Fly-Fishing, Bottom-Fishing & Trolling. (1870). Author: Henry Cholmondeley-Pennell (1837-1915). Publisher: Frederick Warne and Co, London. References to Teme pages 137-8:. *"Leintwardine on the Teme may be considered as the centre of the grayling country; and from Leintwardine to Ludlow is the best piece of grayling water in the kingdom; so far as my experience goes." "When I last fished the Teme, the limit of size under which the Leintwardine Club wisely prohibited the taking of Grayling was 10 inches. I hear, however, the club rules have been recently revised.* "(This phrase and the one above is an exact repeat of the words used in his book The

Modern Practical Angler which was published in 1870 (The LFC rule from 1870 was: *"No Grayling exceeding ½ lb weight shall be killed between December 1 and August 1 and no Trout or Grayling shall be killed at any time less than 8 inches in length, i.e. ¼ lb in weight"*. The same rules remained in place until at least 1883)

23.   Flies and Fly Fishing for White and Brown Trout, Grayling....With Hints On Using The Minnow And Grasshopper Bait. (1873). Author: Harris Saint John Dick. Publisher: R. Hardwicke, London.

"I have fished most of the grayling rivers in England, and give the palm to the Lugg, in Herefordshire, for the size and number of its fish, with the exception (perhaps) of that portion of the Teme preserved by the Leintwardine Club, which was some years ago quite the best."

24.   Fly-Fishing and Worm-Fishing for Salmon, Trout and Grayling. (1876). Author: Henry Cholmondeley-Pennell. Publisher: G. Routledge, London.

"The Wye, Dee, Lugg, and Teme are the only Welsh rivers holding Grayling that I am acquainted with. Leintwardine on the Teme may be considered as the centre of the Grayling country; and from Leintwardine to Ludlow is the best piece of Grayling water in the kingdom; so far as my experience goes. ...... When I last fished the Teme, the limit of size under which the Leintwardine Club wisely prohibited the taking of Grayling was 10 inches. I hear, however, that the club rules have been recently revised."

25.   Recollections of Fly Fishing for Salmon, Trout, and Grayling: With Notes on ... (1884). Author: Edward Hamilton, MD. Publisher: S Low, Marston, Searle, and Rivington.

Contains a woodcut of Leintwardine Bridge by the author. There are excellent descriptions of his sixteen years of fishing on the Teme, over a forty year period prior to 1884.

26.   The Badminton Library (of Sports and Pastimes). (1885). Volume 2. Fishing: Salmon and Trout. Author: H. Cholmondeley-Pennel and others. Publisher: Longmans Green & Co, London.

27.   Fresh Woods and Pastures New. (1887). Author: Edward Marston. Publisher: Sampson Low, Marston, Searle and Rivington, London.

The book contains a series of letters that Marston wrote for the *Fishing Gazette* in 1886 when he decided to take a holiday in Herefordshire to fish the rivers there. He did not fish on the Club waters but on the Teme on Harley water, the Lugg and Arrow. He provides some useful contemporary background comment on the area. Letter IV describes his day on the Teme below Buckton Park Farm, having gained permission from *'Squire Harley'*.

28.   The Book of The Grayling: Being a Description of the Fish and the Art. (1888). Author: Thomas Evan Pritt. Publisher: Goodall and Sudick.

29.   Fishing Reminiscences Of The Late Archdeacon Lea. (1892). Author: William Lea. Publisher: Shuttle Office, Kidderminster. 53 pages. Published for his most intimate friends and relations. 100 copies printed for private circulation. The ten chapters include *"A Day at Leintwardine"*. See Appendix Five for the complete chapter.

30.   Grayling And How To Catch Them. (1895). Author: Francis Walbran. Publisher: *The Angler* Co Ltd, Scarborough.

31.   Elements Of Angling; A Book For Beginners. (1908). Author: Hugh Tempest Sheringham (1876-1930). Publisher: H. Cox, London.

 Comment on fishing clubs: *"The subscription varies from a few shillings in some provincial society up to twenty pounds or more in one of the select clubs which rent really good water, clubs like the Driffield, Dorchester, Wilton or Leintwardine, which fish respectively the Driffield Beck, the Frome, the Wylye and the Teme. These, and a few more like them, are by no means easy to get into; a man has, as a rule, to put his name down, and wait his chance of election for a considerable time, when a vacancy in the limited list of membership occurs."*

32.   Dry-Fly Fishing For Trout and Grayling. (1908). Author: James Englefield (red Quill) 1908. Publisher: Horace Cox, London.

His definition of the dry-fly purist, modelled as he 'humbly' admits on himself, can be read at Appendix Three.

33.   An Angler At Large. (1911). Author: William Caine (W Quilliam of *The Field*). Publisher: Kegan Paul, Trench, Trubener & Co Ltd, London.

Of fly fishing, wet and dry   *"Two things are necessary to both arts: an apparatus and manual skill. But to the wet-fly game must be added knowledge. And the greatest of these is knowledge."*

34.   Haunts And Hints For Anglers. (1925).   Published by the Great Western Railway Co.

"The mention of the Teme always sets the angler thinking of pleasant times amongst the grayling for which it is Justly famous....needless to say the Teme is either private or preserved (fishing)"

35.	*The Field* **– Where To Fish 1955-56. (1955).**	Under the entry for Leintwardine, asserts *"Tickets are available from the Lion Hotel for 2 rods on the Clun over a stretch of one mile. 5/- to residents – All fishing on the Teme reserved."*

36.	**The Green Dragoon. (1957)**. Author: Robert D Bass. Publisher: Alvin Redman Ltd, London. An account of the life of Banastre Tarleton.

37.	**Rod in Hand. (1958).** Author: CV Hancock. Publisher: Phoenix House, London. The author was literary editor of The Birmingham Post and a friend of LFC member HA Hopkins. Long chapter on grayling fishing, with numerous mentions of the Teme and several of the Club. Includes a photo of Hopkins fishing on LFC Water, page 80.

38.	**A History Of Flyfishing. (1992).** Author: Conrad Voss Bark. Publisher: Merlin Unwin, Ludlow.

39.	**The Coventry's of Croome. (2000).** Author: Catherine Gordon. Publisher: Phillimore in association with the National trust.

40.	**Victorian Days In England. (2002).** Author: Anna Fay, with additional material by Julia Ionides and Peter Howell. Publisher: Dog Rose Press, Ludlow.

41.	**Orange Otter. (2006).** Author: Christopher Knowles. Publisher: Medlar Press Ltd, Ellesmere, Shropshire. The story of the Reverend Edward Powell (1888-1972) who was a frequent visitor to the Leintwardine Teme.

APPENDIX THREE

THE GRASSHOPPER

Illustration from *The Rod and Line (1849).* Versions of the grasshopper, No. 2 being the favoured model, top right.

"The grasshopper is not, as may be supposed, that agile little insect that you see hopping about in the meadow grass," so says Francis Walbran in his book *Grayling, and how to catch them,* (1895), *"but an artificial bait which more resembles a large gooseberry than anything in creation. It is made as follows: - on a Limerick bend hook, size about No. 6, Kendale scale, is wound some lead wire in a spherical form; over this foundation bright green Berlin wool is wrapped, with a broad tag of scarlet; a ribbing of yellow completes the monstrosity. Another pattern is as above, with the addition of two strips of straw down each side of the bait, and a small triangle hook, No. 1 , Kendale scale, attached to a loose thread of gut the length of the 'Grasshopper'."*

What has this got to do with the Leintwardine Fishing Club? No one in living memory will have used this lure as the club is strictly fly fishing only and has been for decades. Yet throughout the 19th century there would seem to have been quite a close relationship between its use on the Teme for catching grayling and within the club itself. It is probably no coincidence that one of the leading proponents of its use was an influential member of the LFC and a member of the aristocracy; he found it effective; no doubt so did others. The utility of this lure was soon being discussed in many a fishing publication but as one can see below although most authors were prepared to describe its characteristics and use, they fought shy of actually endorsing it. However, like other useful but distasteful inventions it cannot be un-invented, and the genie once out of the bottle had a good long run of at least a hundred years. Can we be sure even now that it does not put in an occasional clandestine appearance along the riverbank?... Of course we can!

The story, however reminds us of the temptations our fishing forbears had to weigh.

Sir Humphry Davy, who had been fishing the Teme since 1805, refers to the beast in his book Salmonia, (1828) as follows: *"There is no method more killing, for large grayling, than applying a grasshopper to the point of a leaded hook, the lead and shank of which are covered with green and yellow silk, to imitate the body of the animal. This mode of fishing is called sinking and drawing. I have seen it practiced in this river with as much success as maggot fishing"*. NB: he does not say he has actually used it, and by associating it with maggot fishing one could presume that he does not approve. Davy also appears to recommend that a real grasshopper be impaled on the hook which again probably indicates that he has never used the method, given the likely difficulty of finding such an insect during most of the season grayling are at their best.

Although he devoted most of his letter to fishing for grayling with a fly "ER" in Edward Jesse's book, *An Angler's Rambles*, writing of a period in 1833, felt he too must include the Grasshopper in his advice on how to catch grayling: *"And now I will conclude by saying that although I prefer the fly, I must allow that the largest fish are killed by the maggot and grass-hopper. The most destructive way with both, is to sink and draw, and it is not unusual to kill four or five fish in a day exceeding two pound in weight, while you seldom get above 'a pounder' with the fly, and the average may be taken at nearly three quarters of a pound during the day. But 'à chacun son goût', and I for one prefer catching thirty or forty lively fellows of that size with the fly, ..., even if I had the chance of killing the largest fish in the whole river."* "ER" finally comments *"at any rate I shall be happy to show you the best places to use the flies I send should you ever come to Leintwardine"*.

The May 1832 edition of *New Sporting Magazine* included an article on fishing, as it did in most of the monthly issues; On this occasion *"G.S.W"* contributed *"A word or two on trolling."* Trolling is drawing a lure horizontally through the water and is not strictly grasshopper fishing, for that involves raising the bait vertically up and down in the water but the reasons found for adopting it would seem to be much the same. *"GSW"* almost seems to issue an apology in the first sentence of his article: *"Of all the methods of catching the finny tribes it will scarcely be disputed that fly-fishing is by far the most delightful, chiefly because being the most difficult it affords greater scope for the exercise of skill....."* A little later into the article we begin to understand why he is suggesting such a course of action. *"But though fly fishing is far superior to any other, yet it cannot always be adopted......too windy....stream too narrow...overshadowed with trees...in short there may be many other circumstances which will prevent the angler from using the fly. The plan that affords the next best sport is that of trolling; and if the size of the fish is more regarded than the quantity, it is in general superior to fly fishing...."* The reader could hardly misunder-stand the message; fly fishing is what is expected but if it all gets too difficult or you need to catch a larger fish you might get away with using other methods...maybe.

Hewett Wheatley wrote extensively in his book *Rod and Line* (1849) about lures and devoted a chapter to *The Grasshopper, Cabbage and Other Grubs*. He also felt it was necessary to say that he was a lover of fly fishing but probably showed his true colours when he wrote, *"Though fly fishing is the most elegant part.of the anglers art, yet is it often annoying enough to go forth on an expedition, and not find a single fin inclined to raise the body whereto it belongs... .And even when fish are rising, a well-filled basket often rewards him who uses them. (Baits)"* He justified the use by commenting that using the artificial lure requires *"quite as much skill as, in the successful use of the fly."*

Probably one of the most distinguished angling writers of the day was Henry Cholmondeley-Pennel (1837-1915). He edited his own fishing magazine for a while and wrote many books. As might be expected he weighed into the fray with his contribution to the book *Fishing Gossip* (1866) which he edited. His article was entitled *Puff Piscatorial*. This chapter amounts to a dignified rant at the fishing tackle shop proprietor, Mr Frederick Allies, of Worcester. What excited Cholmondeley-Pennell's ire was the way in which Mr Allies claimed to be the main supplier and inventor of the Grasshopper *"as we happen to know that the invention* (the grasshopper) *was first introduced to the Teme grayling-fishers, by Mr Jones of Ludlow, some five and forty years ago...".* That would be 1821, but we know from *Salmonia* that it may well have existed earlier. He also accused Mr Allies of hypocrisy for advertising his stock of Grasshoppers through letters to *The Field* but in the same letter counselled buyers not to over use them for fear of destroying the fishing. Henry concluded: *"Now is it not funny? Here is poor Mr Allies, who has got to get his grass-hoppers, like so many unmarriageable daughters, off his hands, and at the same time to maintain an elevated and pure standard of sporting morals in the midst of the first grayling county in the world."*

The first written confirmation in the Leintwardine Fishing Club rules mentioning use of the Grasshopper occur in 1870; Rule VII. States the members may fish with the Grasshopper from October 1st to the end of the season. It seems quite likely that the rule was in force earlier as Cholmondeley-Pennel would seem to imply in *Fishing Gossip* that he knew of the rule: *"Well grasshoppers are deadly things, no doubt, and Mr Allies makes them: so far it is all plain sailing: but if the clubs won't have them – forbid them, in fact, except on certain days – what is to be done? So Mr Allies, poor man, finds himself between... 'carpet-bag on one side, and the tongs on the other".*

In fact in the same year, 1870, Cholmondeley-Pennell, in yet another book *The Modern Practical Angler* makes clear that he is familiar with the Leintwardine water: *"Leintwardine on the Teme may be considered as the centre of the grayling country; and from Leintwardine to Ludlow is the best piece of grayling water in the kingdom; so far as my experience goes."* He further indicates that he has fairly close links with the Club, *"When I last fished the Teme, the limit of size under which the Leintwardine Club wisely prohibited the taking of Grayling was 10 inches. I hear, however, the club rules have been recently revised."*

The following year, 1871, the LFC reworded the rule; "*Members may fish with the Grass-hopper from October 1 to December 31, but a member and his friend may not use two grasshopper rods on the same day, unless the friend be provided with a Grasshopper ticket*". This refers to Rule IV which stated that each member was entitled to twelve tickets, four of which could be used during the Grasshopper season. It is clear that use of the Grasshopper was becoming more common necessitating the tightening of the rules.

Even the famous Cholmondeley-Pennel would now appear to have accepted that gentle-men could fish with the Grasshopper, should circumstances permit His next publica-tion *Fly-fishing and worm fishing for Salmon, Trout and Grayling* (1876) devoted a whole section to the Grasshopper. Here he stated, "*The lure known by the name of the artificial grasshopper, is really a rough imitation of the caterpillar, and not of a grasshopper. The best are imitations made as follows*". He goes on to describe the lure in much the same terms as above, i.e. green and yellow with strips of straw, "*It should be baited for use with three or four large gentles (maggots) put on the hook so as to make a bunch and partly cover the bend and point."*

In 1878 the LFC rules were relaxed a little by bringing forward the start of the grasshop-per fishing season by two weeks to September 15. Also at this time 'trolling' was permit-ted from June 15 to September 30.

Edward Hamilton in his *Recollections...* (1884) has very definite views on the subject: "*Maggot and grasshopper fishing for grayling, in my opinion, is worse than any worm fishing – and it is destructive beyond measure to future sport. It is no excuse to say that these big fish do not and will not rise at the fly. Of course they will not, because the greater part of them are taken by the grasshopper. What sport there can be in lugging up a big grayling with tackle that would hold a twenty-pound salmon I cannot imagine. I can recollect a certain captain, a member of the club, who never came to fish till he could do so with the grasshopper, killing in one day thirty-five grayling – all caught in this poaching fashion. . Fortunately for the river, the captain was got rid of, and the bye-laws altered*". We can probably identify this individual as one Captain Frank Corbett as he appeared on the members list for 1863 but was not invited to join in 1870 when the club was reconstituted and the rules were altered.

Thomas Evan Pritt, *The Book of the Grayling*, 1888, was a man who fished the northern rivers and demonstrated a little northern disdain for the south, probably reflecting the views held by many when he stated "*There are four methods of angling for grayling – with the fly, the worm, the grasshopper and the maggot. I propose to dismiss the two latter summarily: the grasshopper which resembles nothing in the wide realm of Creation, though it is said to be a wonderfully killing lure on some of the south country rivers – because it appears to be of little use...in our shallower rivers... and the maggot, because this type of fishing as practiced on* *certain northern rivers is to be discouraged as much as possible. A man who wanders forth in search of game and handsome fish like the grayling, armed with quarts of maggots for ground baiting purposes, **is not a sportsman: he is only a fish catcher,** and ought to be suppressed in every club to which he is accidently admitted."*

1888 saw the production of the *Badminton Library of Sports and Pastimes*, and our familiar author, Henry Cholmondeley-Pennell, was asked to edit the volume dealing with fishing. He includes a chapter on *Fly Fishing for Trout and Grayling* by another famous angler, Henry Ralph Francis. He too would appear to have intimate knowledge of the Teme and the Leintwardine Club water, as well as a good sense of humour as these extracts indicate. *"The very name of fly fishing carries back my fancy to many a pleasant hour- many a lovely scene…..knee deep in a ford of the Teme where he (the roe deer) lingers lovingly in many an encircled sweep round the ivied cliffs and oak clad slopes of Downton, I wave a potent, and in that well proportioned stream, 'all commanding wand' over the rough eddy, sentinelled with watchful trout, or where the quieter run deepens into the haunts of the Grayling."* And, *"Though I care little for grayling fishing except with the fly, I ought fairly to mention that the heaviest fish are caught with other lures…..the artificial grasshopper….the heaviest basket I ever heard of was made at Leintwardine by the late Sir Charles Culyer…the exact weight I cannot recall, but the best nine fish weighed twenty seven pounds."*

He goes on to tell a revealing little story that tells us all what was really going on: *"I remember early on a July morning mentioning this (pointing the fly hook with an ant's egg) to a friend who was driving me over to Leintwardine. W- had little hope of sport; the river was low, the fish shy; the grayling especially, he told me, were sulking in shoals at the bottom of the deep pools. 'Were it not for your club rules' said I, 'which you tell me are so very strict, you might pick out a few of those fellows by pointing your hook with an ant's egg.' He replied it was not to be heard of, yet methought was rather curious as to the forbidden process.*

We parted shortly after at the waterside, and before we met again in the afternoon I had a grand basket of trout. The river was so low that every stake showed; the fish came strong on the feed, and behind every stake I could see the suck of a goodly snout, so that a long cast up-stream with my two-handed rod was absolutely murderous. W- had done very little with the trout, not having fished 'so fine' or so 'far off', and having been unlucky in his choice of water. But there were two or three really handsome grayling in his basket, against which I had nothing to show. I had killed the only one of decent size which I had seen rise during the day, and even he was no great thing. Could it really have been mea maxima culpa that I had taken no fish like those before me? W - answered my question as to the fly he had used with an admirable steadiness of countenance : but when " still I gazed, and still my wonder grew," he could stand it no longer, and burst into that cheery ringing laugh which his many friends around the Clee will recall so well and regretfully. It was impossible not to join chorus as he just articulated, 'Ant's eggs."

The last decade of the 19th century saw a huge increase in the number of books written about sport and fishing. The instructional books mostly included all manner of means of catching salmon, trout and grayling. They recognized that not all methods would be universally welcomed on the water but nevertheless their use was discussed and described in minute detail. As some of the above examples show most authors made it very plain to their readers that their own preference was for using the fly rather than a lure. One cannot help but suspect that the experience recorded above by Henry Francis was quite typical.

By the turn of the century conservation was not only necessary but increasingly of concern to those who spent their recreational time in the countryside. There was much less desire to 'fill the creel' or boast of the numbers or weight of fish taken. By 1903, the Leintwardine Fishing Club was essentially fly fishing only; trolling had been reduced by two weeks to the period June 15 to August 15, and although the grasshopper was still permitted it was now restricted to just the fifteen LFC members between October 1 and February 1. Although there are no further copies of the rules available for this period Lord Coventry's diary tells us that he continued using the "*hopper*" until he stopped fishing in 1910. It is quite likely that when he died so did the use of the grasshopper on the Leintwardine water.

Fishermen were generally becoming more discerning and this in turn lead to new distinctions amongst anglers: the dry fly purist, or the '*chuck it and try it*' wet fly fisherman. So yet again the inattentive angler could find himself considered beyond the pale of acceptability. Naturally there were books to educate and inform. James Englefield in 1908 produced his book *Dry Fly Fishing for Trout and Grayling.* His definition of the dry-

JAMES ENGLEFIELD

("Red Quill")

fly purist, modelled as he 'humbly' admitted, on himself, is as follows:

He (the dry fly purist) is a man who *" has gradually arrived at perfection in his fascinating art, first of all and chiefly by constant practice and experience; by watching the methods of experts by the riverside, and avoiding the mistakes of some not yet expert; by the discriminating choice of suitable rods, lines, casts, and flies, landing net, &c. ; also by hints and knowledge gained in reading the current angling literature of the day, and modern books on the subject. To the dry-fly purist no other sport can vie with it; he cares for no other sort of fishing (in my case for no other sport), never resorts to the wet fly lure, although finding no fault with those good fishermen who do use it. He kills no small fish, nor any out of condition: is content with moderate sport, especially if obtained under adverse conditions proving his patience and skill. Therefore it need hardly be said, he is no pot-hunter, save in the limited sense that he nearly always presents his spoil to his friends. Further, he prefers small flies to large: consequently (and for other reasons) he often does not join the throng of Mayfly enthusiasts, whose sport is sometimes like mere slaughter. He is humane to a degree in carefully unhooking and also in returning a fish to the river so as to avoid injuring them; in need, supporting them at its side until they recover from the shock of being pulled out – so contrary to the practice of many anglers who toss them through the air, when, on falling, they are often injured by concussion with the water. In fact, dry-fly fishing reduces the cruelty of angling to a minimum, and is a good argument in its favour. The dry-fly purist is a contemplative man, always in love with nature in her varying beauties, and not least so when in his delightful environment by the river-side the weathers is favourable for his sport; but even then his skill is at fault until there is a 'hatch-out' of flies on the water (as the metamorphosis of nymphae to sub-imagines is often erroneously termed), and fish are taking them. Then he makes the best of his opportunities. He does not, however, 'hammer away' for long over a particular fish, but, leaving him for a time, quietly retires from the bank so as not to scare him and other fish away."*

Clearly we have now travelled many miles from even contemplating the use of a maggot or even a grasshopper! The whole idea is unthinkable! Isn't it?

APPENDIX FOUR

LORD COVENTRY'S FISHING JOURNAL

This article was written by Barney Rolfe-Smith and appears as it was published by The Leintwardine History Society Journal;

In the Worcester Record Office is a cardboard box labelled, *Family Box 20 (yellow)*. Inside, amongst a collection of papers, is a brown paper parcel marked *F75/8*. This turns out to be a quarto sized, black, hard backed notebook, with ruled lines on the pages. There is no title but on the first page is written:

"August 1880

Rented Warden Villa ....Unfurnished"

Underneath this note someone else has written, *"Bought the property, through Meredith of Graham's Cottage, when it was sold by auction for £387:10:0: the other cottage then rented by Mrs Catstree was bought subsequently from H.A.Price, who had secured it at the auction for £95:0:0."*

The next sentence is *"The purchase of Warden Cottage was made on the 3rd of March 1891. And the following was the description of the property bought by the Earl of Coventry"* [Then follows a full description of the property. This can be found in the full transcription of the journal available from the Leintwardine History Society].

The journal turns out to be a record of the visits made by Lord Coventry and his family to Wardens House in Leintwardine over the period 1891 to 1921. Lord Coventry, George William, 9th Earl Coventry (1838-1930) lived at the family home at Croome Court. The estate had been in the hands of the family since the late 16th century and lies about 7 miles south of Worcester. Anyone wanting to find out more about this interesting family should read *The Coventry's of Croome* by Dr Catherine Gordon. She describes the 9th Earl as : *"Jovial and rather vague, and known to his close friends and family as 'Covey', he posed proudly for photographers alongside his wife, his prize bull or his racehorse, his clothes always a little awry and a benign and a rather bemused smile playing across his face. No county function was complete without his presence, no hunting party nor race meeting seemed so successful in his absence. His popularity amongst his tenants was unprecedented, and he seemed to be regarded with genuine affection wherever he went."*

So what was the Coventry connection with Leintwardine? The second entry of the journal on Monday 28th September 1891 gives several clues: *"A lovely day. Mother, Father and Barbara drove to Ludlow for the agricultural show held in the*

Castle grounds.   Father judged hunters, and won first prize with his bull Rare Sovereign and second with Tarragon.   They returned in time for luncheon.   Reggie fished without much success only killing two small fish; Father joined him in the afternoon but caught nothing."

Lord Coventry was a member of the Leintwardine Fishing Club and we can only assume that he had been fishing on the Teme for sometime before he rented Warden House in 1880 and subsequently bought it in 1891. Fishing was certainly the principal reason for his interest in Leintwardine.   However, he also bred Hereford cattle, having started his herd with animals from Mr Tudge, of Adforton, in 1875. The journal clearly shows that Lord Coventry appreciated the standard of husbandry in this area for he bought horses, bullocks and many sheep from this district to be sent back to Croome.   He went to many of the local cattle shows and was often asked to judge horses – he was the owner of two winners of the Grand National.   Amongst many other positions he was one time President of the Hereford Herd Book Society and was asked to preside at many luncheons for retiring breeders in and around Leintwardine and found it useful to spend the night before at The Wardens.

The journal was written by several members of the family.   Much of it is in the third person and is started by his wife, Lady Blanche Coventry, Lady Blanche Craven (1842-1930).   She was the third daughter of William Craven, 2nd Earl of Craven, of Coombe Abbey, Warickshire.   Whilst it was rare that any stay was longer than 4 or 5 days in any one year it is clear from the comments they added to the journal that everyone from the family who came to The Wardens enjoyed their stay.   Lord and Lady Coventry were keen to make their home in Leintwardine as comfortable as possible and when in residence would involve themselves in the community and make note of the goings on. The journal must have been kept at The Wardens with a clear family rule that it was to be filled in!   Later the journal may well have been used as an 'aide memoire' for the housekeeper, Mrs Castree, as there are specific directions for where fish are to be sent and which piece of furniture she should expect to be delivered from which shop.

Two entries for September 1892 indicate the family's involvement in Leintwardine life:

*"**Sept 27th Tuesday**   Very stormy day.   Scarcely stopped raining.   Father and Reggie started for the river at 10.30 and fished all day, the former catching eleven (one over a lb) the latter seven.*

The mother (sic) superintended the fixing of the new looking glass and pictures, which father had bought at Cheltenham, over the chimney piece: ordered a screen for her room and made a lamp shade which was very much wanted.   Barbara strongly recommends S Meredith's "bath buns". The Rev Colvin called in the afternoon and accepted father's and mother's annual subscription to his Harvest Thanksgiving Fund.

The Skye terrier "Wasp" is no longer resident at Warden Cottage.

Mrs Castree has announced her intention of paying "The Lord" her rent in person.   Her house has been repaired.

Sept 28th Wednesday   A lovely day but cold towards evening.   Father and Reggie started fishing but the river was too high and dirty.   Father managed to kill two small grayling.

Mother and Barbara started at 12 o'clock to walk to Downton Castle.   They went by the footpath across the hill to the Lime Avenue and Price's farm and arrived at Downton in time for luncheon where they discovered that Mr and Mrs and Miss May Knight had been to call at Warden Cottage soon after they had started.   As the whole Knight family had to start for Hodnet to see the christening of Mr Grevilles firstborn Mother and Barbara had only just time to see the gardens and start for home.   They returned by the river, a beautiful walk, and joined the Lime Avenue again at Price's farm getting back soon after 4 o'clock.   After tea Father, Reggie and Barbara went to Walford to see a cob belonging to one Goode.   The Father liked the cob and arranged to see it again the next day at five o'clock."

Judging by the hand writing Lady Blanche makes most of the entries until 1902 when Lord Coventry drops the third person style as in the entry for 27 June 1902;

"I came to Leintwardine from Euston but as it was a Bank Holiday my telegrams were not delivered and in consequence Mellings did not meet me at Craven Arms, and I had to hire – I got, however, a very nice horse and trap which brought me over capitally, but I did not arrive until 11.15, and Mrs Castree had gone to bed.   However I knocked her up, as I had fortunately dined at Shrewsbury, I wanted nothing for supper.   On the 28th I drove to Burrington Bridge and fished up.   It was very bright and hot but I caught 6 trout with the minnow and of these 4 were quite 13/4 lbs each – in the evening I went out again."   Throughout the journal Lord Coventry always records how he travels, where from and by what means.   It would seem that as far as railway journeys were concerned he had much more choice than we have now.

When both Lady Blanche and Lord Coventry travel to Leintwardine they take the opportunity to do a little shopping for antiques.   The entry for 9 Sep 1903;

"Father and Mother came from Croome.   Left Worcester at 12.40 and reached Hereford about 1.30.   We went to Parkers and Mrs Stephens shops and bought a Sheffield silver bread basket from the former and a lovely carved Adam flower stand from Mrs Stephens.   We left Hereford 3.30 for Leominster and Kingsland.   At Kingsland Mellings son met us with the waggonette.   It rained in torrents when we started from Kingsland but cleared before we got to Wigmore.   A very keen strong wind.   Found Mrs Castree very well and a delightful fire in the sitting room and we had tea.   Rufus came to say it might be possible to catch a trout the river much too high for grayling – so Father went off to fish and Mother unpacked her bags.   Father caught 2 good trout for dinner."

The Wardens also sees the arrival of Lord Coventry's children and grandchildren in one of the first visits by motorcar in 1906.

"Tom, Barbara, Tobe and Obby came here by motor from Strensham. They left home about 4 o'clock and got here about 6.45 travelling by way of Worcester, Bromyard, Tenbury, Ludlow, a lovely journey but roads too winding to be able to let car out much till you get to Ludlow. Crowds of children came to see us get out of the motor; we brought a small portmanteau of Tom's with all our things in it. Barbara has not been here since Sept: 1893. Mrs Castree does not look a day older. She insisted on giving us a cup of tea which was excellent after our long motor. We have come here so as to attend the Knighton pony show tomorrow. After tea went to see Mellings, watched him feed pigs, then went to a meadow some way down to see the pony he hopes to win with tomorrow – beautiful mover, he bought her as a sucker. Came back all alongside river, walked over wooden bridge with handrail, climbed over bridge, and were stopped at Mellings' house to see his stables which used to be the old shop. Obby wished to mix his pigs food for him. Got home about 8 o'clock put children to bed. Obby sleeps in Tom's room. Tobe in Barbara's. They are both wild to help Mrs Castree cook in the morning and want to bathe in the river. We drank Dada's health at dinner in a bottle of the finest Cliquot found in the cupboard under the writing desk. Went to bed early as there is every prospect of having to wake early. Sent motor to Swann as advised by Father."

Lord Coventry continued to buy furniture; his entry for 1908:

"I came here on Tuesday 7 Jan 1908, and was glad to find Mrs Castree better. I got to the house in time for dinner having travelled by Hereford to Shrewsbury, and back to Hopton Heath. At Hereford I bought of Mrs Stephens one old urn stand <u>4:0:0</u>; 1 old stool <u>1:15:0</u>; 1 nice old bureau <u>7:0:0</u> and these I mean for Leintwardine. At Shrewsbury I bought of Mrs Pye 1 Sheraton Secretaire <u>16:0:0</u>; 1 Banner screen <u>2:10:0</u>; a pair of old brass candle sticks <u>1:15:0</u>, and these are to go to 1 Balfour Place. At Wynn's I saw a very beautiful Queen Anne marqueterie cabinet for which he asked £30 which I don't think out of the way." Many of these items appear again in the catalogue at the sale of his furniture when he sells the house in 1921 and for all we know could still be here in Leintwardine.

As time passes, Lord Coventry in 1910, now 72, still fishes but has more interest in spotting good animals to buy. He notes in September of that year:

"<u>Friday 16th Sep 1910</u> Blanche and I came driving from Kingsland. Dull, gloomy, weather, and a cold wind from the N.E. Found everything in apple pie order. There appears to be a good many fishermen, but I hear they have had no sport at all and the fish seem quite sulky. At Kingsland station I saw 10 good bullocks property of Mr Whiteman of Buckton Park. [Lady Blanche adds] Father, Mother had a walk after tea. Mrs Castree cheerful, and fares well. Saturday 17th September 1910. Cold but no rain in the morning. Father went out fishing with great perseverance he managed to get 4 fish. I went to meet him after luncheon and we met Mr Colvin and had a long gossip with him.

On Sunday 18th Sept   We went to church in the morning and after luncheon went to Mr Whiteman's to look at 10 bullocks which I had seen at Kingsland station and liked.   I agreed to give him £20 apiece for these.   They are three parts fat, and, tho' I considered them dear, still, as it was my first deal with him, and strong cattle are difficult to find, I thought it best to take them.   Then we drove on to Stanage to have tea with Mr and Mrs C Rogers who welcomed us very warmly and showed us over the grounds which are full of good timber – particularly fine beech and oak trees, and I looked at the ponies.   We got back to Leintwardine a little before 7.   We took away with us a Sheffield plate tea pot for use at Croome."

By 1911 Lord Coventry has given up fishing because of rheumatism and would seem to come on his own to stay only a night at The Wardens before going to either Knighton or Pennybont Fair to buy animals.   He always notes who he has bought from and the price he has paid.   The health of Mrs Castree is always commented upon.   Mellings invariably meets him at the station and if he cannot make it then 'young' Mellings will attend and in extremis Miss Mellings will turn up in the 'dog-cart'.   Finally in 1918 we see the last entry in the journal.   Unfortunately the realities of war impose a sour note, as follows:

"On arriving here on Wed 28 Aug.   I found 2 soldiers, hay balers, had been billeted in my house.   I called at the Constable's house, and said I wished to see him, but he never deigned to come to my house and when I met him in the street afterwards, his manner was very disrespectful.   Mrs Castree informs me that he came to the house and said he wanted lodgings for 2 men, who are hay balers: her granddaughter told him that it was Lord Coventry's house, and that lodgers were not taken in, whereupon he said he could commandeer the house if permission was refused, and so they were frightened into taking them in."

Lord Coventry sold his house at auction, at The Lion Hotel, on July 6th 1921.

To see the entire journal, of some 26 pages, complete with explanatory notes, and to find out how much and to whom the house was sold, and the sales catalogue of furniture and effects, you will need to apply to The Leintwardine History Society:

teepee@hatherly.orangehome.co.uk

or johnleint@btopenworld.com.

A DAY AT LEINTWARDINE

EXTRACT from "Fishing Reminiscences" by the late Archdeacon Lea, which was printed Kidderminster at the Shuttle Office, 32 Worcester Street in 1892.

———— ————

The extract relates to "A Day at Leintwardine" on the River Teme.

A SCAN OF THE ARTICLE WRITTEN BY ARCHDEACON WILLIAM LEA

A DAY AT LEINTWARDINE.

THE River Teme is certainly one of the best, if not the best, river in England for trout and grayling. There may be longer trout in some of the Cotswold and South country streams, and even better grayling fishing in the Lugg; but for the union of these two, gamest of all fishes, I doubt if the upper portion of the Teme has any equal. The river may be said to commence its course at Leintwardine, at the junction of the little Teme with the Clun, immediately above the village. It then runs under the old historic walls of Ludlow, and thence leaps on its way rejoicing, through rich meadows which will feed an ox, and orchards famed for cider, and hopyards whose produce exceeds the far-famed Kentish ones in flavour, till it joins the Severn a few miles below the city of Worcester. Its feeders, too, whether brooks or rivers, are all notable for trout; but I believe that the grayling confine themselves to the main stream of the river, and never diverge from it. I have never heard of them being taken in any of the lower feeders of the river. The chief of the feeders of the Teme are the Oney and the Corve, which join it above Ludlow; the Letwidge and the Rea below. In this stream, which rises in the Brown Clee Hills, and worms its way through rich red lands to its destination, the trout are particularly fine, and their flesh is often of a deep pink color and unusually firm.

At Leintwardine for many years there was a Fishing Club, of which I was sometime a member. To my sorrow it has now come to an end, as far as I am concerned, for when the lease expired in '69 the proprietor of the river took the water into his own hands, and formed a new club of his own. I have thus lost a pleasant outing for the inside of two or three weeks in the year. which was all the time I could manage to spare for it. I may remark here that if a river contains both trout and grayling the fishing season is delightfully prolonged. From the 1st of March to the beginning of September trout were in season in the clear open streams of the higher Teme; and the grayling fishing, in one shape or other, continued from March till the end of November, first for the smaller grayling, who were too young to spawn—and I believe they do not begin till the third year of their age,—and after July for the larger fish, who have then recovered from their spawning and who reach their highest condition in October and November. These larger grayling, whether from the club water being over-fished or from their preference for ground bait, rarely rose well at a fly, but at times, especially after a sharp white frost in November, they ran freely at what was called the "Grass-hopper," which is a leaded hook wound round with green silk with strips of straw at the sides and the barb covered with gentles. Some members of the club were dead hands with this bait, and almost fabulous baskets, thirty or forty pounds weight in the day, are said to have been taken by them, the fish running from three-quarters of a pound to two pounds, but very rarely exceeding this latter weight. Personally I never cared much for this kind of fishing, which is best effected by keeping to one spot all day; but preferred strolling, rod in hand, from one end of water to the other.

In the Club water, at the time I speak of, the grayling had greatly out-numbered the trout, in fact they had almost driven them from parts of the river. There might be several reasons for this. The grayling is a hardier and more prolific fish than the trout. He is, too, always routing with his snout in the gravel, which must be very annoying to such a gentleman as the trout, who likes elbow room and hates a bustle, and consequently gets out of the way: but I myself expect that there is a better reason than this. I more than suspect that the grayling eats the trout spawn, and that in water where he is getting the better of the trout, the keepers' work should be to hatch trout as they do in many parts of the Continent, on the plan shown in our Zoological Gardens, and turn them into the river when old enough to take care of themselves.

And now for a day on the Club water at Leintwardine. It was the end of August, for I always chose a time for my visit when the water was likely to be tolerably clear of rods, and avoided the seasons, such as the May fly blossom, when members most did congregate. I took a companion with me, who like myself liked roving along the water. We had fished for three days with but moderate sport, taking about thirty fish between us each day in pretty equal proportions. This was our last day; the Friday of the week. My companion, whom we will call Forester, elected to walk to the bottom of the water, and fish his way up with the minnow. I was to fish down from the top water with a fly, and work my way back home with the minnow; but seeing two rods on the upper streams I gave them a wide berth and walked on to the weir before I began to fish. It was a heavy dull morning, and thunder was evidently about, and the fish were in the sulks, for I whipped for four hours for three small grayling, going over the loveliest streams which it is possible to imagine and not seeing a fish move in the water though I knew there were cartloads lying somewhere on the bottom. At last, when I neared the rocks or narrows where the river had cleft its way through some rocks of Silurian formation, where at times you picked up a trilobite, the rain began to fall. This was always an event to be welcomed, for while the drops danced down on the water the fish usually rose well. Whether it was that the rain beat down some of those invisible midges in which grayling delight, or whether they could not so easily discern the difference between the natural and artificial fly, or between the artificial flies of different makers—for we always considered that the fish, from long use, knew whose make it was when they saw the fly, and had their preferences—I know not; but the fact remains that they always rose best and truest in the rain. So, when I had cleared the narrows I saw symptoms in some shallow water at the head of the "Horse-shoe Meadow" that the grayling were on the rise; so wading across the stream, I began to throw. Yes; it was a shoal on the blossom. Once, twice, thrice, and two fish at least rose each cast at the flies. Sometimes both were landed, sometimes one. After about ten minutes the blossom as suddenly subsided, and not a fish was to be seen; but in those ten minutes fifteen fish, varying from "shuck" to half-a-pound, had been drawn out, and were kicking about on the gravel. The streams in the meadow were fished for nine more—these, however, all good fish—and then I came to a shallow pool at the end of the meadow, where from the movement of the water on the other side, some large fish were evidently sporting. At the first cast I had two on, each quite one pound in weight, a trout and a grayling, but the trout only came to land; and for another five minutes I rose one or two large fish at every cast, and landed four. Then suddenly the big fish ceased, and the "shuck" began to rise. I had caught five or six, when I heard a voice behind me, "You've got enough of them little ones, and they are no use to send away. I should stop now." it was the voice of Rufus, so called for the same reason as our second Norman king, and in his way equally devoted to sport. He was called "keeper"; his better name would have been "killer," for a deadlier hand never threw a line. Whatever the weather he could always catch fish; and I have a shrewd suspicion that for the heavy baskets which sometimes were brought home, members were partly indebted to his aid. Well, I took his advice, and took stock of the fish. They were 36 in number: 33 grayling, 22 of them "shuck" and 11 larger fish; and 3 trout, one of them weighing a pound.

It was now three o'clock. The boy was sent home with the fish; and I changed my fly for a minnow and set out to fish up the river home.

I fished my way very carefully, making sure from the look of the water that at every bend I ought to have a fish. Such water for spinning could not be found in all the kingdom, I am sure; and most of it can be reached without wading, if you fish under your own bank all the way; but for more than two hours not a fish did I move. The rain was over, and a fresh wind had sprung up. At last, on rounding a corner, on a shallow gravel bed just above a large tree which had fallen across the river, I saw a trout splashing about, with his body out of water. He had been too eager in following the minnows, and had stranded himself. I sat down and watched his struggles for a minute or two, till at last he regained the stream. My companion, Forester, came up at this moment. He had fished all the lower parts of the river, and had taken nine good fish, the largest weighing one pound eleven ounces, with the artificial Exeter minnow —the same as I was using myself—but not having run a fish since the rain ceased at 3 p.m., he had put up his rod and was walking home. We held a court-martial to decide the tactics to be pursued with regard to this trout; and it was agreed that as he was so eager as to strand himself he would probably take the minnow if it were offered. So I crept cannily on hands and knees to within reach of the stream, and scarcely had my minnow touched the water when my friend seized it greedily, but after one rush, being tired, we concluded, with his efforts in extricating himself from the gravel bed, he allowed himself to be drawn on shore like a log. He proved to be a fish one pound three ounces in weight.

A little above this was a bend of the river, where the stream had excavated a small hole which ran some way under the bank on the other side. So casting across I let the stream carry my minnow well under before I began to draw. When I did there was an obstacle. Then a great spluttering and splashing on the surface, and in due time a trout of one pound five ounces was drawn up upon the gravel. While Forester took the hooks out of his mouth, "Why not have another cast," he said: "another may be there." To oblige him I said I would, though doubting whether two fish would feed together in so small a hole; and accordingly another cast took my minnow to the very head of the stream. When it reached the same point it was taken again, and the companion fish, one pound six ounces in weight, was in due time drawn up upon the shelving bank.

We now came to the great weir hole, "Temptation Hole" as it was called, because it looked so likely that everyone stopped to fish it; and consequently the fish were so shy that though they would come up to look at the fly they generally turned down again without opening their mouths to take it, or perhaps tried to drown it with a blow from their tails, which sometimes turned out fatally for them.

Now it so happened that two famous trout inhabited this hole, and used to come up into the stream immediately below the weir to feed. They had had their adventures, especially during the May-fly season, when they had been hooked more than once, but had always managed to escape. The bigger of the two had been hooked by old Stock, the keeper, with an artificial May-fly, and had twice been brought up to the side, and twice run out again after his finger and thumb had been across his back, the second time breaking his hold. Now we had seen these fish ourselves during the week. The first day we saw both rolling their broad yellow sides in the stream. They saw us too, and fell down quietly into the big deep pool below. The second day they were not in the stream, so I cautiously made a cast into the boil, and to my surprise, whether after my minnow or whether as an intimation that they knew what we wanted and were not going to be caught, one of them jumped out of the water right over the line. On the Thursday we had both tried for them, but without any result, and now it was Friday evening after six o'clock, and our last chance for the season. So we agreed that at any rate one final attempt should be made.

So I crept quietly along the weir, with the water running into the tops of my boots, till I came within reach of the boil. There were several stakes with their tops just out of the water, and I threw the minnow between them, well under the bottom of the weir, where the stones seemed washed away so as to form a hole. "Oh, what a bore! I am fast on a stake! No, it moves. It is the fish." And sure enough it was. As luck would have it, he must have been lying in this hole as we came up, and consequently did not see us, and took the minnow for the last time. I wonder how many minnows— aye, and small trout and grayling too, he had eaten in his time. Well, out he ran, close under my feet, along the weir, fortunately missing the stakes, and then down into the deep pool below. Forester was in a great state of excitement, was for rushing in wildly—for we had no net—into water far deeper than his six-foot stature; but I restrained his ardour till, after some ineffectual attempts to reach some snags and roots under the willow bushes on the side, where doubtless his wife—or rather her husband, for this proved to be the female fish—was reposing, her circles became narrower and narrower, and then first one broad side came up, then the other, till at last fairly killed and floating on her back, she was brought to the foot of the weir, and with Forester's strong finger and thumb firmly clasped on her wigand, was triumphantly carried to land. When we reached home she weighed exactly three pounds four ounces; and had still the dint on her upper lip where she had broken away from old Stock's fly. That great authority had put her weight at three and a half pounds; and probably she was that weight at the end of the May-fly season, but had fallen away somewhat since.

The next year, as luck would have it, I got the companion fish. It was the first day of the minnow fishing, and the May-fly was still on the water—not that particular day, for it was one of the roughest days I ever remember, and it was as much as one could do to stand by the river side. I hooked him in the very same boil under the stones of the weir, where I had taken his wife in the previous August; but I had not the same trouble in bringing him to land, for the big alder bush which stood by the side of the pool had been cut down in the winter. So, after one or two turns round the hole, I led him down to the gravel bed at the foot of the hole, and, walking backwards, gently drew him out. He was a smaller fish than his companion, and weighed two ounces under three pounds. He, too, had had his adventures. I took him on the Wednesday morning. On the previous Saturday he had broken one member of the Club, and on the previous Saturday carried off a portion of the line of another; and when I took him he had still the hook in his mouth and a yard of gut attached, which were restored to their rightful owner, who happened to pass by soon after he was caught.

The evening of the day of which I have recorded the result there was great excitement in the quiet village of Leintwardine. It seems there were certain Sadducees there, who doubted the existence of any large trout in the river, and who talked in the tap rooms of the good old times when they were taken by the score, and chaffed old Stock on his inability to show such now. So that evening he had his revenge. The big fish was first placed on a thin deal board, and his outline carefully traced and cut out, and his weight and the place and date of his capture duly recorded upon it. Then the ten best fish were picked out, washed, and laid on a plank in the back-yard—I am not sure that sundry small grayling were not crammed down their throats, in case any should wish to weigh them,—and the Sadducees were invited to call. In they came, headed by a saddler, a cobbler who had a reputation of knowing something about the fish, and other gossips, frequenters of the various taps. They went away convinced, I hope, by old Stock's argument, founded on that day's sport, that there were just as good fish as ever in the river, only they were grown too knowing to be caught.

I could not myself subscribe to this view of the case, for I was of opinion that the grayling have completely gained the mastery over the trout, and that the only way to restore the proper proportions is to hatch trout for turning in.

Such was the pleasant conclusion of what was, as far as I remember, the best day's fishing I had during my term of membership of the Club. Doubtless to the "good hands" or to members who could pick their days it would not be a great day; but it was ample for sport according to my ideas of it; and now that there is an end of those pleasant wanderings by the sparkling Teme, I have amused myself by fishing my fishings over again on paper, which, though by no means to be compared with the reality, is not without its pleasure.

OFFICERS OF THE LEINTWARDINE FISHING CLUB 1848-2010

DATE	PRESIDENT	SECRETARY AND TREASURER
1848-1856	*Sir William Rouse Boughton*	James Ackers
1856-1868	James Ackers	James Ackers
1868-1870	*Benjamin St John Ackers*	*Benjamin St John Ackers*
1870-1909	Andrew Rouse Boughton Knight	Andrew Rouse Boughton Knight
1909-1918	Charles Andrew Boughton Knight	Charles Andrew Boughton Knight then A R Beale Secretary & Treasurer 1912-19. CABK always communicates with Major Wood and treats him as the 'President.'
1919-1922	HL Heber-Percy	Heber-Percy appears only a titular President. Major Wood seems very much in charge and Colonel Westropp Secretary/Treasurer
1922-1930	Major HC Ackroyd	Ackroyd elected in his absence, Maj Wood ex-officio President for 1922 and probably to 1930. Westropp Secretary & Treasurer until 1927
1930-1936	AR Beale	1936 minutes note that Beale was re-elected President and CF Drake as Secretary.
1937-43	Major CE Wood elected but all meetings from 1837-1842 chaired by AR Beale as Vice	Drake Secretary to 1942 then Colonel HD Marshall Secretary 1942-1945?
1943-46	AR Beale	Major H Sykes Secretary 1945-46
1946-51	Major HR Sykes, AR Beale Vice	CS Asbury Secretary 1946-52

1951-67	Sydney Guy	J Ash Garland Secretary 1952-60.
		WRJ Heatley Secretary 1960-67
1967-77	AA Mitchell	WR J Heatley Treasurer 1967-78, Col HB Watkins, Secretary 1967-77, DW Plant , Secretary 1977-81
1978-1998	Colonel F Walter James	J W Bannister Treasurer 1978-86, AW Henn 1986-98.
		DW Plant, Secretary 1977-81, K Armstrong, Secretary1981-95, J Mawdsley, Secretary 1995-2000.
1998-2002	AW Henn	Dr PJ Beckenn Treasurer 1999, RG Brown 1999-2004
		Cliff Gammon, Secretary 2000-2004
2002-2004	Jack Mawdsley (At this point the club decided to re-designate the President position as Chairman)	Roger Brown Treasurer 1999-2004 Cliff Gammon, Secretary 2002-2004
2005-2008	Cliff Gammon	W Hiscocks, Treasurer 2005-2010
		Daniel McDowell, Secretary 2004-2006
		Nick James, Secretary 2007-2008
2009-	Daniel McDowell	M Hollands, Treasurer 2011-
		Richard Bowen, Secretary 2009-

APPENDIX SEVEN

LFC RIVER-KEEPERS/WATER BAILIFFS

DATE	RIVER KEEPER	COMMENTS
1849 -1907 58 years	Edward Meredith	Lived at Criftin Ford Cottages and later at Graham's Cottage. On pension Oct 1907. Dies 19 May 1910, buried Leintwardine. Underkeepers: 1871-77 Thomas Picking 1877-79 E Langslow 1880 E Howells 1884 Cruxon 1894-7+ E Steadman (May well have continued beyond 1897)
1909-1911	E Griffiths	Serious accident falling off bicycle, 1911.
1913-16	William Bullock	Kelly's Directory 1913 lists him as Water Bailiff and living at Graham's Cottage.
1916-1917	HS Burmingham	Burmingham is a stand in river keeper whilst managing The Lion, until he is dismissed.
1917-18	Dimmer	
1919-20	J Watts July - Oct '19	
	C Lane Oct '19 - Jan '20	
	T James Jan'20-Feb '20	
1920-1935	T James?	
1936-1941		An unknown keeper was employed during this period but not in 1942.

1943-1956 13 years	E Holloway	First employed in 1943 for only 20 weeks then resigned. 1946 minutes, agreed to retain him for 'time being'. Carried on to 1956 when it was reported he had died.
1956-1978 22 years	George H Morris	He Lived at Brockley Villa. 1969 LFC Minutes noted he had been ill.
1979	Ian Laurie	Departed 28th January.1980.
1980-93 13 years	Fred Banks	He retired at 80 and presented with an inscribed salver. Continued to help and give advice. after retiring.. Lived in Downton and later at Nacklestone bungalows. He died
1993-2000	Colin Barr	He lived at Trippleton Cottage.
2000-2009	Tony Jones	Associate of the Advanced Professional Game Angling Instructors Association. Lived in Bucknell.
2010	John Ramsay	
2011	Quentin Eardley	

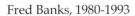

LFC River Keepers and Bailiffs

George Morris, 1956-1978

Fred Banks, 1980-1993

Tony Jones, AAPGAIA,

2000-2009

APPENDIX EIGHT

LIST OF MAPS AND ILLUSTRATIONS

(all photographs by the author unless noted)

PAGE NUMBERS   ILLUSTRATIONS

End papers Detail of Downton Estate map, surveyed 1832-34, printed 1835.

Front piece Leintwardine Bridge by Edward Hamilton.

4   Trout and Grayling, 1839, *The Fly-Fisher's Entomology*, Alfred Ronalds.

8   LFC Members List 1863.

11   Source of the Teme and the Teme at Milebrook.

13   Leintwardine Bridge.

14   LFC Sketch map of the Club water.

17   Richard Payne Knight, c 1830

18   Castle Bridge at Downton by Thomas Hearne, c 1785, Private Collection.

19   Downton Castle. Cartouche from estate Map[1], James Sheriff, c 1780.

20   Humphry Davy.

22   Thomas Andrew Knight, by kind permission of P Wiggin, Downton Hall.

25   Fishing Tackle, a sketch[8] by Banastre Tarleton.

26   Downton Castle from a sketch by Frances Stackhouse Acton, *Salmonia*.

29   Billy Jones, photo courtesy of David Edwards.

31   Sir William Rouse Boughton, by kind permission of P Wiggin, Downton Hall.

35   Leintwardine from a sketch by Frances Stackhouse Acton, *Salmonia*.

36   Lady Langdale, courtesy of Edward Harley.

39   Sketch of Bow Bridge, c 1860, by William Lea.

43   Downton Castle, c 1870.

46   LFC Invitation[7]1870.

48   LFC Accounts 1870.

49   Dining Room at Downton Castle[3].

54   1884 map[3] showing the weir at Graham's Cottage.

59   LFC Logo, 1886.

62   Lord Coventry[6].

62   The Wardens, by kind permission of Jane Wells.

65   RWD Harley, courtesy of Edward Harley.

67   Birmingham Corporation Map[3], 1898.

70   LFC Ticket[3].

71   Lord Coventry's Fishing licence.

76   Graham's Cottage, Map 1903[3] .

78   Graham's Cottage, courtesy

L Bromage.

81   LFC Headstone subcribers[6].

82   Edward Meredith's Headstone.

Colour Section pages 83-98

83   LFC Rules, 1863-4

84   LFC Upper Beat, the village concession.

85   LFC Upper Beat, Trippleton and Wide World.

86   LFC Upper Beat, towards Standledean and Aqueduct Bridge.

87   LFC Upper Beat, above and below Black Bridge.

88   LFC Middle Beat, Burrington Bridge.

89   LFC Lower Beat, below Burrington Bridge and Owney Cottage.

90   LFC Lower Beat, Owney Meadow.

91   LFC Lower Beat, Downton Bridge.

92   LFC Lower Beat, Bow Bridge.

93   Graham's Cottage and Criftin Ford Cottages.

94   Trippleton House and The Wardens.

95   The Lion and The old Swan Inn.

96   Leintwardine House, courtesy of Craig Adams and LFC river-bank sign.

97   Andrew Rouse Boughton Knight[3].

98   Downton Castle.

99   Maps, 1883 and 1903[3].

100   Charles Andrew Boughton Knight[3].

101   Helen Dupré Boughton Knight[3].

101   Pools farm.

104   Geoffrey Harley, courtesy of Edward Harley.

106   Downton Castle Fishing Ticket book[3].

109   RGG Harley fishing on the Nile, courtesy of Edward Harley.

112   Postcard of The Lion[8].

118   Knackleston Meander, 1903 Map[3].

124   Photo of JRH Harley and RWD Harley courtesy of Edward Harley.

127   1935 Minute Book[7].

129   Francis Brett Young.

133   Postcard of The Swan Hotel[8].

135   Major Kincaid Lennox[3].

139   HA Hopkins from the book *Rod in Hand*.

142   Sydney Guy

143   Sydney Guy and *'feathers in our cap logo'*.

147   Cormorant skull.

148   George Morris, courtesy Mr Morris.

149   Scott-Atkinson and Sydney Guy on the Teme.

153   'Sydney Guy' LFC map c 1960.

155   Dennis Lennox[3].

197   The Grasshopper.

202   James Englefield.

223   River-keepers, George Morris, Fred Banks, Tony Jones.

Index to Fishing in Time

A

A Day at Leintwardine, 38,177,195,210

Ackers, Benjamin St John, 45,47,162

Ackers, James, 32-45,70,75,78,162

Ackroyd, Major H Cecil,117-127,162,219

Addiscote, William, 163

Aldenham Hall,164

Allsopp, Sir Henry,45-58,163

Allsopp, Samuel C, MP,163

Angler's Co-operative Association,137

An Angler at Large, (1911),195

An Angler's Rambles,27,151,191,198

Angling in All its Branches, (1800), 21,190

Apreece, Mrs,22

Arrow, Fishery,69

Arrow, River,64,195

Asbury, CS,132-136,164,219

Atkinson, G Scott,149,152,164,226

Attwood-Mathews, Benjamin St John,,164

B

Badminton Library, The (1885),58,121,194,201

Bagot, Lt Col, Ponsonby,55,164

Bailey, RC,107,110-119,164

Baily's Magazine…,40

Banks, Fred,156,159,222,223

Banks, Sir Joseph,21

Barber-Starkey, William Joseph,164

Barker, RG, 136,164

Barracks, The, Leintwardine,75

Bartholomew, Colonel, HJ,164

Beale, AR,108-145,165,187,219

Beale, Rev Theodore,168

Beckenn, Dr PJ, 220

Bedstone, Court,114,116,118,122,177,180

Berkeley, Major,53,114,119,165

Bevan, G (E) H,117,119,122.165

Birmingham Water Corporation,67

Bishton Hall,109,114,122,188

Blanche, Lady Coventry,63,170,205-207

Black Bridge, Criftin Ford Bridge,16,19,31,32,37,38,41,48,54,56, 75,79,106,117,119,126,128,129,134,136, 144,145,157,226

Blackmoor Park,176

Bodenham,115,164,185

Book on Angling, A, (1867),192

Boote, James B,118,122,165

Boosey, Thomas,27,191

Boswell, MA,165

Botfield, Beriah,33

Boyce, Colonel, C,127,165

Bow Bridge,18,19,27,31,37-39, 42,67,126, 128,135,144,155,156,225,226

Bowen, Richard, 220

Bowlker's Art of Angling, (1854),25,193

Bowlker, Charles,25,190,192

Bowlker, Richard,21,25,27,161,190

Bowstead-Wilson, Rev J, 165

Brampton Bryan,6,7,12,13,15,16,32,65,105,
117,122,140,141,144,165,174,175,182

Branogenium,12

Breadalbane, Earl of, 45,48,50,58,165

Brett Young, Francis,129,130,132,166,226

Bringewood,6,15,16,52,100,141,

British Angler's Manual, (1848),32,34,192

British Zoology, (1776),21,190

Britten, Admiral RN,104,166

Broad-Bissell, J, 167

Brown, CC, 167

Brown, Henry, 45,167

Brown, RG,220

Bucknell,40,114-116,122,165,122,165,174,177
181,184,222

Buckton Park, Farm,64,195,207

Bullock, William, river keeper,117,119,120,
221

Burford House,180

Burmingham, HS, Lion proprietor,112,118,
119,221

Burrington,16,28,31,191

Burrington Bridge,15,41,119,135,148,152,
206,226

C

Canada,75,125,163,178

Carden Park,176

Carlton Club,162,178,187

Castree, Mrs,63,79,205-208

Chapel Lawn,130

Charnock, Head Leintwardine
School,72,107

Chippenham Hall,180

Cholmondeley-Pennell, Henry,40,58,192,
193,194,199,200,201

Clay, Mr,52

Clerke, Captain Charles L,58,71,73,115,167

Clerke, Mary Dora,115,116

Clerke, Lady Georgina,116

Clerke, Lt Col Sir William, 9th Bt,115,167

Clerke, Sir William, 10th Bt,116

Cleobury, Fishery,116

Clive, Edward, Lord Powis,16

Clive, Hon RH,15,27,31

Clowes, Major,50,51,53,55,56,167

Clun, Point of,118

Clun, River,12,23,25,28,118,145,149,152,196

Clun Rural District Council,149

Clungunford House,43,45,50,182

Cook, Rev James,45,48,51,53,56,167

Colby, Major, 167

Collins, Lt Col, Neville,167

Colvin, Colonel John, 34,38,43,45,48,167,168

Colvin, Rev,63,168,205,207

Comber, Rev EP,130,132,167

Combermere Abbey,185

Compton Court Farm,188

Connel, F,169

Connel, JSM,169

Connelly, Mr, Downton Agent,135

Coops, James,33,162

Corbett, Captain Frank, 45,111,169,200

Corbett, ERT, 111,114,119,169

Corbett, J, Agent,31

Cormorants,148

Corser, G Bryan,169

Corser, FG, 136,169

Corsham Court,179

Cottesbrooke Park,

Coventry, Lord, 9th Earl,53,61,62,63,68,71,
    72,78,79,102,103,106-110,124,128
    169,170,175,179,202-208,225

Coventry's of Croome, (2000),63,196,204

Cowrie, Mr,118

Craven, Earl of,15,16,205

Craven Arms,116,124,174,184,206

Crawshay, Herbert, 44,45,50,54,108,170

Crawshay, Miss,107,108

Criftin Ford, Bridge, see Black Bridge,

Criftin Ford Cottage (s),74,226

Croome, Court,62,169,204

Cruxon, river keeper,58,221

Curtler, LM,53,170

Curtler, WT, 170

D

Daniel, Rev William Barker,21,190

Davies, Mary,75

Davies, Priscilla,75

Davy, Sir Humphrey,6,20-22,26-28,30,31
    150,190,191,198,225

Deerfold,15,16

Devereux, Hon, Humphrey,45,57,165,170

Devonshire Works,181

Dixey, Dr, Sir Harry Edward, 107,122,170

Douglas-Pennant, Hon George, 170

Downton Castle,19,25,26,28,30,31,36-38,43
    48,49,55,63,67,69,73,100,101,126,138
    178,183,206,225

Downton Estate,6,15,16,18,27,28,31.34,37,42
    100,101,105,117,128,141,144,156,157
    160

Downton Gorge,16,17

Downton, Hall,31,38,100,106,183,225

Drake, Charles Flint,126-128,132,143,171,
    219

Drummond, General, John,45,73,171

Drummond's Hole, Pool,41,119

Dry-Fly fishing For Trout and Grayling,
    (1908),195

Dublin,

Duck, Fund,125

Ducie, Lord,59-61

Dudley, Earl, William Ward, 45,48,51,55,171

Dulas, River,130

E

Earle, W,58

Edwards, Mr,16,24

England, JEL, 132,143,172

Elan Valley,67,80,130

Elements of Angling:…, (1908),195

Elton,16

Elton Hall,22,58,181,186

ER,27,28

Essington, WE, 45,53,172

Eton,52,169,170,171,174,177,179,181

Eywood,111

Eyton, Colonel Philip, 172

F

Fallings Park,142,143

Fay, Anna,37,180,196

Fenn, Thomas,66,101

Ferney, Fearney, Hall,43,45,114,122,175,184

*Field Magazine, The,*145,147,199

*Field Book of Country Questions,*138

*Fisherman's Magazine,*40

*Fishing Gazette,*38,64,147,177,194

*Fishing Gossip, (1866),*192,199

*Fishing Reminiscences, (1892),*38,77,177,195

Fitton, Colonel GW, 127,172

Fletcher, JA, 172

Flies and Fly-Fishing…, (1873),194

Fly-Fishing and worm-fishing…, (1876),194

Forge Fridge,18,31

Frances, Fanny Stackhouse Acton,
   (Knight),22,26,225

Francis Francis,149,152,193

Freeman, Francis, 45,172

*Fresh Woods and Pastures New, (1887),*64,194

G

Gammon, Cliff,6,160,220

Gardener, H,58

Garnett, Frederick William, 45,172

Garland, MG, 172

Garland, J Ash, 142,172,220

Gentlemen of Worcestershire,53,165,169,170

George, King IV,24

Goodall, Harriet,75

Gordon, Dr Catherine,63,109,196,204

Gordon-Forbes, Cosmo,173

Gouldbourn, Mrs,145,149

Gouldbourn, Miss G,150

Gibbons, Colonel W, 173

Graham's Cottage,53-56,67,75-
   78,80,81,117,119,130,135,204,221,225

Grasshopper, Grass-hopper,32,47,49,51,63
152,192-194,197-203

Grayling, Greyling,4,40,51,64,66,137,200

Grayling and How to Catch Them, (1895),195

Great Western Railway Company,126,195

*Green Dragoon,*24,196

Green, Mr,71

Greville, Captain A, RN, 122,173

Grierson-Clayton, J, 173

Griffiths, E, keeper,81,107,221

Guards Club,164,187

Gurney, Mr RG, Harley Agent,135-139

Guy, JMB, 174

Guy Motors,142

Guy, RS, 132

Guy, Sydney Slater, 134-137,142-153,174,
220,226

Guy, TM, 174

Guy, WRE, 174

H

Handbook for Travellers, (1867),193

Handbook of Angling, (1847),191

Ham Court,178

Hamilton, Edward,9,40-42,159,194,200,225

Hamilton, Sir William,30

Habershon, KRH, 174

Halstead, Major,110,111

Hampton Hall,169

Hancock, CV, Birmingham Post,137,196

Harley, Alfred, 6th Earl of Oxford, 37

Harley, Christopher Charles, 145,146,174

Harley, Edward, 2nd Earl Oxford and
Mortimer, 16

Harley, Estate,19,28,37,44,145,160

Harley, John Ralph Henry, 124-129,136-141
144,145

Harley, Robert George Geoffrey, 73,104-123

Harley, Robert William Daker, 49,64-72

Harley, Sir Robert,16

Harley, Thomas,16

Haunts and Hints for Anglers, (1925),126,195

Hearne, Thomas,17,18,225

Heatley, WRJ, 155,175,220

Heath, The,33,162

Heber-Percy, HL,73,106,107,110,113-116,119
122,125,175,219

Henn, Alan, W,158,220

Hereford Herd Book Society,169,205

Hereford Record Office,6,128,161

Herons,77,125,134,146,147

Hinton Admiral,101,183

Hocken, Colonel CAF, 175

Hodson, Mr D, Downton Agent,136

Hofland, Thomas,32

Hollands,M,220

Holloway, E, river keeper,133-
135,137,146,222

Hope Court,114,185

Hopkins, HA, 131,137,138,139,175,196

Hopps, Bernard, 119,122,176

Hopps, JA, 176

Hopton Heath, Station,40,80,207

Hornyold, Thomas Charles Gandolfi, 176

Horseshoe Meadow, 117,118,137

Hill, Major William C, 58,65,66,68,72,73,79
102,111,175

Hindlip Hall,50,163

Hiscocks,W,220

History of Ludlow,25

Hurlestone-Leche, John,55,176

I

Ibbotson, Rev C, 45,50,176

India,15,34,52,122,168,170

Inglis-Jones, Elizabeth,26

J

James, Nick,220

James, T, river keeper,123,125,127,221

James, Colonel, Walter,156,157,159,220

Jesse, Edward,27,32,150,191,198

Jobling, G, 176

Jones, William, Billy,28,29,31,32,36,225

Jones,Tony, 222,223

K

Kelsall, Mr, Fishery Officer,148

Kelly's Directory,108,164-168,176,183-186,221

Kempsey,177

Kennard, Rowland SE, 114,117,177

Kenny, Lt Colonel DEC, 132,176

Kenswick,166

Kent, SM, 176

Kenya,72

Ker, AG, 176

Kerry Hills,12

Knacklestone,117

Knight, Edward,16

Knight, Frances,31,36

Knight, Richard,16,31,128

Knight, Richard Payne,16-18,30,31,49,225

Knight, Rev Thomas,16

Knight, Thomas Andrew,22,26,28,31,33,34
36,183,225

Knights of Downton Castle,26

Knightwick Rectory,165

Knighton,12,40,123,165,176,181,186,206,208

Kingsland,40,162,176,180,186,206,207,208

Kington,111,177,186

L

Langdale, Lady Jane Elizabeth, 32,33,36,37
42,44,45,47,49,175,177,186,225

Langham, Herbert, 57,58,177

Langley, HW, 110,114,116,117,118,177

Langslow, E, river keeper,53,221

Lea, Archdeacon William, 38,39,40,42,77
79,81,137,159,177,195,210,225

Lechmere, Anthony Hungerford, 177

Leigh, H, 177

Leintwardine, Bridge,7,12,13,16,19,32,42
44,64,119,128,129,134-137,146,149,156
160,194,225

Leintwardine History Society,6,9,161,204,
208

Leintwardine, House,23,34,70,168,176,226

Lennox, Major William Mandeville
Peareth Kincaid,135,137,138,144,145
146,155,178

Lennox, Dennis Peareth (Hornell), 155-157

Letters To Sir Henry Plowden re origin of
LFC, 70

Levett, Major E, 178

Life of Sir Humphrey Davy, (1831),191

Lion, The, Hotel, Inn, 22,35,40,46,69,72,79
105,112-120,124,127,128,131,138,145
149,151,159,163,193,196,208,221,226

Little Teme,28

Lloyd, Major, DSO,123,124

Lloyd, Mr, Maltster,120

Longnor Hall,114,133,185

Lovett, JN,134,135,136,178

Ludlow,6,13,15,16,21,25-28,31-34,40,51
105,114,120,151,168,172,179,181
183-186,199,200,207

Ludlow Natural History Society,33,34,37,
163,182

Lugg, River,64,65,137,186,194,195

Lyon, Major AC, 119,122,178

M

Marlow,80,184

Marrington Hall,173

Martin, George Edward, 58,178

Martineau, Brian,145

Martineau, Sir Philip,109,113,128,129,141,144

Marshall, Colonel HD, 127,132,133,143,163,
178,219

Marshall, RP, 178

Mary Knoll, House,101,172

Maslem-Jones, Dr Samuel Walter, 136,178

Mathews, Mr,68

Mawdsley, Jack,159,220

McDowell, Daniel,6,160,220

McMicking, Colonel H, 179

Meade-King, E, 179

Mellings,61,79,206-208

Meredith, Edward, river keeper, 38,39,51,53
58,72,74-82,106,204,221,226

Meredith, Harriet,75,76,78,80,81

Meredith, William Rufus,76,77

Meredith, Ellen,76

Methuen, Colonel (later Field Marshall)

Hon Paul, 60,179,185

Meysey, Edmund,72

Milman, Sir William, 179

Milking Bridge,41,117

Minute Book 1870,73,116

Minute Book 1912, 74,114,119

Minute Book 1935,127,131,143,226

Minute Book 1946,132,133,222

Mitchell, AA,149,150,151,155,156,180,220

Mocktree,15

Modern Angler… (1864),192

Modern Practical Angler, (1870),193,194,199

Moor Park,45,179

Moorhay,178

Morgan-Vane, Sir Henry, 180

Morris, George, river keeper,146,148,157
    222,223,226

Mr Lucton's Freedom,(1941),130,166

Mustrapp, Lt Col, 180

N

Newbould, Dr JC, 180

Nicholson, Dr WA, 180

Northwick, Right Hon Lord George, 45,180

O

Oakly, (Oakley)
Park,15,16,18,21,27,28,31,32,41,143,151

Onibury,80,114,175,184

Orange Otter, (2006),131,196

Overtons,80

P

Park Hall,188

Parkes, Cyril W,136,180

Parker, John, 45,50,180

Parsons, Major WG, MC,148,180

Patterson, Mr W,135,136,138,140,141

Peebles, Brigadier EC, CB CMG DSO, 181

Pennant, Thomas,21,26,190

Penrhyn Castle,170,171

Peters, Thomas, 45,181

Picking, T 51,53,76,221

Pilkington, W, 181

Pike,47,49,76,77,116,125,126,128,146,147
    148,152

Piscatorial Reminiscences and Gleanings,
    (1835),27,191

Plant, DW,220

Plowden, Sir Henry,70,71,116,165

Poaching,36,80,145,146,200

Pontrilas Court,164

Pools Farm,101,102,183,226

Porter, HM, 59,61,73,181

Powell, Rev Edward,131,196

Price, HA,204,206

Prinknash Park,34,43,162,163

Q

R

Radcliffe, Gerald,181

Radley School,115,165

Recollections of Fly Fishing for salmon,
    Trout. (1884),41,194

Red Indian Logo,143

Redlake, River,149

Reid, KG, 181

Richardson, Dr,45,181

Ripley, G, 181

Ripley, Sir HWA, Bt,
73,110,114,119,122,175,181

River's Side, The, (1866),192

Rocke, John, 38,43,45,48,50,152,181

Rocke, Rev John,33,48,57,152

Rocke, Rev T Owen, 43,45,182

Rod and Line, (1849),32,34,192,197,199

Rod in Hand, (1958),137,175,196

Rogers, Coltman,208

Rogers, Rev John, 44,45,48,53,167,182

Rollason, Dr NJL, 132,152,182

Rouse-Boughton, Edward
    Shuckborough, 182

Rouse-Boughton, Sir William Edward, 31
    33,36,183,219

Rouse-Boughton-Knight, Eliza née

Severne,36,100,183

Rouse- Boughton-Knight, Andrew
    Johnes, (ARBK), 36-38,42-81,101
    116,165,183,219

Rouse- Boughton-Knight, Charles
    Andrew, (CABK), 100-134,145,178
    183,219

Rouse-Boughton-Knight, Edmund
    Meysey,72

Rouse-Boughton-Knight, Helen, Dupré,101

Royal Society, The,21

Rufus,76,78,79,80,82,206

Rural Sports, (1801),21

S

Salmonia, (1828),6,27,31,35,151,190,199

Seedley, House, 58,116,122,128,164,167,171

Seg-Fly,32

Severn, River,13

Severn River (Catchment, Fishery) Board,
    71,134,147,148

Severne, Eliza,36,100

Shaw, TW, 122,184

Shooting Times, The,147

Short, Rev Thomas, 184

Shorthouse, HS, 184

Shropshire, Fishery,117

Sidebotham, Rev,131

Sitwell, William Willoughby George

Hurt, 110,112,114,116,184

Sitwell, Willoughby Hurt, 38,43,45,48,50 51,55,57,184

Smythies, George, 57,184

Somerset, Vere Francis John,57,184

Sparrow, GE, 185

Stamp, Police Constable,146

Stanage Park,53,45,182,208

Stapleton-Cotton, Colonel Hon Richard, 58-61,179,185,188

Starey, John Helps, 111,113-116,118,185

Steadman, E, river keeper,81,221

St Giles, Church, Downton,43,73

Stonebrook House,126,174

Stormer Hall,50,108,170

Sunderland, Bryan, 110,114,185

Surrey Trout Farm,134,135

Swan Hotel,133,135,136,138,226

Swanson, JL, 185

Sykes, Major Herbert Rushton,114, 116,119,122,127,132,133,136,142,185 219

T

Tarleton, General Sir Banastre,22,24,25,34 196,225

Tarleton, Lady Susan,23

Taylor, Samuel,21,190

Taymouth Castle,166

Teme, River,12

Temperance Arms, Hotel,116,125

Temptation Hole, Pool, 39,41

Tenbury Wells,13,40,45,51,180,185,207

Thomas, SV, 186

Thompson, Arthur H, 151,186

Threlfall, RE, 131,186

Tin Mill,18,31,155

Tipton's Row,81

Trinity College,33,34,52,162,165,176,181,182 183,184

Trippleton,16,51,54,116,119,120,122,134,141 226

Trout and Salmon, The,148

True Treatise on the Art of Fly-Fishing, (1838) 191,

Twyford Abbey,188

Twyford, Colonel LTC, 116,119,122,186

U

United University Club,43

Universal Angler…, (1766),21,190

USA,75

V

Vale-King, W, 79,167,186

Vaughan, Brigadier E, CMG DSO, 186

Victorian Days in England,196

Villiers Bayley, C, 186

W

Ward, John George Rodney, 37,42,44,47,186

Wardens, The, Villa, House, Cottage,62,63
79,124,168,170,204-208,225,226

Watkins, Colonel HB, OBE DL, 155,186,220

Watkins, Police Constable,146

Westropp, Colonel FM, DSO, 122,123,125
126,127,131,132,187,219

Westropp, FGM,152,187

Weyman, Mr,109,128,141

Wheatley, Hewett,32,192,199

Whitchurch, 50,77,185

Whiteman, Mr,207,208

Whitmore, Colonel Francis Alexander
Woolryche, 45,59,60,61,69,187

Whitmore, George (Geoffrey), 45,187

White, Harry, 134,150,132,187

White, RF, 138,132,187

Whittington, Richard (Dick),53

Whitton,16,114,172,182

Whymper, Frederick H,53,187

Wigram, ER, 58,187

Wigmore, Abbey,19

Wigmore, Castle,15

Wigmore Hall,117,122,163

Wigmore Magistrates Court,31,36,146

Willcocks, WG, 187

Williams, Mary Anne,33,162

Willows, The, Farm,120

Wilson, Rev TB, 187

Wingfield, Colonel Charles Ralph
Borlase,114,119,122,188

Withington, TS, 188

Witley Court,171,172

Wood, Major CEW, 81-128,188,219

Wood, John, 188

Wood, Thomas, 45,188

Woolley, Wing Comd RE, 188

Worcester,13,40,45,53,62,105,106,161-172
177,180,183,199,206,207

Wright, J Leslie, 132,188

Wright, Thomas,25

Wye River Board,152

Wynne-Corrie, Alfred,188

X

Y

Yates, Mrs P, 188

Yates's Fancy, 64

Z